HAVING IT
Y'ALL

HAVING IT Y'ALL

ANN BARRETT BATSON

RUTLEDGE HILL PRESS
NASHVILLE, TENNESSEE

Published in Nashville, Tennessee, by Rutledge Hill Press, Inc., 513 Third Avenue South, Nashville, Tennessee 37210

Typography by Bailey Typography, Nashville, Tennessee

Library of Congress Cataloging-in-Publication Data

Batson, Ann Barrett,
    Having it y'all.

    1. Southern States—Social life and customs—
1865-   . I. Title.
F216.2.B393 1988 975'.04   88-11351
ISBN 0-934395-76-4 (pbk.)

Printed in the United States of America
1 2 3 4 5 6 7 8 9 — 94 93 92 91 90 89 88

Acknowledgements

Heartfelt thanks are due to the many folks, all paragons of Southern Style, who lent their advice, knowledge, and support during the arduous process of bringing *Having It Y'all* into the world. God bless you all (as we're fond of saying in Dixie), including:

Dale, Bill, and Brian Prentiss; Cindy Seibert; Pam Brown; Barry Landsman; Alan Ethridge; Katherine Koshewa; Helon Winn; Soo Peer; Sheila Murray; Malcolm Douglas; Nancy Wood; Allison Lucas; David Newell; Barbara Barrett; Elizabeth B. Barber; Sandy and Doug Mickle; Joy Dillingham; Dawn Carpenter; Mary Wis Estes; Ann Welch; Laura Anderson; Susan Storey; Val Kersey; Brenda Davis; Tim Seibert; Marvin Seibert; Mrs. James M. Hirs; Mrs. Tommy Praytor; James Levatino; Jocelyn and Frank McGuire; Deanna Conner; Renee Busby; Susan Fincher; Tara Prince.

Landsman Photography; the Country Music Association; the Association of Junior Leagues, Inc.; tourism and development boards of the states of Alabama, Arkansas, Georgia, Kentucky, Louisiana, Mississippi, North Carolina, South Carolina, Tennessee, and Virginia; Atlanta Public Library, Buckhead Branch; The Coca-Cola Company.

Credits

Sources for the artwork reproduced in *Having It Y'all* are: Tonya Pitkin, pages 1, 3, 8, 19, 38, 39, 43, 63, 64 (top and middle), 97, 127, 133 (bottom), 134, 135, 163, 186, 189, 213; Barrett Batson, 9, 10, 15, 31 (top), 35 (middle right), 66 (bottom), 110, 112, 160, 161, 167, 217 (bottom), 218 (bottom), 223 (top); Webb Garrison, 20, 21, 22 (top), 25 (bottom); 27 (left), 28 (top and middle left), 32 (bottom), 33 (bottom), 35 (middle left), 169, 205 (top), 223 (top); *Lee's Illustrated Weekly*, 22 (bottom), 23; Barry Landsman Photography, 25 (top), 32 (middle), 37 (middle right), 40, 42, 65 (top), 73 (bottom), 76, 77 (bottom), 115, 122, 128, 132 (bottom), 133 (top), 147, 151, 162, 178; Library of Congress, 26 (left), 27 (right), 34 (left), 205 (left); New York University, 26 (right); *Harper's Weekly*, 28 (right); The National Archives, 30 (top); courtesy of The Coca-Cola Company, 30 (bottom), 37 (bottom), 70, 71, 72; courtesy of Georgia Peanut Commission, 31 (bottom); Extension Service, United States Department of Agriculture, 32 (top); Tennessee Tourism Development, 33 (top), 41, 58, 65 (middle), 73 (top), 82, 241; Kentucky Fried Chicken, 35 (top); Federal Express, 36 (top); Courtesy of New Orleans World's Fair Authority, 37 (top); Virginia Division of Tourism, 40, 44, 90, 118, 244, 245; Allison Lucas, 49; Will Owen, 51, 100–101, 119, 130–131, 132 (top), 148, 185, 196, 211; Louisiana Office of Tourism, 64 (bottom), 129, 141, 156, 230; Mississippi Department of Economic Development, 65 (bottom), 232, 233; Smithfield Ham and Products Co., Inc., 75; Courtesy Original Appalachian Artworks, 77 (top); *Mobile Press-Register*, 78 © 1987, 109 © 1986, 113 © 1986; Kentucky Department of Travel Development, 80, 226, 227; by permission, Estate of Elvis Presley, 85, 86; courtesy Houmas House, 88; Office of State Parks, Louisiana, Audubon State Commemorative Area, 89; Lance, Inc., 123; Days Inns of America, 124; Maurice's Gourmet Barbeque, 144; The Catfish Institute, 145; Courtesy of the United Methodist Publishing House, 174 (bottom); *Sacred Harp*, 175; Office of Alumni Relations, Vanderbilt University, 192, 194, 195; NFL Properties, Inc., 202; Sports Information, University of Alabama, 204; Tennessee State University Department of Public Relations, 205 (bottom); Arkansas Department of Parks and Tourism, 206, 220, 221; State of Alabama, Bureau of Tourism and Travel, 209, 217 (top), 218 (top); Georgia Department of Tourism, 223 (bottom), 224; Elizabeth B. Barber, 229 (bottom); Shreveport-Bossier Convention and Tourist Commission, 229 (top); North Carolina Travel and Tourism Division, 235, 236; Charleston Trident Convention and Visitors Bureau, 238; South Carolina Department of Parks, Recreation and Tourism, 239; courtesy Museum of Appalachia, 242 (top); The Peabody Hotel, 242 (bottom).

Contents

HAVING IT Y'ALL

Southern by the Grace of God

Hold on to your watermelon, because you're about to take a rollicking ride through the Southland and a frolicking look at Southerners and things southern! Whether you're a bonafide Southerner or just passing through, this is your guaranteed guidebook to life, southern style. Now you can learn about Southernness, the tie that binds everything and everybody down South. Find out why Southerners have reason to smile so contentedly and so often and why so many passers-through decide to stay a lifetime.

If by God's grace you were to the southern manner born, here's the "Official Handbook for Citizens of the South" like you. Or if you were less than blessed to know the southern experience firsthand, then this book's just what you need to make up for what you've missed all these years.

Life's too short to live without Southern Style, so welcome to the Gates of Dixie!

Chapter One

Elements of Southern Style

We could tell you that Southern Style is a state of mind (which it is) and we could also advise you that Southern Style is a state of grace (which it is), but you'd be working two bricks shy of a full load were we to leave it at that.

Rest assured, however, we're not inclined in the least to so leave it. There's too much to tell you. Why, we'd surely split a seam if we couldn't go on any further about this treasured commodity of ours.

Having Southern Style is the down-South equivalent of having it all. It's the *ne plus ultra* of attitude, habitude, longitude, and latitude. It's all the style you'll ever need.

Once you understand the basic wisdom and whimsy behind Southern Style, then you, too, can be well on your way to Having It Y'all. It's all yours for the asking.

THE SOUTHERN BIRTHRIGHT

Of all the millions of people in the world, only a relatively small number will have the divinely conferred destiny to be a born Southerner. And since life in the Southland is pretty darn close to heaven on earth, those of us who were blessed with this birthright quite naturally feel like the Chosen People. This explains why words such as *angst* and *ennui* have near-obscure status in the southern vocabulary and why, instead, we're inclined to deliver such spontaneous proclamations as "I'm as happy as a pig in . . . ," "Southern by the grace of God," or "Take me now, Jesus."

Being a divinely granted privilege, the Southern Birthright cannot be bought, sold, or transferred. You either have it or you don't. If you do, no doubt you thank the good Lord daily for your great fortune. If you don't, but wish you did, don't despair. There's a whole slew of happily naturalized Southerners down here, and thousands more arrive every day.

Here's how to get yourself situated in our ever-swelling ranks of inductees:

1. First and foremost, high-tail it to the Southland, *pronto*. Set up a homestead and learn firsthand about the Southern Style of life.

2. To expedite the assimilation process, consider marrying into a southern family, thereby inextricably immersing yourself into the southern way of life. Should this be impractical, the best alternative is to find a sponsor family to "adopt" you (consult local churches or community organizations for names of donor families).

3. Permanently write yourself into southern genealogy by parenting a passel of southern young'uns. Your efforts will assure you perpetuity in the Dixie roll call, and your progeny will be the ordained beneficiaries of the ultimate gift of life: a Southern Birthright.

SOUTHERNER'S CITIZENSHIP QUIZ

So you say you're a citizen of the South and proud of it? Then put your reputation where your mouth is with this Southerner's Citizenship Quiz. In five minutes you can prove whether you do indeed hail from the Southland or you're just whistlin' Dixie.

1. What is "The pod of the Gods"?
2. What Pray-TV evangelist and country music troubadours are cousins?
3. What was the name of Scarlett O'Hara's first husband?
4. Which southern state was the first to secede from the Union, and which was the first to be readmitted?
5. What is a "green front" store?
6. What is pot likker?
7. Who was the "First Family of Country Music"?
8. Which Southerner founded the Girl Scouts of America, and in which southern city did this occur?
9. Name the two winningest collegiate football coaches in history and the universities at which they claimed their records.
10. Who from the Southland was the world's first rock and roll star, and what was his middle name?
11. What Dixie state is known as the undisputed "Catfish Capital of the world"?
12. Which southern baseball hero broke Babe Ruth's lifetime record for home runs, and for what team was he playing when he made history?
13. List the ingredients in a mint julep.

14. *Vidalia* refers to
    A) a speckled bird indigenous to the Carolina coast
    B) an onion revered for its sweet taste
    C) the site of a famous Civil War battle in Arkansas
15. Where did the world's first powered aircraft flight occur?
16. In which southern state was Walton's Mountain, of prime time television fame, situated?
17. What action did Rosa Parks take on behalf of the nascent civil rights movement in 1955?
18. For what literary contribution is Joel Chandler Harris best known?
19. To what insect did the town of Enterprise, Alabama, erect a monument, and why?
20. What famous general of the Confederate States of America was accidentally shot to death by one of his own troops?

(Answers on page 6)

Scoring:
9 or less correct answers: *Plumb Puny!* Either you're fibbing about your allegiance, or you're a visitor.
10–15 correct answers: *Sakes Alive!* You need to study up on your homeland or, we hope, you're an admiring fan of ours.
16 or more correct answers: Bodacious! You know the South like the back of your hand.

WHERE'S THE SOUTHLAND?

No one seems to agree exactly where the Southland starts and stops. Of course, it doesn't help matters that we don't even officially exist (that point was conceded over one hundred years ago). So depending on who is pontificating, the exact whereabouts of the Southland are guaranteed to vary six ways to Sunday.

Most of the prevailing methods used to define the Southland are all wet, but one is guaranteed to hold water. It works like a charm. Find out for yourself how to handily resolve the speculation once and for all.

DRAWING THE LINE AROUND DIXIE

METHOD # 1: HISTORY

Bogus. There's no disputing that the War Between the States transformed a region into a nation for four difficult years. But since that single idea was never enough to unite all of the southern states or sustain the nation that came to be, the Confederate States of America is a dubious way to designate the Southland, especially 125 years later.

METHOD # 2: GEOGRAPHY

Unreliable. If you think that the Mason-Dixon line will tell you where to find the Southland, you're plumb out of luck. Location below the line can fool you for sure, as the following evidence will attest.

South Florida: These days, the only remaining toe-holds of the Southland in Florida are to be found in and around the Panhandle. Due to the irreversible effects of the New York migration and the Cuban occupation, it's a sight easier to find an egg cream or fried plantain around there than a mess of collard greens.

Texas: Our distant relatives in Texas spend a lot of time insisting that the Lone Star State is a world unto itself, and we're inclined to agree. These are a people who prefer to drive Cadillacs with steerhorns mounted on the front grills and who wear their cowboy boots to church. Clearly, they

Answers to "Southerner's Citizenship Quiz" on page 5
1. Okra. 2. Jimmie Lee Swaggart, Mickey Gilley, and Jerry Lee Lewis (all are first cousins). 3. Charles Hamilton. 4. South Carolina (December 20, 1860); Tennessee (July 24, 1866). 5. A state-owned and operated liquor store. 6. The broth formed by cooking beans, peas, or turnip greens with a hambone, which is usually ladled over these vegetables when served, then sopped up with cornbread. 7. The Carters (A. P., Sara, and Maybelle). 8. Juliette Gordon Low; in Savannah, Georgia. 9. Eddie Robinson, at Grambling State University; Paul ("Bear") Bryant, at the University of Alabama. 10. Elvis Aaron Presley. 11. Mississippi. 12. Henry ("Hank the Hammer") Aaron, in 1974 while playing for the Atlanta Braves. 13. Sugar water, mint leaves, crushed ice, and bourbon whiskey. 14. B. 15. On Kill Devil Hill at Kitty Hawk, North Carolina. 16. Virginia. 17. She refused to relinquish her seat in the front of a Montgomery, Alabama, bus to a white man, thus sparking the beginning of an organized mass transit boycott by blacks and civil rights sympathizers. 18. His Uncle Remus stories (Uncle Remus. His Songs and His Sayings). 19. The boll weevil beetle. The insect's infestation and devastation of the region's cotton industry prompted the area to try peanut farming, which brought prosperity for the formerly destitute economy. 20. Thomas Jonathan ("Stonewall") Jackson.

have substituted the more mainstream conventions of their southern roots with an indisputably Wild West flair and a culture to match.

Others: Additional exclusions to the below-the-line theory are the so-called Border States of Maryland and Kentucky, neither of which cast its lot with the Confederate States of America and both of which still devote a lot of time to debating whether or not they claim the Southland. While we'll side with Maryland's position that its mindset is actually mid-Atlantic (a sort of soft-core Yankee), Kentuckians are fooling only themselves as they savor the bite of frosty mint juleps and merchandise their decidedly southern charm to tourists.

METHOD # 3: UNITED STATES GOVERNMENT

Useless. It may be "official," but it's for sure that the U.S. government is no voice of authority on this subject. What Uncle Sam calls the South is an arbitrary catch-all of the sixteen states (plus Washington, D.C.) that just happen to be in the lower right-hand corner of a U.S. map. This alleged region may provide a convenient repository for statistics peculiar to the "South," but it will leave you clueless as to what, if any, connection it has with the Southland.

METHOD # 4: CULTURE

Absolutely failsafe. The most unimpeachable way to determine the boundaries of the Southland is to forsake all else you've heard and tune yourself in to the telltale signs of southern culture. We say "tune in" because if you just look for it, you won't come up with much for your effort. Being the product of two centuries of intense emotional involvement, you'll know you've located the real thing only when you *feel* it.

It may seem paradoxical that such a dispersed citizenry could be united by something you can't even see. But just toss out words like *camellia, red-eye gravy,* or *Vacation Bible School* around any suspected southern locale, and you can get verification in no time flat. If you're met with indifference, you had better go down the road apiece and tune in elsewhere. But if you're greeted with a look of understanding and anticipation, then go no farther. You have indeed found yourself a genuine province of the Southland.

Authentic map of the South-land.

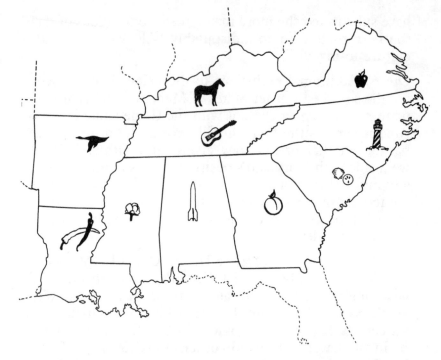

THE SOUTHERN MYSTIQUE DEMYSTIFIED

Have You Mistaken Our Identity?

Now that you know where to find us, do you know whom you're looking for? Perhaps not.

It may be the late-twentieth century, but an amazing amount of folks Not-From-Here still imbue Southlanders with the intriguing and legendary "Southern Mystique." This mysterious, inexplicable force is assumed to reside in each of us, an alter ego scripted around gothic tableaux of moonlight and magnolias or moonshine whiskey, *et cetera, ad nauseam*. You get the all too familiar picture.

Hopefully, you know better than to believe it. Fact is, these overworn notions miss the idea of the Southern Mystique by a country mile. Now, you can bet your britches that there is indeedly such a thing as the Southern Mystique, but you'll have to look far beyond the bygone era of the Lost Cause lamented and deeper than the florid romance pulps and relic movies to discover it.

What's really behind the enigma of the Southern Mystique? Look at our singular way of life, and you'll need to seek no more. Plain and simple, it's our *lifestyle* that distinguishes us from others and unifies us in spite of our differences. Often called a "relaxed state of grace," our southern lifestyle is known and admired the world over and revered in home territory.

We call this precious asset *Southern Style*. It's a way of life we don't take lightly, are downright proud of, and don't aim to ever give up. Intriguing? Yes. Mysterious? Not at all. To know us is to love us, and we predict you'll be doing both in no time flat.

THE SOURCE OF SOUTHERN STYLE

We didn't just luck up on our inimitable Southern Style in the turnip patch. No, it emerged over two kaleidoscopal centuries, the natural outcome of a mindset known as "Southernness."

Southernness is the operative culture of our land, the tie that binds us together. Credit Southernness for our unparalled worldview and identity. It's the psyche of the South, the source from whence all things southern cometh.

We want you to understand this phenomenon of Southernness because unless you do, you are going to be hard put to make sense of the South and Southern Style. So we've fixed you up with a look at the psychology of our sociology.

THE ABCs OF SOUTHERNNESS
A. Southerners have a "sense of place."
Eudora Welty, one of our famous authors, spoke with the voice of a true native daughter when she penned this phrase. Southerners *do* have a proprietary sense of belonging and allegiance to the Southland and their people. Steeped in tradition, strengthened by a heritage of setbacks and hard-ups, and bound by a fierce love for God, family, and the land, this "place" is located in the collective heart and soul of all Southerners, wherever they may be.
B. Southerners live by Godly precepts.
Religious affiliation or predilection may or may not have much effect on a Southerner's standards of behavior today (although it usually does), but our typically benevolent and

unpretentious ways are deeply rooted in the God-fearing teachings of countless church sermons and Sunday school lessons. Oft-repeated prescripts such as "Thou shalt love thy neighbor as thyself," "Do unto others as you would have them do unto you," and the always-reliable "What would Jesus do?" helped spawn such admired southern social conventions as a kind word, a pleasant smile, and a good turn to friends and strangers alike.

C. Southerners live for today and have faith in tomorrow.
We've learned from experience to enjoy what we have while it's ours, because the only thing we know for sure is that nothing is for sure or forever (scholars are right fond of calling this the "southern sense of tragedy"). We also know from experience that if our somethings indeed become nothings, why it's a fact that you can't keep a good old boy or gal down for long.

In the immortal words of Scarlett O'Hara, who well knew the value of this ABC: "I'll think of it all tomorrow. . . . I can stand it then. After all, tomorrow is another day." While scholars and shrinks like to call *this* "the South's heritage of denial," it's really the epitome of southern-style pragmatism at its best.

Or in plain-folk talk: Relax. Don't worry yourself sick. Enjoy life; don't fight it. Ain't no never mind; everything's going to work out just fine.

THE TEN QUINTESSENTIAL ELEMENTS OF SOUTHERN STYLE

We Southerners really are a breed apart from the rest of the world. To us there's the South, and then there's everything else. Likewise, there's the southern way of doing things, and then there's everybody else's way. This means that even though the Southland is smack dab in the middle of the age of Esprit, McDonald's, and MTV, these things don't amount to a hill of beans unless they're accessorizing our own special Southern Style.

'Most everybody knows about our rightly famous Southern Style. It's our biggest asset and our star attraction.

Often accoladed and imitated, but never equalled, Southern Style is the registered trademark of the Southland.

Although you'll find as many variations on our Southern Style as you'll find Southerners, you'll also learn that we're all using the same ten basic ingredients. They're what make having it our way the only way to have it.

1. Friendliness.

Southerners just can't imagine going through life aloof and poker-faced. We were raised to behave in a sociable, neighborly fashion to our fellow man, even if we don't particularly like them or know them from a hole in the ground. First-time visitors to the South invariably receive our wholesale friendliness with astonishment, if not with guarded suspicion, but are soon eager to adopt our amicable ways for themselves.

If you've a hankering to, you can learn some southern-style friendliness for yourself with the following guidelines. But remember our fair warning: Use your newly found skills with discretion when you venture outside the Southland. Since your contemporaries may be unusued to such kindliness, they probably will wonder just what in the Sam Hill has got into you.

Being friendly to unknowns: Unless the strangers you encounter are most unsavory characters, behave as if you've known them since they were born. This means waving or smiling when passing (depending upon distance) and always greeting ("How you doin'?") if within earshot.

Being friendly to knowns: If the passerby is friend, family, or even mere acquaintance, the encounter should become a reunion of sorts. All participants should avidly discuss the weather, their health, and (always) any newly-discovered tidbits of gossip or scandal. Always conclude the get-together with a fond farewell, such as "Now, you tell your sweet mama I said hello."

2. Relaxed Lifestyle.

We Southerners are content to proceed more slowly, leaving the frenetic ways of life to those Not-From-Here. Even in big cities like Atlanta we're liable to keep things to a slow trot. Taking it easy is our form of preventive medicine and pop psychology—good for what ails you and good for the mind.

We were raised to behave in a sociable, neighborly fashion to our fellow man, even if we don't know them from a hole in the ground.

Even in big cities like Atlanta, we're liable to keep things to a slow trot.

If you are a non-Southerner conditioned to feed upon frenzy, we highly recommend our *modus operandi*. Once you've relaxed southern style, you'll think twice about ever working yourself into a tizzy again. After all, since life is a journey, what's the use of not enjoying the ride?

3. Languid locution.

Just why do we Southerners loll our words around so? Not because we're lazy. Shucks, no. It's because they *taste* good. Being communicative sorts, we take our time when we talk so we can prolong the pleasure of the moment.

While one has to be raised down South to "speak southern" authentically, it *is* possible for others to do a commendable job by keeping the fundamentals of southern speech in mind:

- Speak s-l-o-w-l-y. Savor the flavor of your words.
- Adopt a nasal twang and add a lilt to your tempo.
- Resist any inclination to enunciate precisely.
- Recognize that you must drop your jaw before your dipthongs can do likewise.
- End your sentences with a lift to your voice, as if you're asking a question.
- Incorporate the southern vernacular ("She's as cute as a speckled pup") into your everyday speech.
- Refer to chapter 3 for further tips.

4. Brothers and Sisters All.

We Southerners not only belong to our homeland, we belong to one another. This is because the Southland is actually one massive extended family of relations and associations. Nearly every one of us can present some sort of connection, direct or distant, to almost anyone else from the Southland we have a mind to. The effects of all this connectedness are considerable and worth pointing out to students of Southern Style:

a. If you are a Southerner, someone in a crowd will invariably know you, your mama, your daddy, your grandparents, and Lord knows who else in your family. Depending on your behavior, this fact of southern life can either give you a comfortable sense of belonging or make you uncomfortably paranoid.

If you are a Southerner, someone in a crowd will invariably know you, your mama, your daddy, your grandparents, and Lord knows who else in your family.

b. Everyone in town (and back home, too) knows about your current state of affairs, or will before the week is up. Southerners are duty bound to follow up vigilantly on their brethren and inform everybody else about what they've learned.

c. No one goes alone in the Southland, because somebody's always there to help out at the drop of a hat. Thanks to our closely knit, family-oriented lifestyle, we've got the best kind of social security anybody could ever hope to have.

5. *Good manners.*

Down South, we're justifiably famous for our gracious manners. Having good manners means being unfailingly polite, courteous, respectful, and helpful to relations, friends, and strangers. Having good manners qualifies one as "good folk," the designation of choice for all self-respecting Southerners. Having bad manners means not exercising diligence in the above and qualifies one for such nomenclature as "common," "rude," or (worst) "trash," all of which imply a fall from the good graces of the social order. Since only a thin line separates the Haves from the Have-Nots, those who are less-than-skilled in the protocol of good manners are urged to study carefully chapter 3, "Profiles in Classic Southern Style."

Having good manners qualifies one as "good folk," the designation of choice for all self-respecting Southerners.

6. *Larrapin' Good Food.*

If you think southern-style cooking is best exemplified by grits and greens, you've been watching too many "Beverly Hillbillies" reruns. Truth is, the mouths of the South delight in an enviable array of acclaimed cuisines which, though they may be homegrown, are definitely not just down-home.

That our ingenious forebears were passionate gastronomes is evidenced in such legendary southern cuisines as Creole and Cajun, Low Country coastal, Gulf Coast specialties, barbecue, country-style hams, burgoos and stews, and, of course, our honest-to-goodness homestyle and soul-food cooking.

For a true view of this Southern Style incarnate, spend some time at the supper table. It'll be a tribute to the bounty of our land, lakes, and seas, a shared celebration you'll not see the likes of outside the Southland.

7. *Have a Way with Words.*

Like the mighty Mississippi, the oral tradition of the Southland runs deep and wide. In fact, it wouldn't be too much of an exaggeration to say that our vocal chords are connected to our hearts. This helps explain our long-standing and intensely emotional love affair with words spoken, sung, and written.

Southerners have such a proclivity for self-expression that the First Amendment could well be the most inalienable right of them all.

Outlets for our affection are easy to find. Just step into an evangelical church service for a firsthand encounter with sermonizing oratory or heavenward testifying. Ten minutes in the Piggly Wiggly grocery store or Singing River Mall offer plenty of chances to observe the gift of gab personified.

From gospel songfests to storytelling competitions, from our legislative chambers to our inimitable narrative literature, Southerners have such a proclivity for self-expression that the First Amendment could well be the most inalienable right of them all.

8. *A Touch of Country.*

While the majority of Southerners now live outside of agraria, few of us will ever discard all the vestiges of our rural heritage, even should we be rash enough to try. You'd be hard pressed to find a Southerner who neither grew up in the country nor spent a childhood vacation with a country cousin, where more than a few hot afternoons were dedicated to picking and shelling snap beans, tending barnyard animals, or fishing in a pond.

While the majority of Southerners now live outside of agraria, few of us will ever discard all the vestiges of our rural heritage, even should we be rash enough to try.

The carry-over effects last a lifetime. Take a look, for example, at our penchant for pick-up trucks (Jeep Cherokees and Chevrolet Blazers are just citified variations on this theme). Or at our innate hankering for fresh vegetables via backyard gardens, roadside vegetable trucks, farmers' markets, and home canning. And at our yearnings for lazy summer evenings on a front porch replete with rocking chairs, sofa swing, and the serenades of crickets and cicadas.

We could get even more long-winded and maybe a little misty-eyed about all this, but we think you get the message. There's a touch of country in us all down South, and we figure it's one of the nicest touches to lay claim to.

9. *Jesus Loves Us.*

Welcome to the Holyland Down South, a.k.a. the Bible Belt, Land of Pray-TV, the 10-percent tithe (that's gross income, mind you), and fundamentalist fervor. To millions of Southerners, religion is a subject that's taken *very* seriously. After all, eternal damnation ain't nothin' to laugh about. So for folks of this persuasion, spreading the gospel goes on like there's no tomorrow since, according to the Holy Word, there may not be one.

With such almighty consequences at stake, it's not surprising that so many of our other-worldly brethren ceaselessly strive to promote the cause of the kingdom. And since most Southerners like things family style, crusading for the family of God is something that comes naturally.

Should you be a dyed-in-the-wool unbeliever, all this carrying-on might make you a little hot around the collar. Better take it as a foretaste of the ferocious fires of hell, brother. If you mend your ways now, you can make your way to the sweet bye and bye in the twinkling of an eye.

10. *Loves the Southland.*

Southerners are so unabashedly devoted to Dixie that the mere mention of The South prompts a warm feeling in our chests. To us the Southland is a metaphor for everything that's quintessentially southern. The South is our homeland, our heritage, our collective identity. Small wonder, then, that so few of us have left the Southland behind for long and that most of us who have sojourned have also returned to the family fold like eager prodigal children.

It may sound trite to anyone who doesn't hail from here, but it's undeniably true: You can take a Southerner out of the South, but you'll *never* get the South out of the Southerner. Our land is in our blood, and it's always on our minds.

THE SOUTHERNER STEREOTYPED

If you're Not-From-Here, you're liable to be toting around some of those exaggerated notions about Southerners and Southern Style. So off and on, we're going to set you straight with the lowdown on the stereotypes and clichés that frequently accompany our fair land and folk.

Some southern stereotypes are like kudzu—all over the place and just as hard to shed. Most notorious of these celebrated characters are the Southern Aristocrat, the White Supremacist, and the Fanatic Fundamentalist. According to those who should know better, one can expect to find a goodly portion of the Southland represented by these archetypes.

We're not going to claim that such sorts are entirely fictitious, since most of us Southlanders have seen or known a few of them. We will, however, insist that their reputation looms larger than their numbers and that the majority of us have more in common with Adam's house cat than these farcial characters.

SOUTHERN STEREOTYPE #1: THE SOUTHERN ARISTOCRATS

Baptized with a Jefferson cup and raised by colored mammies, the Southern Aristocrats know that—one day—the South will rise again. They while away languid hours at their Taraesque mansions, planning lawn parties and barbecues. She's as pale and fragile as bone china, as high-strung as a Kentucky racehorse, and an irrepressible flirt. He's a bourbon-swigging, cigar-smoking poker player who likes to bag quail, ducks, and women every chance he gets. For them, time is permanently suspended in a vignette of nineteenth-century provincialism predating the arrival of the Recent Unpleasantness.

SOUTHERN STEREOTYPE #2: THE WHITE SUPREMACIST

He's got Red Man tobacco in his cheek, a Confederate flag in his fist, and white sheets in the closet. He knows that—one day—the South will surely rise again. This character's the unrepentant racist who has little respect for anyone who's not white, southern, and male. A heart of stone and a narrow mind are standard equipment on this model, whose mission in life is to restore the South to the former glory days of the old order and whose idea of a joy ride entails firebombs, threats, and other similar recreation.

SOUTHERN STEREOTYPE #3: THE FANATIC FUNDAMENTALISTS

They're the flash and brash of the Bible Belt, and they know that—one day soon—Jesus will come again. In anticipation of that out-of-this-world event, all the tent's a stage of hellfire-and-brimstone sermonizing, holy rolling and prophesying, faith healing, and snake handling. Every street corner's a pulpit for delivering stoked-up invocations and condemnations ("Get right with God!" "Repent and be saved!"); every passerby's a recruit to be plucked from the clutches of Satan. And because the end is near, there's never an end to this heavenly action on earth.

THE SOUTH ON CELLULOID

To what do we owe the perpetuation of some of the most familiar stereotypes of Southerners? Frankly, my dears, much of it is owed to Hollywood.

When it comes to cinematic portrayals, the South and Southerners invariably fall into the same category as cowboys and Indians or cops and robbers—heavy on the hyperbole, light on the variety, and short on substance. Now this may be entertainment (of a sort), but it ain't the gospel. When you consider that Hollywood has yet to reproduce a halfway-decent southern accent or significantly vary its genre of "southern" films in the last fifty years, you can see why we tend to get a little fractious about how we're inevitably depicted.

Here's how the South usually looks on celluloid:

THE ANTEBELLUM SOUTH.

The cinematic version of the Southern Aristocrat. Often an epic tragedy, the orderly and halcyon life of southern landed gentry is felled at the hands of Yankees. You can count on women to be presented as either coquettish southern belles or saintly southern ladies, men as hot-headed but weak-willed idealists, and blacks as loyal, obedient slaves. Most familiar examples: *Gone with the Wind; Shenandoah.*

Clark Gable as Rhett Butler in *Gone with the Wind.*

THE FALLEN SOUTH (a.k.a. Southern Gothic).

Melancholy moral tales about the decay and collapse of the southern social order. Eccentric and flamboyant characters despair their circumstances but are unable to accept change. Most familiar examples: *The Long, Hot Summer; A Streetcar Named Desire; Jezebel; Wise Blood.*

THE BACKWOODS SOUTH.

Spoofs of southern country bumpkins crossing paths with city folk. A big fixture on prime time television during the 1960s and, to this day, on syndicated reruns. Most familiar examples: *The Weavers;* "The Beverly Hillbillies"; "Green Acres."

THE GOOD OLE BOY SOUTH.

Modern-day Johnny Rebs race cars, chase women, and plot to outsmart state troopers. Waylon and Willie, chewing tobacco, six-packs, and sassy good old girls are ever-present fixtures in this genre. Most-familiar examples: *Smokey and the Bandit (I, II, III); Macon County Line; Cannonball Express;* "Dukes of Hazzard."

KNOW THY SOUTH

Since to know us is to love us, those who are strangers to our Southland have, sadly, been denied one of life's finest pleasures. As you can already tell, we certainly don't believe that those of you in this unfortunate circumstance should do without. Lord, no.

Our sage advice to natives and aspiring hopefuls alike is to Know Thy South. As you can never be too rich or too thin, you can never know too much about Southern Style. This explains why we've had more than a mouthful to say about the subject already. Too, it explains why what we've said so far is only the *warm up.*

Our advice also is to keep reading. So even if you're not already one of the family, with our help you'll be able to pass for one in short order. Which is precisely what having it y'all is about.

Chapter Two

A Look Back

Even before Charles Mason and Jeremiah Dixon were knee-high to a surveyor's level, there was history aplenty being made down this way. We've never had it otherwise, either.

Where else but the Southland could such all-American institutions as bourbon whiskey, Coca-Cola, and the Moon Pie have been inspired? Who else but Southerners would have the spunk to insist, "Give me liberty or give me death!" and, nearly 200 years later, "I have a dream!"? And from where else but the South could both the father of our country and the king of rock and roll hail? The answers are, of course, nowhere, nobody, and nowhere.

The same goes for many more of our claims to fame (and our fair share of claims to shame)—so many, in fact, that we'll just let history speak for itself.

SOUTHLAND TIMELINE

A march through Southern history.

BEFORE THE WAR: The first of the South's three historical epochs.

1607. First permanent English settlement in America is established at Jamestown colony, Virginia.

1693. Academia arrives in the South with establishment of Virginia's William and Mary College.

1775. Virginian Patrick Henry declares, "Give me liberty or give me death."

1775. Acadians are expelled from Canada; they later migrate to Louisiana territory to build Cajun communities.

Right: Patrick Henry. *Far right:* Eli Whitney.

1776. First U.S. scholastic fraternity, Phi Beta Kappa, is founded at Virginia's William and Mary College.

1776. Congress adopts Declaration of Independence, drafted by Virginia planter Thomas Jefferson.

1792. Yankee Eli Whitney invents cotton gin while in Georgia; he helps cotton become king in South.

1795. America's first state university is founded in Chapel Hill, North Carolina.

1801. Virginia planter Thomas Jefferson is inaugurated third President of the United States.

1803. France cedes Louisiana Territory to United States for fifteen million dollars.

1814. General Andrew Jackson defeats Creek Indians at Battle of Horseshoe Bend.

1828. U.S. Congress passes "Tariff of Abominations"; South Carolina's protest begins sectionalism in South.

1828. Nation's first gold rush begins near Dahlonega, Georgia.

Davy Crockett at the battle of the Alamo.

1829. Tennessee statesman Andrew Jackson is inaugurated seventh U.S. president; South Carolinian John C. Calhoun enters second term as vice president.

1830. First parade by a mystic society is held in Mobile, Alabama; America's Mardi Gras tradition is born.

1831. Black preacher Nat Turner leads bloodiest slave insurrection in southern history.

James K. Polk

1831. Virginian Cyrus McCormick invents reaper and revolutionizes grain harvesting.

1835. James Crow of Kentucky, perfecter of sour mash bourbon distilling method, gives world his namesake whiskey.

1836. Tennessee frontiersman and politician Davy Crockett dies in battle at the Texas Alamo.

1842. Dr. Crawford Long of Georgia is first to use general anesthesia for humans.

1844. James K. Polk of Tennessee defeats Kentuckian Henry Clay for U.S. presidency.

1850. Henry Clay proposes Compromise of 1850 in Congress to mediate the growing North–South slavery disputes.

1857. U.S. Supreme Court denies Missouri slave Dred Scott his freedom; the controversy builds.

1859. Abolitionist John Brown hanged for insurgent efforts to liberate slaves.

THE WAR BETWEEN THE STATES: Southern Epoch #2.

December, 1860. South Carolina unanimously adopts Ordinance of Secession from United States; ten other southern states soon follow.

February, 1861. The Confederate States of America convenes in Montgomery; Jefferson Davis is elected president.

The *Monitor.*

The *Virginia*.

April, 1861. The War Between the States begins as Confederate guns fire on Fort Sumpter, South Carolina.

May, 1861. Confederate Congress declares war on United States.

March, 1862. First ironclad battle ends underwater as C.S.S. *Virginia* and U.S.S. *Monitor* are both sunk at Hampton Roads, Virginia.

WAR NOMENCLATURE

What to call the War.

Southern culture dictates the use of historically and socially correct nomenclature to refer to the Blue–Gray conflict. Southerners who have been raised right will employ any of the following:

The War Between the States
The War of the Rebellion
The War for Southern Independence
The War of Seccession
The War
The Lost Cause
The Late Unpleasantness
The Recent Altercation

What NOT *to Call the War.*

There is one sure way to immediately cast doubt upon your citizenship (or your upbringing), and that is to employ the erroneous term *Civil War* when referring to the War. Those who know better know that there's a big difference.

Historians will tell you that the whole ruckus came about because many southern states wanted sovereignty, freedom to run their own affairs without outside interference. Their goal denied, eleven southern states seceded and fought for independence as the Confederate States of America, *not* to overthrow the U.S. government. To many Southerners the distinction between the two is enormous, which explains why some Dixie citizens still get a little bent out of shape when they hear the War Between the States called the Civil War.

WHY WE LOST THE CAUSE

You can read about this subject till the cows come home, but after all is said and done, the defeat of the Confederacy boils down to six fundamental issues:

1. Since the preservation of slavery was essential only to a very small but very wealthy and powerful group of Southerners, most who fought the War were defending a cause that had very little, if any, effect on their livelihood. The honor of this ideal eventually paled for many Confederate soldiers in the face of death and destruction. By the War's end, almost one-third of the Confederacy's troops had deserted their duty.

2. "There was more of them than there was of us." The Confederacy's population numbered about eleven million, contrasted with twenty-two million northerners and non-aligneds. Additionally, slaves made up nearly one-third of our nation, making it pretty clear that we were outnumbered from the moment we commenced the conflict.

3. We initiated the War with plenty of zeal but were nigh empty handed of such assets as an operational government, organized militia, a financial system, an industrial base, foreign trade relations, and, well, you get the gist.

4. Ironically, the pragmatic necessity of a sovereign government was handicapped by the South's own doctrine of state's rights. As a result, many efforts to build a more effective Confederate government were vetoed for the sake of separatism.

5. The primarily defensive military strategy of the Confederacy became its nemesis. War tacticians theorized that the North could be repelled repeatedly enough so that eventually it would abandon its attacks and that England and France would support the Confederacy to maintain the import trade from the Southland. However, neither theory panned out, and the North's offensive strategy to geographically divide and conquer the South proved successful.

6. Being a religious folk and believing in predestination, many Southerners came to interpret the Confederacy's inability to defeat the Union as God's will. Finding it increasingly difficult to justify the staggering loss of life and land in the name of slavery, a humbled Southland finally confessed its errancy and surrendered the Cause forever.

September, 1862. Key Confederate offensive at Antietam Creek, Maryland, is thwarted by Union troops; 26,000 die.

September, 1862. President Lincoln issues Emancipation Proclamation, proclaiming freedom for all slaves.

July, 1863. Confederate army suffers decisive defeat at Gettysburg, Pennsylvania.

Confederate currency.

July, 1863. Vicksburg falls to Union forces; control of Mississippi River follows.

May, 1864. U.S. General Sherman starts rapacious march to the sea through Georgia.

August, 1864. Admiral Farragut urges "Damn the torpedoes, full speed ahead" during his attack on Mobile Bay.

April, 1865. General Robert E. Lee surrenders to General Ulysses S. Grant at Appomattox Court House, Virginia; the War Between the States officially ends.

Robert E. Lee surrenders to Ulysses S. Grant.

LEADERS AND HEROES OF THE CONFEDERACY

They're the legends of a past long gone, the icons of abandoned ideals. They nobly served their nation and gallantly defended a cause. Those standing tallest in this historical drama include:

General Robert Edward Lee.
Commander-in-chief of the Confederate army. Although he personally abhorred secession and was offered field command of the Union army, Lee chose to defend the honor of his homeland. It was Lee who surrendered the Confederacy to Ulysses S. Grant at Appomattox Court House ending the war. He later became the patriarch of Washington & Lee University.

Right: Robert E. Lee. *Far right:* Thomas J. ("Stonewall") Jackson.

Thomas Jonathan ("Stonewall") Jackson.
One of the Confederacy's most brilliant tacticians. Stonewall Jackson led several key defensive Confederate campaigns; at the Battle of Bull Run, he earned his nickname after his troops unyieldingly held their line "like a stone wall." Tragically, in the confusion of battle at Chancellorsville, he was shot in the left arm by a Confederate soldier and died a week later.

Jefferson Davis.

President of the Confederate States of America and former U.S. senator and U.S. secretary of war. Faced with the ultimately impossible task of building a nation from a cause, Davis strove to organize and equip the Confederacy for self-sufficiency. Imprisoned for two years after the war and denied his U.S. citizenship, he "carried the sins" of his people as the figurehead of the fallen Confederacy.

Far left: Jefferson Davis. *Left:* J.E.B. Stuart.

General P.G.T. Beauregard.

Louisiana's legendary military hero, most admired for directing the assault on Fort Sumpter, marshalling the victory at Bull Run, and defending Charleston and Richmond.

Major General Nathan Bedford Forrest.

Tennessee's expert military tactician who often resoundingly defeated or repelled Union attacks (including Shiloh and the battle of Nashville).

Lieutenant General Wade Hampton.

South Carolinian Chief of calvary for the Confederacy. He prevented President Jeff Davis's capture at War's end and became governor of his home state.

Nathan Bedford Forrest.

Brigadier General J.E.B. Stuart.

Virginia military officer whose clever leadership forged victories at Bull Run and Chancellorsville. As commander of the Confederate Army, his army's failure at Gettysburg sealed the fate of the Confederacy.

VILLAINS OF THE LOST CAUSE

Union General William Tecumseh Sherman.

Sherman is indisputably the scoundrel primo and damnedest Yankee of them all. After reducing Atlanta to ashes in the fall of 1864, he engineered wholesale devastation with his march through Georgia to the sea (thoughtfully, however, he spared Savannah, presenting the lovely old city to Lincoln as a Christmas gift). Understandably, Sherman's name is still despised in many parts of Georgia, and nowhere in the Southland is it likely to arouse a gracious reception.

Right: William Tecumseh Sherman. *Far right:* Ulysses S. Grant.

Ulysses S. Grant.

Supreme commander of the Union army, Grant was the mastermind of the Union campaigns that ultimately forced the surrender of the Confederacy. His tenure as president further ensured his villainous stature in the South; Reconstruction and his corrupt administration further worsened the post-war Southland's dire straits.

Yankee carpetbaggers and southern scalawags.

Opportunistic parasites who capitalized upon war-torn Dixie's reduced circumstances, they were viewed down South as some of the most despicable, contemptible, and downright low-down excuses for humanity in history. Not surprisingly, this opinion has changed very little over the last hundred years.

WAR TRIVIA

• The South's first major offensive effort, which occurred in 1862 at Antietam, was likely lost due to the carelessness of a Confederate soldier. An observant Union soldier found three cigars, either dropped or discarded, wrapped in a CSA order. The information enabled Union General McClellan to successfully rout Lee's army.

• Over two billion dollars' worth of Confederate currency was distributed during the War Between the States. As well, there were countless issues by states, counties, cities, railroads, and businesses, plus plenty of counterfeits. When the Confederate "blue backs" were first issued in 1861, they were valued at ninety-five cents on the U.S. dollar. By the War's end at Appomattox, their value was about one and one-half cents to the dollar.

• Confederate General Nathan Bedford Forrest had twenty-nine horses shot from under him during the war.

• Mary Todd Lincoln's brother was a Confederate surgeon, and each of her three sisters was married to Confederate officers.

AFTER THE WAR: SOUTHERN EPOCH #3.

1865. Slavery is declared illegal with ratification of Thirteenth Amendment.

1867. Ku Klux Klan ("the Invisible Empire") is exposed in Tennessee newspaper story.

1868. Reconstruction begins with readmission of most southern states to Union. Carpetbaggers and scalawags emerge.

Early members of the Ku Klux Klan.

1868. Edmund McIlhenny of Louisiana first bottles Tabasco sauce.

1873. Tennesseans Randolf McCoy and Floyd Hatfield squabble over hog stealing; escalates into family feud of the century.

1875. First Kentucky Derby is held at Churchill Downs for $2850 purse.

1877. Carpetbag governments flee north with final removal of Federal troops.

1878. Most extensive yellow fever epidemic in nation's history ravages the Gulf states and Mississippi valley.

1881. Tuskegee Institute, vocational school for blacks, is chartered in Alabama under tutelage of Booker T. Washington.

1881. Br'er Rabbit and Tar Baby are introduced to America by Georgian Joel Chandler Harris in *Uncle Remus*.

Coca-Cola syrup keg, 1890.

Sip and Judy slave house near Wiggins, Mississippi.

1886. Henry Grady, Atlanta journalist, makes "New South" appeal to New York financiers.

1886. Atlanta pharmacist J. S. Pemberton concocts "delicious and refreshing" potion, calling it Coca-Cola.

1892. Tennessee salesman Joel O. Cheek's ready-to-perk coffee blend is a hit at Nashville's Maxwell House hotel.

1894. United Daughters of the Confederacy is founded in Nashville, Tennessee.

George Washington Carver.

1896. Southern agriculture is revitalized by George Washington Carver, who finds new uses for sweet potatoes, soybeans, and peanuts while at Tuskegee Institute.

1897. The Father of Country Music, Jimmie Rodgers, is born in Meridian, Mississippi.

1897. Jazz comes of age in New Orleans' Storyville district.

1900. Casey Jones dies at the throttle of the Cannon Ball Express in Mississippi; he's later immortalized in a popular ballad.

1901. Booker T. Washington's *Up from Slavery* is published; it becomes a best seller.

1903. Orville and Wilbur Wright make history in North Carolina with first flight of a heavier-than-air machine.

1907. William H. Smith of Mississippi organizes the "Corn Club," precursor of 4–H Clubs of America.

1909. William Du Bois helps found National Association for the Advancement of Colored People during his tenure at Atlanta University.

1911. Alabamian and jazz great W. C. Handy composes "Memphis Blues."

1912. Juliette Gordon Low founds American Girl Scouts in Savannah, Georgia.

1913. Virginian Woodrow Wilson is inaugurated twenty-eighth U.S. president.

1913. North Carolinian Phillip Lance cooks up a snack food dynasty by selling roasted peanuts for five cents a bag.

1919. First Moon Pie is made by a Chattanooga bakery.

1919. Candler family sells Coca-Cola Company to Robert Woodruff for $25,000,000.

1919. Alabama town of Enterprise honors boll weevil by erecting first monument to an insect in United States.

Girl Scout pin.

Woodrow Wilson.

"The Grand Ole Opry" in full swing.

1923. "The Grand Ole Opry" begins broadcasting from WSM in Nashville; it becomes longest-running continuously aired radio show in America.

1925. Tennessee schoolteacher John Scopes is convicted in "monkey trial" for teaching concepts of evolution.

1926. Virginian Richard Byrd is first to fly to North Pole and back.

1927. Almost 700,000 are homeless after worst Mississippi River flood in history.

Clarence Darrow at trial of John Scopes.

1929. Delta Air Lines of Georgia begins passenger service and starts steady ascent to success.

1930. Kentuckian Robert Penn Warren's statement of southern agrarian ideals, *I'll Take My Stand,* is published.

1934. First Masters Golf Tournament is held at Augusta National Golf Club, Georgia.

1934. Notorious bank robbers Clyde Barrow and Bonnie Parker bite the dust in Louisiana.

1935. Senator Huey P. Long of Louisiana is assassinated.

1935. Rural South is electrified by REA.

Right: "Kingfish" Huey P. Long. *Far right:* Margaret Mitchell.

1936. Atlantan Margaret Mitchell's *Gone With the Wind* is published; sales top one million by year's end, and Pulitzer Prize follows.

1939. The movie *Gone With the Wind* opens at Loew's Grand in Atlanta.

1946. Kentucky's Duncan Hines helps pioneer cake mixes.

1947. Mississippi dramatist Tennessee Williams receives Pulitzer Prize for *A Streetcar Named Desire.*

1953. Hank Williams, "King of Country Music" and Alabama native, dies.

1954. U.S. Supreme Court rules racial segregation in public schools violates Fourteenth Amendment, in *Brown v. Topeka Board of Education.*

1954. Son of Mississippi Elvis Presley records first hit, "That's All Right."

1954. Meteorite strikes woman in Sylacauga, Alabama.

1955. Rosa Parks is arrested for refusing to relinquish her seat on a Montgomery, Alabama, bus to a white man.

1956. "Colonel" Harland Sanders makes fast food finger lickin' good with his Kentucky Fried Chicken.

1957. Nine black students attend Little Rock's Central High School under protection of Arkansas National Guard.

1960. U.S. manned space flight program takes off at Marshall Space Flight Center, Huntsville, Alabama.

1963. Martin Luther King, Jr., writes history with "I Have a Dream" speech on steps of Lincoln Memorial.

"it's finger lickin' good"®

Far left: Dr. Martin Luther King, Jr. *Left:* George Wallace became symbolic of white resistance to the Civil Rights movement.

1965. Over 25,000 civil rights supporters march from Selma to Montgomery to protest voter discrimination.

1966. Foxfire project debuts in Georgia; it documents the lives and customs of Southerners in Appalachia.

1968. Martin Luther King is assassinated in Memphis.

1969. Hurricane Camille wreaks havoc on Mississippi coast, 150 die.

1970. Ted Turner starts his superstation television dynasty.

1971. U.S. Supreme Court rules in favor of busing to achieve desegregation.

1972. Alabama politico George Wallace is paralyzed by assassin's bullet during his second campaign for presidency.

1973. Charles Hickson and Calvin Parker of Mississippi claim to be examined by aliens in a cigar-shaped spaceship.

1973. Tennessean Frederick Smith's expeditious Federal Express opens for business.

1974. Alabamian and Atlanta Brave Hank Aaron breaks Babe Ruth's home run record.

1976. Plains, Georgia peanut farmer Jimmy Carter, Jr., is elected thirty-ninth president of the United States.

1977. The King of Rock and Roll, Elvis Presley, dies at age forty-two.

1977. Courageous Ted Turner wins America's Cup race.

1977. Georgian Bert Lance resigns from Jimmy Carter's cabinet amid accusations of monkey business in banking.

Right: The South's populist president Jimmy Carter and his wife Rosalyn. *Far right:* Ted Turner, a.k.a., "Captain Outrageous."

1979. Coca-Cola magnate Robert Woodruff makes history with $105 million endowment to Emory University.

1980. President's brother, Billy Carter, is investigated by U.S. Senate for possible political ties with Libya.

1982. Knoxville hosts World's Fair; most of the world stays home.

1984. New Orleans gives a World's Fair a try; it's another financial misfire for Dixie.

May, 1985. New Coke is presented to America amidst great fanfare.

July, 1985. New Coke goes flat; Coke "Classic" revived.

1986. Professor Jan Kemp wins suit against University of Georgia's "athletics first" practices; gets $1.1 million.

1986. *Southern* magazine debuts; sheds new light upon the mind of the New South.

March, 1987. Holy wars of television evangelism commence when Jim and Tammy Bakker admit their unholy indulgences.

TRIBUTES TO THE OLD SOUTH

Many Southerners periodically take time out to commemorate the Old South, making honorable mention of an epic chapter in our history and proudly admiring treasured artifacts of our antebellum heritage. While the Old South you'll encounter today is a once-removed relative of the original article, what endures are sterling heirlooms of early southern style, as these rituals will attest.

PILGRIMAGES

A return to the Old South in the truest sense of the word, each spring the landmarks of antebellum prosperity are opened for a circuit of open houses. Known in some parts of Dixie as "pilgrimages," the heartlands of pre-War staple-farming (cotton, sugar cane, and so forth) showcase their legacies with an annual tour week.

Enjoy

Coca-Cola

Trade-mark ®

CLASSIC

Grand flourishes of Southern Gothic preserved, the Deep South's pilgrimages make a conventional open house look like child's play. Awesome examples of the Greek Revival and Italianate styles (post-War homes excluded, thank you), situated on stately lawns and impressively furnished, draw disciples from all corners of the world to pay homage. Ladies in prewar finery (often descendants of old Southern families) conduct the tours of these Deep South treasures with a mother's pride, an archivist's knowledge, and a commandant's authority.

Everybody takes it all *very* seriously. See for yourself.

Mississippi

Natchez (early March—early April; October): The grand dame of pilgrimages reveals the splendor of one of America's formerly wealthiest cities with thirty examples of antebellum splendor. Don't miss the Confederate pageant (topped off with a coronation of its annual king and queen) and other theatrical tributes to the Old South. The Pilgrimage is repeated in the fall. Contact: Natchez Pilgrimage Tour Association, P. O. Box 347, Natchez, 39120.

Columbus (mid-April): Never attacked by Union forces, this city opens fifteen of its over 100 impressive antebellum homes for two weekends. Contact: Columbus Chamber of Commerce, P.O. Box 1016, Columbus, 39703.

Vicksburg (late March—mid-April): Nine homes are included in the pilgrimage of this once thriving port and site of one of the Civil War's most important sieges. Contact: Vicksburg–Warren County Tourist Commission, P.O. Box 110, Vicksburg, 39180.

Port Gibson (mid-April): The town that General Grant reputedly declared "too beautiful to burn" opens eight historic homes for its annual weekend pilgrimage. Contact: Port Gibson–Claiborne County Chamber of Commerce, P.O. Box 491, Port Gibson, 39150.

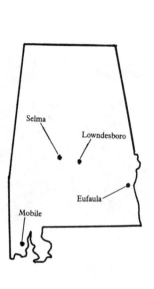

Alabama

Eufaula (early April): Rivals Natchez in magnificence of antebellum heritage; over ninety structures in this former river town are listed in the National Register of Historic Places. Contact: Eufaula Heritage Association, P.O. Box 486, Eufaula, 36027.

Selma (late March): Visit antebellum homes dating from Selma's days as a flourishing riverboat and railroad center. Contact: Selma and Dallas County Chamber of Commerce, P.O. Box 586, Selma, 36702.

Lowndesboro (mid-March): Often called the jewel of Alabama's planter villages, it has some of the state's finest Old South homes and churches for touring. Contact: Lowndesboro Pilgrimage, P.O. Box 11, Lowndesboro, 36752.

Mobile (mid-March): Amidst blooming azaleas, tour an array of nineteenth-century Federal-style townhouses, Creole cottages, and plantation homes. Contact: Historic Mobile Homes Tours, Inc., P.O. Box 2187, Mobile, 36652.

Georgia

Madison (mid-May; December): Spared Sherman's torch during his march through Georgia, twice a year Madison welcomes guests to many of its beautifully preserved antebellum homes. Contact: Madison Tours, Box 571, Madison, 30650.

Savannah (mid-April): Walking tours of this port city's Federal-style homes and Greek Revival mansions have been a favorite spring ritual for over fifty years. Contact: Savannah Tour of Homes & Gardens, 18 Abercorn Street, Savannah, 31401.

Louisiana

St. Francisville (March): Relive an early chapter in antebellum architectural history by visiting some of Louisiana's loveliest "cottage" style plantations during the annual Audubon Pilgrimage. Contact: West Feliciana Historical Society, Box 338, St. Francisville, 70775.

South Carolina

Charleston (March—April; October): Twice-yearly walking tours in one of America's oldest cities showcase admirable examples of Adams-style and Greek Revival architecture. Contact: Festival of Houses, 51 Meeting Street, Charleston, 29401 (spring tours); The Preservation Society, P.O. Box 521, Charleston, 29402 (fall tours).

Georgetown (April): Elegant river plantations and historic city town homes attest to the antebellum bounty of indigo and rice. Annual plantation tours are a forty-year tradition here. Contact: Annual Plantation Tours, Prince George Winyah Parish, 300 Broad Street, Georgetown, 29440.

Beaufort (April): In a town settled over 400 years ago, striking examples of pre-Revolutionary and antebellum style architecture are featured in its annual Candlelight Tour. Contact: Historic Beaufort Foundation, Beaufort, 29902.

THE LOST CAUSE REMEMBERED

Should you believe that the War holds fascination primarily for historians and senior citizens, you must have just fallen off the back of the turnip truck. Plenty of Southerners are avid students of the Lost Cause, and to some of them the saga of the Confederate States of America is akin to a Greek tragedy. Reminders of the Recent Altercation are abundant (there are *thousands* of war markers and memorials across Dixie), and often they're as large as life itself:

Re-enactments.

The hue and cry of battle breaks forth on spring and fall weekends across the South, when re-enactments of the War Between the States are staged on historic battlefield sites. Replete with period uniforms (some descendants even sport family heirlooms) and antique munitions, re-enactments are the manly version of pilgrimages.

Two of the most spectacular: In May, when over 1000 Blue and Gray soldiers converge upon Virginia Military Institute to restage the Battle of New Market in the Shenandoah Valley, and in October, when 500 participants re-enact Kentucky's most decisive battle at Perryville Battlefield State Shrine.

Artifacts Fairs.

Those with a hankering for military memorabilia from the War Between the States can experience hog heaven several times a year at commemorative military shows and artifacts fairs. Enthusiasts and scholars alike will find a bonanza of uniforms, equipment, paintings, books, and other relics for sale or trade. Two premier shows are the Southeastern Civil War Relic Show (Marietta, Georgia, mid-August) and the Mid-South Civil War and Antique Military Show (Memphis, spring and fall).

Between fairs, dyed-in-the-wool collectors can be found combing battlefield trenches with metal detectors or paging through the latest issue of *Blue and Gray.*

Social Aspects.

Don't fret if your ancestors didn't come over on the *Mayflower* or fight in the Revolutionary War. You're in Dixie, remember? If your forebears fought for the Confederate States of America, you've automatically qualified for a far more noble distinction. You can stake your place in the social register with membership in one of three stalwart salutes to the Lost Cause: *United Daughters of the Confederacy* (27,000 members), *Sons of Confederate Veterans* (6,000 members), or the more venerable *Military Order of the Stars and Bars,* for Sons of Confederate Veterans members whose ancestors served as commissioned officers (700 members).

Should you belong to these organizations, you're entitled to participate in activities ranging from the genteel (annual conventions and benevolent efforts) to the more controversial (such as the Daughters' successful block of North Carolina's 1979 decision to cease raising the Confederate flag on Confederate Memorial Day).

College-bound young southern gentlemen can pledge lifetime allegiance to the Old South through membership in *Kappa Alpha fraternity.* Founded at Washington and Lee University shortly after the War, Kappa Alpha brothers are sworn to emulate the integrity of Robert E. Lee, the noble icon of the Lost Cause. Each spring, KAs across the Southland celebrate the penultimate southern frat party, Old South, during which uniformed youths and hoop-skirted belles revel in the name of antebellum tradition and under the influence of Rebel Yell whiskey.

Re-enactment scene.

THE STARS AND BARS OF DIXIE

Paying tribute to the Old South also comes in more controversial forms, namely the song "Dixie" and the battleflag of the Confederacy, the Southern Cross. Seems somebody is always giving or getting a lot of flap about why so many folks down here still wave that flag and sing that tune after so many years.

Whether you look at them as the symbols of regional pride or as the up-to-no-good badges of twentieth century Johnny staunch Unionist, Daniel Decatur Emmett of Ohio, for a minstrel show in 1859. Soon "Dixie" was popular on both sides of the Mason–Dixon line, and it's even said that both presidents, Abe Lincoln and Jeff Davis, were partial to the lively tune which, to this day, never fails to cause a commotion when it's played.

Confederate flags.

Above all, know that there's no such thing as a "rebel" flag or *the* Confederate

Rebs, it's for sure these reminders of the Old South won't go away, away from Dixieland, any time soon. Seeing as they do belong to our heritage, you had better bone up on how they came to be a part of Southland culture.

"Dixie."

The song that has been called "the doxology of the Southern religion of the lost cause," as well as "the best pep song ever written," actually was penned by a flag. What you see in the Southland today (as commonly brandished by the if-your-heart-ain't-in-Dixie-get-your-ass-out set) is the Confederate battle flag, called the Southern Cross. One of *five* flags that Confederate States of America armies waved, it was never designated the official CSA flag. Although the Southern Cross might have been retired at Appomattox along with Lee's sword, it's still on active duty down South.

Chapter Three

Profiles in Classic Southern Style

Granted, the South is smack dab in the middle of the high tech revolution and on the front porch of the twenty-first century, but one thing will never change for us as long as we have our druthers: Classic Southern Style. You'll recognize it as the persona we present to each other and the rest of the world, the visible and audible embodiment of our cultural conventions. Think of it as the down-South version of Emily Post, graced with a southern accent and figures of speech.

The Classic Southern Style stays in vogue in Dixie because not only do we wear it well, we've impressed the whole world with it. For us this style has become timeless attire. We wouldn't hear of parting with it or changing it, either. So today, as in generations past, we wear the Classic Southern Style with pride and hand it down in the same way.

Should you aspire to make a welcome entrance into southern culture and remain in its good stead, then you should dress like we do—in the classic Southern Style. If you've a mind to do just that, read on and heed the advice.

DEPORTMENT DOWN SOUTH

Make no mistake about it: Manners matter in Dixie. You can be as poor as a church mouse or ugly as a mud fence, but don't ever be found empty-handed of good manners. It's the fundamental tenet of classic Southern Style to religiously respect and scrupulously practice good manners. They're the fixed price of admission into the fellowship of southern good folk.

Long before young Southerners can spell *black eyed peas*, they're proficient at the rudiments of deportment, southern-style. They know why they are, too, because:

1. The Bible says so (don't forget the Golden Rule and setting a Christian example; this *is* the Bible Belt);

2. Good manners make life more pleasant for everybody;

3. Good manners are democratic ("manners will get you where money won't");

4. Good manners are what make Southerners different (a euphemism for "better") from those who Aren't-From-Here, a distinction of which Southerners are *very* aware and *very* proud.

You simply can't take good manners too seriously down South. While an occasional trifling with the law of southern manners can be tolerated (but not excused), those who blatantly defy it will soon find themselves about as warmly received as secular humanists or carpetbaggers. After all, we Southerners wrote the bible on good manners and believe in practicing what we preach.

THE FIVE COMMANDMENTS OF GOOD MANNERS

Do you need to bring your manners up to snuff? Then these five commandments should give you something to chew on. Just remember this first of all: Good manners are extended to everybody, regardless of whether you know them, on which side of town they live, or whether they tithe. No exceptions.

1. Be humble.

Others first; yourself last. Self-denial and deference to others ("After you") are the cornerstone of good manners; acting selfish or uppity is not. This commandment is indisputably rooted in Bible Belt theology ("The first shall be last, and the last shall be first").

2. Be courteous.

Remember the Golden Rule. Go out of your way to be helpful and kind to everyone you encounter ("Why, it wouldn't be no trouble a'tall to carry you on up to the Jitney Jungle, Miss Sally").

3. Behave yourself.

Don't be uncouth, rude, brash, loud, coarse, or cause a commotion in public. Only trashy types and Yankees do such things . . . and obviously this is because they weren't raised to know better.

4. Be friendly.

Put your friendliest foot forward, whether you've been properly introduced or don't know the person from a hole in the ground. Be sociable and neighborly, just like you learned in Sunday school ("Thou shalt love thy neighbor as thyself").

5. Be modest.

Never be high falluting. Practice modesty in all situations. "Why, shucks, I guess I was in the right place at the right time" would work just fine upon learning that you had won the Pulitzer Prize. "Of course I won it, I deserved to" would absolutely categorize you as too big for your britches.

COMMON COURTESIES IN DIXIE

Too much is never enough.

1. Say "please" without fail.

Please, always say "Please" when you make a request, no matter how trivial or important.

2. Always ask, never tell.

The only way to make a request is to ask for it; directives are much too surly. "Would you please carry me up the road a piece?" is correct. "Give me a ride to the market" is most assuredly not.

3. Say "Thank you" without fail.

Upon being granted your request—be it a personal favor or impersonal transaction—always look the other party in the eye, give them a pleasing smile, and cheerily say, "Thank you." To show them you're really grateful, dress it up with "Thank you kindly," "Thanks a whole lot," "'Preciate it." If your request is denied, say "Well, thank you anyway," using your best turn-the-other-cheek manner.

4. Say "ma'am" and "sir" without fail.

If any adult your senior addresses you (or vice versa), automatically attach the appropriate title to your response ("Yes ma'am"; "I reckon so, sir"; "Pardon me, ma'am"). Neglecting this rule is apt to be interpreted as arrogance or insolence and is a sure fire way to deny yourself the good favors of those you've been disrespectful to.

5. Always refer to those of the female gender as ladies.

The descriptive *woman* is usually reserved in Dixie for females of questionable repute. If you are a gentleman, then treat all ladies with the courtliness, deference, and respect you'd accord members of the royal family since, in the South, ladies occupy such status. This is an immutable rule of order in Dixie, no matter what may be happening elsewhere on this planet.

LADIES AND GENTLEMEN OF THE SOUTH

While good manners are the common denominator among Southern good folk, some of our good folk represent the gold standard of social grace down South: Southern Gentility. Part tradition, part Protestant ethic, part breeding, and a tad pretense, Southern Gentility is synonymous with unimpeachable deportment and propriety in Dixie.

Membership in the ranks of Southern Gentility earns you such designations as Southern Lady, Southern Gentleman, and Fine Young Lady/Man (the latter being generously applied to anyone not yet over the hill). It means you're a shining example of Southern Style, grace, charm, and finesse (no matter what or where the circumstances) and a living testament to the virtues of a respectable southern upbringing.

If you must ask, money has absolutely *nothing* to do with gentility. In fact, the reverse often applies. In a land where worldy possessions have frequently come and gone ("The Lord giveth and the Lord taketh away") over the last 130 years, Southern Gentility is defined by the ownership of the intangible. Money may buy privilege, but it won't get your big toe in the door when it comes to Southern Gentility.

Remember, "A good name is rather to be chosen than great riches." Amen.

Archetype of a Southern Lady

The Southern Lady is living proof of southern values and ideals. If you can't pass the following muster, you won't pass for a Southern Lady. The following attributes are standard equipment on the genuine article:

- Is a Southerner by birth who loves God, her family, and the Southland.
- Was brought up "right" (southern upbringing); is usually "well-educated" (likely at a girls' school).
- Is a paragon of good taste, refinement, and prudence.
- Is gracious and accommodating.
- Is adept at protecting the male ego; avoids overt competition with men (academics excused).
- Is a charming hostess.
- Is actively involved in volunteer work, often of staggering proportions.
- Does not flaunt her elevated position.

Options:
- Is an independent thinker (frequently considered an eccentric).
- Employed outside the home in a full-time "real" job (invariably the province of the younger generation, divorcées, or old maids).

Archetype of a Southern Gentleman

Becoming a southern Gentleman is the unwritten expectation, if not aspiration, for almost every son of the South. Joining the fellowship of this fraternal order of gentility is a long-standing rite of passage for a southern male, and few pass up the opportunity to belong. He:

- Is a Southerner by birth who loves God, his family, and the Southland.
- Was brought up "right" (southern upbringing); is usually "well-educated" (likely at a military or boys' school).
- Is self-assured, relaxed.
- Is a paragon of good taste and manners.
- Is gainfully employed in a respectable profession and lives a comfortable lifestyle.
- Takes a *very* traditional view of women's roles.
- Is a master at the social graces with women of all ages: courtesy, ceremony, flattery, wit.
- Can hold his liquor.
- Is a proficient outdoor sportsman (probably hunts or fishes often) and a team sports player or fan.
- Is likely to collect prints of wildlife or battles of the War Between the States.
- Does not flaunt his elevated position.

Riding at Sherwood Forest Plantation, Charles City, Virginia.

THE BELLES AND BOYS OF DIXIE

SEPARATING FACT FROM FICTION WHEN IT COMES
TO FAMOUS PROFILES IN DEPORTMENT IN DIXIE.

THE BOTTOM LINE ON SOUTHERN BELLES

If you're new to the ways of the Southland, you might think that the Southern Belle is an exemplary role model for fine young ladies. Maybe you've conjured up visions of little belles-in-waiting earnestly rehearsing their well-bred wiles, impetuous head-tossings, dainty foot stampings, and syrupy southern accents.

Whoa, darlin'! Despite all her honeysuckle charm, most of us don't consider the Southern Belle a worthy maiden to emulate, believe it or not. Let us explain:

1. Like her Motherland lost the War, the Southern Belle lost face, only this time it was on film several generations later. Endless scenes of flouncing pantaloons and petulant exclamations ("Oh, mah *goodness*, you're such a *bad* boy!") made the prevailing notion of the Southern Belle a parody of her antebellum ancestors, even to most Southerners. Her appeal as a role model has now faded to nothing in comic consequence.

2. The most famous Southern Belle of all, Scarlett O'Hara, was not exactly a living testimonial to the lessons of Christian virtue. Recall how deeply those beliefs run in the Southland, and you can understand why it will be a cold day in hell before any right-minded southern mama and daddy will raise their young lady to follow in Scarlett's rather opportunistic and vain footsteps.

3. Unlike earning the designation "Southern Lady," donning the role of latter day Southern Belle doesn't require society's stamp of approval, just good mimicry. Since most Southerners believe that anything free is not worth having, passing yourself off as a Southern Belle these days will probably gain you no more

social distinction than being a Jewish American Princess in New York or a Valley Girl in California.

4. As very few young ladies in the antebellum South ever lived behind the magnolia-shaded porticoes, family legacies of bellehood are actually few and far between in Dixie. So even if being a Southern Belle were a serious aspiration these days, carrying the banner of bellehood into the next century is beyond the reach of most southern girls.

Nevertheless, the Southern Belle *does* occupy a legendary niche in Dixie culture as a fascinating symbol of our antebellum past—and you already know how much we love to toast our Old South heritage. So when it comes to such observances as social events, historical celebrations, buttering the bread of tourism, or just gently pulling a visitor's leg, we're more than happy to oblige with faithful re-creations of fetching Southern Belles, schooled, of course, in genuine ladylike Southern Style.

A GOOD LOOK AT GOOD OLD BOYS

Some legends of the Southland actually do exist, none probably better known than the Good Old Boy. Yes, there are lots and lots of them down South, *thriving*.

There are many dimensions to this business of the Good Old Boy. This is because almost all southern males have a touch of Good Old Boy in their blood, the only real difference being how much. Better get yourself acquainted with him now.

1. Basic Good Old Boy.

The original, authentic model. Garden-variety, middle-class Southerner and contented to be one. A country boy at heart, if not in residence. Hard-working, good-hearted, very traditional. Loves to hunt and/or fish. Likes country music and hymn singing. Genuine and unpretentious, but dumb as a fox. *Universally regarded in Dixie as the living embodiment of basic southern values and ideals.*

2. Quasi-Good Old Boy.

Usually found in southern cities. Adept at assuming the good-hearted-country-boy demeanor of the genuine article on occasion, but wouldn't be caught dead doing it for a living. Uses persona to demonstrate southern origins and allegiance. Wearing it is *de rigueur* for all-male outings (hunting, fishing, sports events, or drinking), when southern accents get so thick you could cut them with a knife.

3. Good Old Boys' Club/Good Old Boyism.

Down-South equivalent of all-male power brokering. Networking with a southern accent and without women, blacks, or anyone else who fails to meet their qualifications (male, white, and southern). This club has been operative as long as the Southland. Members only.

SOUTHERN STYLE #1: THE GOOD OLD BOY
It's deer-hunting season in Dixie.

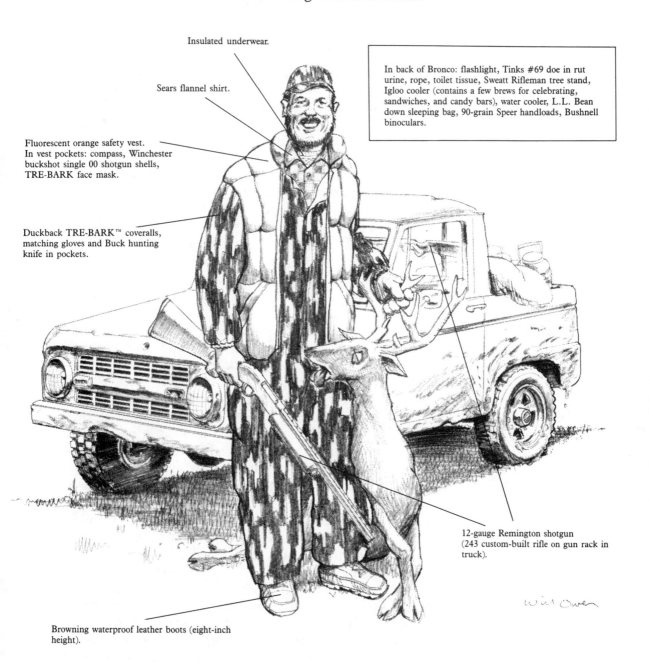

Insulated underwear.

Sears flannel shirt.

In back of Bronco: flashlight, Tinks #69 doe in rut urine, rope, toilet tissue, Sweatt Rifleman tree stand, Igloo cooler (contains a few brews for celebrating, sandwiches, and candy bars), water cooler, L.L. Bean down sleeping bag, 90-grain Speer handloads, Bushnell binoculars.

Fluorescent orange safety vest. In vest pockets: compass, Winchester buckshot single 00 shotgun shells, TRE-BARK face mask.

Duckback TRE-BARK™ coveralls, matching gloves and Buck hunting knife in pockets.

12-gauge Remington shotgun (243 custom-built rifle on gun rack in truck).

Browning waterproof leather boots (eight-inch height).

A FEW WORDS ABOUT ECCENTRICITY IN DIXIE

Somewhere along the line, we Southerners became associated with a decided predilection for eccentric behavior. To hear some folks Not-From-Here tell it, lapses in lucidity are a conventional form of conduct in Dixie, an unfortunate consequence of all that heat and humidity or generations of in-breeding. And it doesn't help matters, either, that an inordinate amount of southern literature seems to contain at least one unforgettably eccentric character.

Well, forget all that hogwash. It does so happen that some Southerners are more disposed than others to indulge their idiosyncrasies, even to the point of slightly bending the rules of social convention. But we will deny til we're blue in the face that there are more eccentrics per capita in Dixie than anywhere else on God's green earth.

The real difference lies in our attitude toward the subject. For most Southerners, an encounter with eccentric behavior is like water on a duck's back. It rolls right off, no trouble a'tall. It's surely nothing to throw up your skirt and scream about. If otherwise refined individuals cross the outer reaches of conformity on occasion, so what? What's a little harmless eccentricity among family or friends?

For some Southerners, having an eccentric in the family can even carry a sort of reverse social cachet. After all, there *is* something downright fascinating about having a second cousin, twice-removed, who is given to spiritedly conducting the church congregation in its hymn singing from his pew on the fourth row or an elderly aunt who has eleven cats with the same name.

Just because we have a healthy appreciation for our eccentrics in the Southland, however, does not mean that showstopping displays of eccentricity are to be found everywhere you turn in Dixie. To the contrary, most Southlanders don't qualify as eccentrics, and such behavior is definitely excluded from our approved codes of southern deportment. But since most of us know an eccentric who otherwise is a well-mannered, well-meaning Southerner, we're inclined to leave that little wrinkle in the social fabric unpressed.

CHOOSING OUR WORDS DOWN SOUTH

There's a lot to be said for the oral tradition of the Southland. And being a loquacious folk, we stand at the ready to oblige it anytime, anywhere.

Having a way with words is a treasured tradition down South. Lending flair to routine goings-on and adding emphasis to serious subjects, it makes everything in between a sight more entertaining.

Folks Not-From-Here usually don't know that the classic Southern Style of speaking is a clear echo of Old World English, with figures of speech from Scotland, Ireland, Africa, and the West Indies folded into southern history. While Noah Webster may have succeeded in making language in the rest of America uniform, we Southerners have remained faithful to our own manner of speaking.

Our way with words is the difference between fair-to-middling and mighty fine, between plain Jane and plumb larrapping. It accounts for why phrases like "I haven't seen you in a coon's age!" and "Don't that just get your gumption?" are as plentiful down-South as fleas on a dog's back. It's the reason we speak with a drawl that's as sweet as honey and as slow as molasses. It's why our politicians, preachers, and storytellers can captivate an audience faster than greased lightning.

Speech is the spice of life in Dixie. No wonder those who taste our linguistic concoctions can't resist adding them to their diet. Sample for yourself the following how-to for putting our words in your mouth.

THE DIXIE DRAWL

The best way to acquire a southern accent is to hear one—over and over, from genuine Southern natives—and to practice it, over and over. Before you start, though, keep in mind that there is no such thing as *the* southern accent. There are all sorts of variations to our celebrated drawl, such as the redneck twang, the Junior League lockjaw, and Lord knows how many regional renderings. All of them are bona fide sounds of the South.

You can, however, get your mouth off and running in our general direction if you keep a few points in mind.

1. Speak musically.

When it comes to speech, every Southerner is a born musician. Let your voice rise up and down the musical scale as you talk and include both upward and downward inflections during the last word of your sentence.

2. Don't rush.

What's your hurry? Let each syllable roll around in your mouth. Prolong the pleasure of monosyllabic words by stretching them out and adding inflections, as in transforming *Hi!* to *Hi-i-i-i!* and *down* to *dow-un-n-n.*"

3. Flatten out and distend your vowels.

Pay special attention to your *i*'s, *o*'s and *u*'s. For example, pronounce the *o* in *roll* the way you would in *ouch.*

4. Avoid precisely enunciating all syllables in a word.

Just let the sounds ease out of your mouth; don't make work of it, for goodness' sake. When you can contract two syllables without a second thought (as in revising *considerable* to *considerble*, then you've got it.

5. Slur or drop an occasional ending consonant.

This is admirably exemplified by dropping the *g* from *ing* endings ("endins") and the *d* from *and* ("an").

6. Pause thoughtfully between phrases.

Imagine you've liberally sprinkled commas and dashes throughout your sentences, as in "Well . . ." (long pause) "that situation . . ." (pause) "got me a little . . ." (pause) "flusterated."

DIXIE DICTION

Nobody can top a Southerner in turning a phrase. No other culture employs more figures of speech and inventive descriptives than we do in Dixie. Most are home grown, and all will do to ride the river with. Why just communicate when you can expressivate Southern Style?

SOUTHERN LEXICON

Words no Southerner can do without.

Abide: tolerate, as in "I can't abide that place."
Act up: misbehave, as in "Her boys sure do like to act up."
Antsy: nervous, fidgety.
Biggety: conceited, full of oneself.
Bodacious: term of expansive approval or appreciation, as in "That's just plumb bodacious of you!"
Chew the fat: discuss, talk at length.

Conniption: fit of anger.
Druthers: preference, as in "If I had my druthers, I'd stay put."
Fetching: attractive, sexy.
Fiesty: spirited, spunky.
Fired up: excited, motivated, as in "The Crimson Tide is all fired up to win!"
Fixing to: about to initiate action, as in "I'm fixing to go over to his house."
Gallivant: cavort, strut.

Give out: tire out.

Gumption: resolve, fortitude, as in "I don't know if she's got the gumption to do it."

Het up: mad, angry.

Hog wild: over-enthusiastic, out of control.

Larrapping: delicious, tasty.

Mosey: amble about in no particular hurry, as in "I guess I'll mosey on home now."

No count: worthless.

Own up: confess.

Peart: perky, full of vim and vigor.

Piddling: insignificant thing or activity, as in "He's just piddling around in the yard."

Play pretties: trinkets.

Plumb: downright, absolutely, as in "Mama's plumb tuckered out."

Pooch: stomach bulge, as in "Jimmy's got himself a pooch from all that Dixie beer."

Puny: sickly, under the weather.

Put out with: aggravated, vexed.

Put up: set aside, prepare in advance, can or freeze.

Rambunctious: boisterous, disorderly.

Recollect: recall, as in "I recollect when your grandmama used to put up toma-toes like there was no tomorrow."

Riled up: angry.

Rot gut: strong, harsh liquor.

Ruckus: commotion, fight.

Sashay: strut, prance.

Scrounge: make something from nothing, scrape together, as in "I'll see if I can scrounge up some supper."

Shuck: take off.

Shucks: exclamatory term of regret, soft-core cuss word.

Smidgin: a little bit.

Splavocate: blow up, explode, as in "I thought he was going to splavocate when she told him she wanted a divorce."

Stand-offish: haughty.

Stove up: bedridden, too ill to work.

Sweet talk: convince someone through flattery.

Swig: a gulp of drink, as in "Give me a swig of your Co-Cola."

Tacky: in bad taste, tawdry.

Tote: carry.

Traipse: trudge around, wander, as in "Odell had me traipsing all over town looking for that rocking chair."

Tuckered out: tired, exhausted.

Tump over: knock over, fall over.

LESSONS IN LOCUTION

Or how to get your point across, Southern Style.

As naked as a jaybird.
As crazy as a bedbug.
As dead as a doornail.
As mean as a snake.
As thin as a rail.
As ugly as homemade sin.
As sharp as a tack.
As smart as a whip.

As blind as a bat.
As right as rain.
As crazy as a loon.
As ugly as a mud fence.
As mad as a hornet.
As wet as a drowned rat.
As limp as a dishrag.
As dry as a bone.

So ugly a train would jump the tracks.
Looks like something the cat drug in (bedraggled).
All bent out of shape; fit to be tied (angry, frustrated).
Like a chicken with its head cut off; all in a flap (agitated to the point of distraction).
Like a bat out of hell (in a hellfire hurry).
Get up a head of steam (work up momentum).
As rough as a cob (uncouth, roughneck).
As high as a cat's back (expensive).
As tight as a tick (miserly).
As scarce as hen's teeth.
Got a lot of gall (bold, presumptuous).

Fix his clock (retaliate).
My hind foot; in a pig's eye (I emphatically object).
In a coon's age; in a month of Sundays (a long time).
Down in the mouth (sad, despondent).
Like a duck on a June bug (without hesitation).
Stuck between a rock and a hard place (in a no-win situation).
Called on the carpet; taken to task (reprimanded).
He'd do to ride the river with (is reliable, trustworthy).
All by my lonesome.
Done done (finished).

THE USE OF *UP* IN SOUTHLAND SPEECH

That Southerners use the word *y'all* as if there was no tomorrow is not a revelation to most people. But you might be surprised to learn that we're partial to attaching the word *up* to our figures of speech. If you're around a Southerner, you'll hear what we mean in no time at all, since we like to tack the word onto the end of all sorts of verbs.

Sure, it's superfluous and has nothing to do with direction, but we just happen to like the comfortable homespun feeling it adds to our speech. Listen up to what we mean: "I'm going to fix us up some supper." "He needs someone to carry him up to the schoolhouse." "Those flowers sure did brighten up my day." "Get on up here, boy, before I break off your leg and beat you over the head with it." "Call up the office and tell them I'm running slow."

To speak Southern Style authentically, you'll need to spice up your speech with an occasional *up*. It's a subtle, but genuine, way to bring your speech up to par in Dixie.

TO TURN A PHRASE AND TELL A TALE IN DIXIE

Whether on podium, pulpit, printed page, stump, or street corner, Southerners are masters of rhetoric. Have been, too, for centuries.

Don't forget, many of our nation's Founding Fathers and patriots were outspoken Southerners. The Bible Belt, of course, was stretched across the Southland with the impassioned exhortations of fundamentalist preachers. The Civil Rights movement was cradled in black southern churches, whose ministers inspired the making of history.

Our gifted southern storytellers have enchanted millions the world over, transforming one of our most plentiful natural resources into art. A classic example of art imitating life in Dixie follows:

Maycomb was an old town, but it was a tired old town when I first knew it. In rainy weather the streets turned to red slop; grass grew on the sidewalks, the courthouse sagged in the square. Somehow, it was hotter then: a black dog suffered on a summer's day; bony mules hitched to Hoover carts flicked flies in the sweltering shade of the live oaks on the square. Men's stiff collars wilted by nine in the morning. Ladies bathed before noon, after their three o'clock naps, and by nightfall were like soft teacakes with frostings of sweat and sweet talcum.

—Harper Lee, *To Kill a Mockingbird.*

Should this illustration merely whet your appetite, you can find plenty more opportunities to savor our linguistic folk art in Dixie, including:

The National Storytelling Festival, Jonesboro, Tennessee.

Every October practitioners gather in the Appalachian mountains to perpetuate the fine art of storytelling. For three days, the South's oral tradition becomes a festival of living history and folklore as stories are swapped to the delight of eager audiences.

The National Storytelling Festival, Jonesborough, Tennessee.

Southern literature.

Southern writers know no equal in their prowess with the narrative style, and we've an abundance of evidence to prove our claim. For classic examples (to name but a very few), read the works of William Faulkner, Eudora Welty, Flannery O'Connor, Thomas Wolfe, Truman Capote, Taylor Caldwell, or Walker Percy. (See "Voices of the Southern Experience" in chapter 4.)

Churches.

The oral tradition is so embedded in the southern psyche that even the staidest of religious denominations are flavored with linguistic morsels during the delivery of the sermon. In many fundamentalist churches (particularly rural ones), rhetorical form is as important as content. To folks of these persuasions, dramatic oratory is regularly dished up in generous helpings.

Government.

Anyone who's ever attended a session of a southern state legislature, or even a hearing in town hall, knows that a podium affects a Southerner like waving a red flag does a bull. Given our innate tendency to loquacity and our belief that eloquence is a God-given gift, you can imagine how we relish speaking our piece to a captive audience.

Prattle.

Our proclivity to prattle at will is sometimes derided by critics as "garrulity," "stream of consciousness garble," or, at worst, "diarrhea of the mouth." This is hardly a kind thing to say about one of our favorite forms of self-expression. Agreed, prattle is by nature verbose and its content frequently inconsequential. But it *is* extraordinarily useful to its many practitioners. Not only is prattle a pleasant pastime and cheap entertainment, it's a reliable way to get things off our chests and to keep our jaws limber. Not bad, considering the price of admission.

WHAT'S IN A NAME DOWN SOUTH

What's in a name? Well, if your name is Betty Sue, Etta Faye, Leola, Vernell, Clyde, Skeeter, or the like, there's not a shadow of a doubt that there's some classic Southern Style in it. Or if you live in a town with a name such as Hard Cash, Hot Coffee, Midnight, Piney Woods, Ozone, Smut Eye, Hushpuckena, or Slapout, there's purely no mistaking that you live in Dixie.

Just as we Southerners are known for our gracious manners and distinctive style of speech, we're no less known for our singular names. Mind you, not all Southerners possess a classically southern-style name, but you can be darn sure that somebody in their family does. And likely as not, at least one of them lives in a town with a name that indisputably belongs in the Southland.

Southland names are one more way we pledge allegiance to the Southland. They're as much a deep-down part of Dixie as kudzu, grits, and 'possums—and equally as unique.

NAME CALLING, SOUTHERN-STYLE

Since we Southerners love to savor the flavor of our words, naturally the same goes for our names (you must agree, names like Edwina or Joella *do* have a lyrical ring to them). And since our names go with us to our graves, it only makes sense that we like the way they sound. Kindly regarded names include:

Double First Names.

Always a popular option for either sex, both the first name (usually two syllables) and middle name (usually one syllable) are used in combination: Billy Wayne, David Earl, Tommy Lee, Jimmy Bob, Clara Jean, Edna Rae, Sadie Ruth, Pamela Georgeann, Nettie Mae, and Mary Margaret.

A and E names.

An amazing number of southern names end with a long *a* or *e* sound. Since Southerners have a penchant for ending their sentences with a lilt, this phenomenon is understandable. Examples: Maudie, Odessa, Loretta, Sadie, Lela, Hattie, Petie, Grady, Jonita, Alma, Leola, Jessie, Lanny, Willie, Callie, Ruby, Ida, Cassie, and, of course, Melanie, and Ashley.

Bible Names.

A standard source for southern names and a favorite of our older generations: Beulah, Esther, Joanna, Mark, Ruth, Obed, John, Seth, James, Mary, Martha, Rachel, Andrew, and Caleb.

Multi-generational Names.

Southern women make the same statement as men do with *junior* and *III* after their names, only with a more downhome approach. The grandmother adds *Big* to her name (as in Big Mary Elizabeth), the mother goes by the given name (Mary Elizabeth), and the granddaughter gets *Little* in front of her name (yep, as in Little Mary Elizabeth).

Initials.

Southern males, particularly those who share at least one name in common with their daddies, often elect to be known by the initials of their first two names, as in J. B., R. A., or K. T.

Surnames As First Names.

A popular choice for old-line southern families. Parents bequeath their little ones with family surnames for first names, a socially approved way to brag on the family tree. Examples: Mackey, Sage, Lee, Avery, Ashley, Stuart, Winn, Dale, Blakely, Lane, and Bolling.

Classic Down-South Names.

For some fitting examples of Southern Style at work, consider these classics: Myrtice, Lavinia, Ernest, Crystal, Luther, Shirlene, Eunice, Lester, Jonita, Everette, Buck, Lula, Loretha, Etta Faye, Bernice, Buddy, and Bubba (the last two, our famous corruptions of the word *brother*).

Terms of Endearment.

Sugar puddin', precious lamb, darlin', cuteness, honey child, sweetness, and sweet thing.

NAME THAT TOWN

Clearly our southern ancestors had a fair share of whimsy when they named our towns; there are more memorable place names across Dixie than Quaker has oats. Some of the best examples of their handiwork, below, should give you more than an eyeful of evidence.

Back-to-Nature-and-Beyond Names.

Muscadine, Petal, Leaf, Grapevine, Tomato, Dewy Rose, Pine Log, Burnt Corn, Pearl, Duck Hill, Turtletown, Hill, Locust Grove, Doe Hill, Bat Cave, Burnt Corn, Turkey Creek, Birdsnest, Flat Rock, Cut Off, Big Flat, Oil Trough, Talking Rock, Six Mile, and Ten Mile.

Biblical and Inspirational Names.

Shiloh, Goshen, Antioch, Corinth, Uriah, Joppa, Beulah, Mordecai, Berea, Friendship, Benevolence, Reliance, Faith, Grace, Excel, Learned, Fair Play, Harmony, Success, and Prosperity.

Just Plain Strange Names.

Eclectic, Normal, Enigma, Nuttsville, Chance, Ball Ground, Hytop, Experiment, Ty Ty, Pooler, Iuka, Kokomo, Lux, Nitta Yuma, Whynot, Soso, Many, Iota, Eastabuchie, Davy Crockett, Ivanhoe, Hortense, Old Joe, Apex, Climax, Hustle, Ether, Husk, Stem, Shongaloo, Jigger, Mayo, Peedee, Finger, Bland, Gore, Nail, Trussville, Extension, Dry Prong, Smackover, and Frankewing.

Chapter Four

Made in Dixie

There's a whole slew of things, places, and faces that we make a proud claim to in the Southland (plus a few we make do with). Not only are they the sights and sounds of life, Southern Style, we're happy to note that they're often a slice of life, American style—probably more often than you ever imagined.

To see for yourself what this bragging is all about, keep on reading. We predict you'll be mightily impressed once you see for yourself what it means to be made in Dixie. So welcome to our southern world as God made it and we've arranged it.

THE GOD-GIVEN AND THE GOD-FORSAKEN

GOD-GIVEN

Magnolia blossom.

Magnolias.

The quintessence of the Old South, *Magnolia grandiflora* is a native Southerner. Each summer, when the large, milky white blossoms of this broadleaf evergreen unfold and fill the air with their sweet fragrance, folks all over Dixie lapse into momentary states of euphoria, nostalgia, and blissful content.

Dogwood blossom.

Dogwoods.

A blooming dogwood is a Southerner's assurance that spring has indeed arrived. For some southern cities (most notably, Knoxville, Atlanta, and Birmingham), the rites of spring focus upon a Dogwood Festival, celebrated midst a fairyland profusion of white and pink dogwoods. Dogwoods have assumed a place in Bible Belt lore, too; their four-petal blossoms are viewed as a timely symbol of Jesus' crucifixion.

Azaleas.

Phooey on those scrawny bushes outside the Southland that masquerade as azaleas. You have to come to the Southland to see how God intended azaleas to look, and there's no better location than the acidic soil of the South's coastal plains. In cities like Mobile, Alabama, or Wilmington, North Carolina, azalea mania takes over each spring as massive banks of pink and fuschia flowers transform the landscapes. In Mobile, a pink stripe is even painted on a thirty-seven-mile route of streets with the showiest arrays.

Spanish moss.

Spanish Moss.

Sightings of Spanish moss, those grey, tufted strands that languidly hang from trees in warmer southern climes, tend to have the same effect on Southerners as magnolia blooms. Spanish moss compels you to cease all activity in favor of a nap under its host tree and to thank the good Lord you're a Southerner. Even its name is mysteriously romantic; so who

cares that Spanish moss is not a moss at all, but a member
of the pineapple family?

Kentucky Bluegrass.

The mere mention of those two words gets plenty of
Southerners plumb excited. Kentucky Bluegrass bespeaks
an idyllic region and lifestyle, of southern gentry and gentility. The Bluegrass means rolling, grassy hills tinted a
bluish hue in springtime, white-fenced pastures, the thrill
of horse breeding and racing at its finest, and the pride of
these Southerners who call it home.

Pecans.

The nutmeat of the *Carya olivaeformis* tree, native to the
Southland, is a favorite treat of folks everywhere. What
would life be without pralines, pecan pie, and fruitcakes, to
name but a few of the delights it's inspired? Hopefully,
you're lucky enough to have a pecan tree in your yard or
know someone who does. If you're out of luck, then run
over to the closest co-op or farmers' market in the fall or
place your mail order with pecan growers in the Deep South
(see chapter 6).

Pecans.

Tobacco.

The New World explorers weren't long in discovering the
pleasurable properties of this southern nightshade plant.
Since then, consuming tobacco has been a popular vice the
world over. Some forms are largely consumed in Dixie;
many a southern granny and grandpappy have been fond of
a pinch of snuff ("to clear the mind"), while a plug of chewing tobacco is a close friend to many a good old boy. The
first southern aristocracy was born from the profits of growing tobacco, and it's an enterprise in which the Southland
still leads the pack worldwide (so to speak).

Tobacco harvest.

Cotton.

Even though cotton isn't native to the Southland and we
no longer lead the nation in its cultivation, at one time cotton was king in Dixie and altered the course of our history.
The South's long growing season, the invention of the cotton gin (by a Yankee in Georgia), and worldwide demand
for cotton textiles put the South on the map as a nineteenth-
century exporter and poured millions of dollars into the

King cotton.

plantation economy (at the height of the antebellum period, over half of the nation's millionaires were cotton-rich Southerners). However, the wealth was controlled by relatively few and at the cost of freedom for many. King Cotton was reined in by the War, later again by the Great Depression and the boll weevil. Unless you're traversing the Mississippi Delta, don't count on seeing endless cotton fields in Dixie these days. Maybe you should look for soybeans instead.

GOD-FORSAKEN

Kudzu.

Kudzu is an everpresent reminder to Southerners that sometimes even we can have too much of a good thing. About fifty years ago, the Oriental weed kudzu was hailed as the panacea for widespread soil erosion in Dixie. The erosion was checked, but the kudzu spread like wildfire over hill and dale and anything else in its path. The result is now a common sight in the Southland: ghostly topiary gardens of kudzu, where the vines have blanketed hillsides and enveloped structures. With a growth rate of up to sixty feet a season, you'd be wise not to stand still too long if you're close to kudzu.

Kudzu gone hog wild.

Fire Ants.

Since its stowaway arrival on a Mobile-bound freighter in 1918, this aggressive pest has steadily infested southern lands. Most Southerners have learned the hard way that dis-

---

Dixie Vermin

Chiggers (Redbugs) • Gnats
Yellow Flies • Mosquitoes • Fire Ants
Roaches (Palmetto Bugs) • Ticks

---

turbing the fire ants' formidable mounds will provoke the wrathful stings of several members of their 150,000- or so strong colonies. With so many of the tenacious little buggers now settled across the Southland, the fire ant is forever a resident of Dixie. Watch your step.

Roaches.

It's our warm and humid climate that enables cockroaches to grow large (up to two inches) and in great abundance in Dixie. Sometimes delicately called "palmetto bugs" by Southerners, roaches invariably are residents of even the most well-kept southern households. Predictably, they make their appearances at socially inopportune times; but nothing short of torching a house will deter them (you can *forget* total extermination). House guests who spot a venturesome cockroach in a Dixie household are advised to grin and ignore the matter.

Climate.

Sometimes the summer heat and humidity in Dixie becomes a sight uncomfortable, even for us Southerners. It gets pretty hot (expect afternoon highs to reach at least 90°) and mighty humid (coastal cities average over 80 percent humidity in the early mornings) during that long summer stretch. Since we prefer bare feet to cold any day of the week, we've learned to manage just fine. Besides, we reap our rewards with a very long crop-growing season, and when winter finally does arrive, we can rest assured it won't wear out its welcome.

THE DIVINELY INSPIRED

SOUTHLAND LEGENDS

Gone with the Wind.

It took Atlanta newspaper reporter Peggy Mitchell nearly ten years to complete her epic tale of the fall of the Old South and its painful rejuvenation. Were it not for the urging of her associates, a visiting New York book publisher in search of the Great Southern Novel would never have learned of her manuscript. The rest is history—of the grandest kind.

Six months after its June 30, 1936, publication, an astounding million copies of *Gone with the Wind* had been sold, despite its then unheard of price of three dollars (many folks pooled their change to afford a pass-around

Vivian Leigh as Scarlett O'Hara.

copy of the novel). By May of the following year, Margaret Mitchell had been awarded the Pulitzer Prize for her 1,037-page masterpiece and Hollywood was well on its way to create the motion picture version. The world's perception of the Southland had become forever intertwined with the greatest selling American novel of its time.

SOUTHLAND LOWDOWN ON *GONE WITH THE WIND*

Not only is *Gone with the Wind* one of the best sellers of all time, many of its admirers believe it's also one of the most misunderstood. Commonly thought to be a dramatic eulogy for the antebellum South, it *did* indeed look back. But Margaret Mitchell's *Gone with the Wind* was more a command to look forward to a New South, with a new culture and new traditions.

Her message was personified in the quandary of Scarlett O'Hara who, like many Southerners, was torn between her ties to the Old South (symbolized by Tara and Ashley Wilkes) and her will to move onward and upward. Scarlett O'Hara did manage to overcome her circumstances, but she had to cast aside the old ways to do it and she paid a price to do so.

Through *Gone with the Wind*, Peggy Mitchell advised the twentieth-century Southland to do the same, but she didn't win many converts. It was a distant notion for most of the book's far-flung audience, and needless to say, the Old Guard was less than enthusiastic about taking her advice (and from one of its own, no less).

COCA-COLA.

No product is more widely sold or recognized in the entire world than Coca-Cola, whose origin lies in the heart of the New South. About two billion ounces of the beverage are consumed daily in over 135 countries; its parent company spends over $150 million annually to advertise Coca-Cola and its sister beverages. Originally concocted in 1886 by Atlanta pharmacist John Pemberton (in a kettle in his back yard) for sale at soda fountains, the Coca-Cola business was bought out five years later by another pharmacist and entrepreneur, Asa Candler, for a total investment of $2,300. Mr. Candler knew what to do with a good thing when he saw it. By 1919 his family was able to sell the business for twenty-five million dollars.

Coca-Cola tray, 1910.

Despite turn-of-the-century flap about the presence of cocaine in its formula (small traces were found until 1905), Coca-Cola has long been a symbol of the wholesome, all-

Advertisement for Coca-Cola, 1914.

American life. Bottling plants accompanied American troops (at General Eisenhower's request) during World War II to boost soldier morale. Coca-Cola's advertising has mirrored America's culture almost as long as it has been around (who could forget the "Mean Joe Green" commercial?). Behind the wholesome product, however, is a very sophisticated parent company and bottler network that takes an aggressive stance to defy competitors (especially archrival Pepsi-Cola) and imitators ("spies" from the company's Trade Research Department test the product in all corners of the world to "protect its integrity" as the Real Thing).

WHEN COKE LOST ITS FIZZ

A few summers ago the Coca-Cola Company got tangled up in its own britches: It shelved master Formula 7X for a new one. New Coke had arrived; "Old" Coke was gone. Despite the big ballyhoo created for its advent, it was hardly an auspicious debut. In less than three months an outraged public and dismal sales of the New Coke had convinced company executives to revive the much-loved Coke of old. New Coke, a hopeful head-on competitor for the smoother tasting Pepsi, was quickly flanked by its predecessor, to the audible relief of Coke bottlers and consumers. A sacred slice of Americana had been returned, but only after its parent corporation had eaten a big serving of crow.

Coca-Cola coupon, 1890s.

Grand Ole Opry.

The Southland is the birthplace of country music, and without a doubt the Grand Ole Opry is country music's cradle and homestead. From its 1925 start as the "WSM Barn Dance" in Nashville (when eighty-year-old Uncle Jimmy Thompson played fiddle for an hour to his niece Eva's piano accompaniment), the Opry has been the world's longest-running live radio show. Performers like Roy Acuff, Minnie Pearl, Hank Williams, Patsy Cline, George Jones, Buck Owens, Dolly Parton, Tammy Wynette, and Johnny Cash have entertained millions of loyal listeners each Saturday evening with the strains of country music and its musical cousins.

The Ryman Auditorium, homeplace of the Grand Ole Opry.

From 1943 to 1974, disciples of the Opry filled the hard wooden pews of Ryman Auditorium, a former gospel tabernacle; the Opry now convenes in the modern Grand Ole Opry House at Opryland USA's fancy complex, also home base for a 120-acre theme park, a hotel, and The Nashville Network's television facilities.

Bourbon Whiskey.

Bourbon is the South's own firewater and has been for over 350 years since early Virginia settlers brewed corn and maize to lift their homesick spirits. Three years before Kentucky was admitted to the Union in 1789, the Reverend Elijah Craig was distilling corn whiskey there; eighty years later, Tennessean Jack Daniels took the whole process one step further, with charcoal mellowing the amber liquid to create Tennessee sour mash whiskey and allowing a somewhat smoother sip.

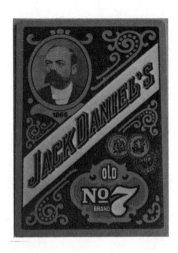

Whether you're high-class, good old folk, or white trash, if you're southern and you drink hard liquor, you love whiskey. Whiskey drinking is firmly fixed in southern culture. Some even liken bourbon, in its brash and vigor, to the South itself. We won't disagree.

Mint Juleps.

Is there a libation more southern than the genteel mint julep? No, least not one that isn't drunk straight from the bottle. And isn't it true that all we do down South is sit on the veranda and sip our mint juleps? No, but it is true that you can buy them at the mint julep concession when you attend the Kentucky Derby. As for concocting them at home, recipes abound, all variations on a legendary theme. Should you not have one committed to memory, this recipe should put some genuine South in your mouth:

ORIGINAL KENTUCKY MINT JULEP RECIPE

Put 12 springs fresh mint in bowl, cover with powdered sugar and just enough water to dissolve the sugar. Crush with wooden pestle. Place half the crushed mint and liquid in the bottom of a crackled glass tumbler or in sterling silver tankard. Fill glass half full of finely crushed ice. Add rest of crushed mint and fill remainder of glass with crushed ice. Pour in whiskey until glass is brimming. Place in ice box for at least an hour (preferably two or three hours, if you can wait that long). Decorate with sprigs of mint covered with powered sugar when ready to serve.

—reprinted with permission from *The Cooking Book*, The Junior League of Louisville

Southern Living *Magazine.*

Every coffee table worth its salt in Dixie carries an issue of *Southern Living* magazine, the monthly house, garden, and travel epistle "For people who love the South." *Southern Living* is an institution of high regional regard; it's Southern Gentility in print. Conservative, refined, traditional, and never controversial, it exudes faith and confidence in Southernness and serves a guide to southern pursuits ("The Long and Short of Okra," "Riding in the Ozarks").

The magazine is such an unavowed success (now over 2.2 million prosperous subscribers) that Time, Inc., purchased it and its sister publications (including *Progressive Farmer*) in 1985. The Yankee purchase prompted warnings of cancelled subscriptions by a few worried Southerners, but fortunately this is one thing Northerners have had the good sense to leave be.

Country Hams.
What the Virginia settlers learned from the Indians about dry-curing meat soon became one of the Southland's best-known gastronomic pleasures: country hams. By rubbing pork with salt and smoking it, the colonists built a savory, 350-year-old tradition that is to this day admired and revered. Although some rural Southerners still cure their own hams (including "Today" show weatherman Willard Scott), most of the delicacies come from a handful of respected producers. Highest on the hog of branded hams are those from Smithfield, Virginia (law requires that they are produced within the city limits), where four makers supply these famous smoked hams with the long-cut shanks.

Some ham makers swear by the smoking process (especially in humid coastal locations), using hardwoods such as apple, oak, and hickory; but around the Appalachians they vow that's just a lot of hot air. In either case, there's no ham like a southern country ham, and no breakfast like a southern breakfast with country ham and biscuits.

Tennessee Walking Horses.

The horse with the springy "rocking chair" canter is the pride and joy of Middle Tennessee. Bred for over 100 years, the high-stepping, over-stepping Tennessee Walking Horse once provided plantation owners with a fast and comfortable ride over long distances; today, forest rangers and the Canadian Mounted Police follow suit. Most of these agreeable, dignified pleasure horses are bred and trained around Shelbyville, Tennessee, home of the Tennessee Walking Horse National Celebration (late August) when over 1,600 walkers perform. The International Grand Championship in nearby Murfreesboro (early August) kicks off the annual excitement for the distinguished Tennessee Walking Horse's devotees.

Tabasco Sauce.

The little bottle and its fiery contents have been relished worldwide for over 120 years. In befitting style, Tabasco sauce has lived an exotic life, lending zest to meals during the excavation of the tomb of Tutankhamen and even on Skylab. The legend began on Avery Island in southern Louisiana when Edmund McIlhenny chopped a special variety of peppers, blended them with vinegar and salt, and then aged them in wooden barrels. From the first 350 bottles, Tabasco sauce was a success; within three years, the family had opened an office in London to handle foreign demand for the condiment. To this day Tabasco sauce remains a family proposition, and a distinguished one at that, as the McIlhennys are descended from twelfth U.S. President Zachary Taylor.

Cabbage Patch Kids.

Once upon a time there was a North Georgia good old boy named Xavier Roberts who stitched together some pudgy-faced, cuddly dollies. He called his friends the Little People and found adoptive homes for them. Very soon, children around the South were visiting Mr. Robert's Babyland General Hospital in Cleveland, Georgia, to adopt their very own Little People.

It wasn't long before a big toy maker decided that girls and boys all over the world should have Little People of their own to play with and love. The doll-babies' names

Cabbage Patch Kids dolls:
Cleveland, Georgia's greatest
claim to fame.

were changed to Cabbage Patch Kids, and the toy maker
found happy homes for over forty million of them. Not only
has this made lots of children very happy, it's made Mr.
Roberts, the toy maker, and other folks very wealthy.

Moon Pie.

If you're a Southerner you can't say *Moon Pie* without
grinning. First of all, even the name is amusing (inspired by
a salesman who declared the world needed a cookie that was
marshmallow, drenched in chocolate, and "as big as the
moon"). Second, the confection itself is a funny-looking,
hamburger-shaped thing made of cake, sugar, and marshmallow goo and coated in chocolate. Then there's the Moon
Pie's humble reputation to consider: together with an RC
Cola, it was once the down-south equivalent of a plowman's
lunch. These days, it's a plain-folk snack, pure and simple
and lip-smacking good.

Despite its less than glamorous image, the Moon Pie is
such a part of the Dixie heritage that Southerners are as
fond of them as Northerners are of bagels. So much, in fact,
that they've even made their way into Mardi Gras tradition,
when parading revelers toss armfuls of the sandwiches to
eager crowds who happily holler, "Moon Pie! Moon Pie!"

SOUTHLAND TRADITIONS

Mardi Gras.

America's own version of pre-Lenten carnival cuts loose for two weeks each year in two southern port cities, Mobile and New Orleans, culminating on Shrove (or "Fat") Tuesday (*mardi gras* in French). Schools and businesses close the last two days before Lent, when the final hours of misrule reach a frenzied climax of parades, balls, parties, and generally sanctioned misbehavior. Even the usually hard and fast codes of southern conduct are relaxed in the name of revelry, much of which occurs behind the anonymity of masks and costumes.

Residents of both cities regularly debate whose observance began first, but most will allow that the first Mardi Gras society was formed in Mobile in 1830 by a group of young and inebriated carousers who dubbed themselves "The Cowbellion de Rakin Society" in honor of their noisemakers (cowbells, rakes, hoes). In both cities citizens take full advantage of the event, toasting the joys of excess in anticipation of Lenten penance. If you've ever participated, you know for a fact that Mardi Gras gets real wild and crazy. It's a two-week party with the intensity of Saint Patrick's Day and the Super Bowl combined.

At the heart of the Mardi Gras tradition are the socially-elite mystic societies (the older, the greater their prestige),

Mardi Gras mystiks on parade, Mobile, Alabama.

whose parades entertain thousands of revelers. Their courts—kings and queens, knights, ladies in waiting, and so forth, who are presented in regal coronations—represent the cities' oldest and most prominent families.

MARDI GRAS LEXICON

Words every reveler should know.

Krewe/Crewe: Refers to a carnival organization (also called a mystic society) and its merrymaking membership. The idea was inspired by a John Milton mask play and first used by New Orleans's Mystick Krewe of Comus in 1857.

Bal masque: Masquerade ball. Every bona fide mystic society has one. Only members have the privilege of wearing costumes and masks. Dress for guests (invitation only) is *de rigueur,* ball gowns for ladies, white tie and tails for men, without exception.

Tableau: A dramatic scene assembled for use at a Mardi Gras ball, coronation, or parade float. Tableaux usually reflect a given theme, such as "Land of Make Believe," which has been selected by its mystic society for a particular year.

Dasante: Dinner dance given in honor of Mardi Gras royalty. Imagine a seated wedding dinner *sans* bride and groom and with a king and queen and Mardi Gras theming instead. Need we say more?

Serpentine: Colorful fettucini-thin streamers of paper which come in rolls and are unfurled in great quantities at Mardi Gras parades and celebrations.

Doubloon: Coins that bear the insignia of a given mystic society and are tossed by their float-riding members to parade-goers.

Flambeaux: Kerosene-fueled torches that are carried by lackeys to light the routes of night parades (artificial lighting is considered bad form).

The Masters.

The enduring legacy of southern gentleman and golf great Bobby Jones is the Masters Golf Tournament. Played each April at the Augusta (Georgia) National Golf Club, the Masters began as an invitation tournament for Mr. Jones and a few of his buddies and is the only pro golf tournament to be played annually in the same location. The Masters has always been peerless. But considering that Bobby Jones and cohort Clifford Roberts were experienced savants of Southern Style, it was inevitable that the Masters would become synonymous with golf's finest.

Its course design has become a world standard for both challenge and beauty, and the most respected names in golf and society comprise its membership (even former President Dwight Eisenhower had a cottage on the grounds). No sporting event is more genteel than the Masters, where gentlemanly protocol and southern hospitality have made all the difference for the game of golf.

The Kentucky Derby.

The world again looks southward (this time in Louisville, Kentucky) on the first Saturday each May, when the prestigious Run for the Roses kicks off the Triple Crown of horse racing. Modeled after the Epson Derby in England, the venerable Kentucky Derby has run with a high profile since 1875, and you can bet your last wager that Kentuckians intend never to lose this distinction. To the horse-racing community, the one-and-one-half-mile race is the penultimate test of mettle for three-year-old colts. To the Bluegrass State, it's a claim to fame *par excellence.*

To race-goers, the Derby is the undisputed crown social event. If your bluegrass roots are also blue-blooded, you can watch the event from Millionaire's Row atop the clubhouse and rub elbows in high style. If your social standing doesn't qualify you for the boxes or grandstand, you can still attend the race, as long as you're willing to share the infield with more than 70,000 other Derby goers and arrive for the five p.m. event nine or ten hours early.

Annual "run for the roses" at the Kentucky Derby.

SOUTHLAND LEGACIES

LEGACY #1: MUSIC-MAKING IN DIXIE.

When the Good Lord measured out musical inspiration, he must have dropped the bucket on the Southland, because we've certainly grown a bumper crop of musical traditions in Dixie. Surely nowhere else on this earth can rightly claim to be the birthplace of so many kinds of music, especially with such widespread appeal. We Southerners are naturally pleased to own this distinction, and we gladly put our money where our mouths are.

The music made in Dixie is the music of Everyman, the kind you can clap your hands to, tap your feet to, sway to, and maybe shed a tear to. You don't have to get too gussied up to listen to it, and you don't have to put on cultured airs (save them for when the symphony is in town). You just have to listen and enjoy yourself, maybe even join right in.

We Southerners are definitely old hands at making music, and no wonder. Our musical heritage came along with our forebears to the Southland. With so many musically minded cultures settling across Dixie, it was inevitable that we'd have enough songs in our hearts to beat the band, as the following will attest:

Traditional Folk Music.

The folk music of the Southland hails from our Scottish-Irish and English ancestors, who settled in the mountains of the upland South. There, folk music came to be truly a family affair. Stories were handed down in ballads like "Barbara Allen" and "Pretty Polly" to fiddle and dulcimer accompaniments, while good old fiddle tunes ("Sallie Gooden") enlivened the tradition. Today the heritage of folk music continues to be passed from one generation to the next. Its legacy rings loud and clear in another southern-grown musical style, country music.

Gospel music.

No old-time religion camp meeting was complete without plenty of harmonizing hymn singing, taught by traveling evangelists and singing-school teachers. To this day, gospel songfests abound across Dixie. Praising the Lord, gospel style, ranges from the traditional (old-time four-part hymns, anthems, and ballads) to the enthusiastic (call-and-response shouting) to the bluesy (spirituals). With the musical ministrations of gospel luminaries like the Speer Family, Mahalia Jackson, the Bill Gaither Trio, and Andre Crouch, gospel music has developed a large and faithful following, both inside and outside the Southland.

Cajun.

South Louisiana's Cajuns are known for their robust and expressive lifestyle, and that includes their music. A melting pot of French, Creole, Celtic, and Anglo-Saxon influences, Cajun music is usually played with an accordion ("squeeze box"), fiddle, and triangle. Sometimes you sing or whoop ("Aiyee!!"); sometimes you don't. But in either case, you most certainly dance to Cajun music, usually with a waltz or a two-step ("special"), and you should always *laissez les bons temps rouler* ("let the good times roll").

Blues.

W. C. Handy statue, Memphis, Tennessee.

The powerful, soulful blues form of music was born in the Mississippi Delta region, a legacy that evolved from plantation work calls and musical ballads. Southern blacks created and nurtured the blues, which recall the frustration and melancholy of life and love, past and present. It didn't take long for blues music to attract a die-hard audience, once the Father of the Blues, W. C. Handy, published such classics as "Memphis Blues" and blues singers like Ma Rainey and others were recorded. It's true that the growing blues culture picked up steam for a while in Chicago, but the best blues you'll ever hope to hear still comes from the Southland, most notably in Memphis and points southward on the Delta.

Jazz.

We wouldn't go so far as to claim that Dixie was the birthplace of jazz, since not even musicologists can precisely settle that trivia question. But we can rightly claim that jazz was pretty much made in Dixie, since the cradle of jazz was most certainly rocked in New Orleans and most of jazz's greatest names are Southerners. Surrounded by the varied musical cultures of the Crescent City—black work songs, spirituals, the music of France and Spain (both were former mother countries of New Orleans), blues, and rag-time—the jazz band assumed its sound and lineup (rhythm, brass, and reed instruments). Under the inspiration of jazz greats and Southerners all—King Oliver, "Jelly Roll" Morton, Louis Armstrong, Dizzy Gillespie, and Bessie Smith—it didn't take long for this musical form to gain international acclaim.

Country.

Country music is the southern psyche in song, our own homegrown style of storytelling and music-making with the southern experience written all over it. Country music was truly made in Dixie, the offspring of such southern musical parentage as folk music, early blues, vaudeville, parlor songs, and old-time religion. Led by its founding family, Virginia's Carter Family ("Will the Circle Be Unbroken?"), and the "Father of Country Music," Mississippi's Jimmie Rodgers, country music struck a familiar chord to its Dixie listeners. Once most Southerners could afford a radio or a Victrola, country music hit its stride and, by the 1930's, country music had taken the Southland, the Midwest, and the West by storm. Since then its appeal has built steadily and shows no sign of letting up.

FIVE OF THE BIGGEST-SELLING COUNTRY MUSIC SINGLES EVER

"Bouquet of Roses" (1948), by Eddy Arnold
"I'm Movin' On" (1950), by Hank Snow
"Sixteen Tons" (1955), by Tennessee Ernie Ford
"Crazy Arms" (1956), by Ray Price
"Stand by Your Man" (1968), by Tammy Wynette
courtesy of the Country Music Foundation

It's not surprising that more than 80 percent of all country—western radio stations are in the South and Southwest. Don't forget, darlin', those songs are *our* songs. You have to possess the down-South heritage to fully appreciate songs like "If You Don't Quit Checkin' on Me (I'm Checkin' Out on You)" or "Stand on My Own Two Knees," and you have to understand the country boy lifestyle, even if you don't affiliate. In a land where the American Dream runs as thick as fleas on a dog's back, country music stardom is proof positive that a good old boy or gal can do swell. By gumption, just look at what Loretta Lynn (the coal miner's daughter), Tammy Wynette (hairdresser), or Merle Haggard (mechanic) did with their God-given talents and a heck of a lot of determination, thanks to country music.

Bluegrass.

While today country music is pretty much an electrified, fancified version of its earlier forms, the old-time pickin' and fiddlin' music of hillbilly string bands has anything but faded away. It's been thriving as bluegrass music since the 1940s, when Kentucky mandolin player Bill Monroe (the "Father of Bluegrass Music") and Earl Scruggs, a North Carolina banjo picker, first put together the classic bluegrass sound: fiddle, rhythm guitar, bass, five-string banjo, and mandolin.

If you've not had the pleasure of hearing bluegrass music, just remember the theme to the television show "The Beverly Hillbillies," particularly the end, when nimble pickers Lester Flatt and Earl Scruggs really got wound up (that's called a breakdown). Then you'll know why folks refer to bluegrass as "country music in overdrive." Lively, infectious, and good, clean fun, bluegrass music is a favorite musical style in Dixie. Hear some for yourself at summertime bluegrass festivals all across the Southland (see chapter 9), and you'll be hooked.

Rock and Roll.

The roots of rock and roll are firmly planted in Dixie, reaching deep down into our black culture's rhythm and blues music. Southerners like Fats Domino and Little Richard crossed the then-steadfast color barrier with their gutsily controversial music and set the stage for rock and roll's official arrival in 1955, when Tupelo, Mississippi, truck driver Elvis Presley turned the music world on its ear with the national hit "Baby Let's Play House." From that day forward, rock and roll was here to stay, a dynamic derivative of rhythm and blues, country, and gospel music, all mainstays of the southern musical repertoire. Modern music has not been the same since.

ELVIS: "THE KING OF ROCK AND ROLL"

His gyrating hips created such a scandal that he was shown only from the waist up on the "Ed Sullivan Show," and his lyrics were equally suggestive to an audience more accustomed to Doris Day and Eddie Fisher. Both only fanned the fires of adoration by his teenaged fans. Almost single-handedly Elvis Presley put sex and spunk into mainstream radio and inspired musicians throughout America and Britain to do the same.

The King of Rock and Roll ruled the pop, country, and rhythm and blues airwaves in the mid-to-late '50s. Classic hits like "Hound Dog," "Heartbreak Hotel," and "Love Me Tender" sold over one billion records in his lifetime. Not bad for a thin-eared Mississippi boy who was born and raised to do without.

As the well-known story goes, Elvis's musical kingdom shrank as the King turned to making broad appeal pop music and white-bread movies (some Elvis students blame this on his manager Colonel Tom Parker). Despite a brief comeback ("In the Ghetto," "Suspicious Minds"), the King's domain was reduced to flashy Las Vegas-style shows across the heartland of America. The man who died in 1977 at age forty-two, apparently from complications caused by drug abuse, was but a bloated caricature of the young man who took the throne of musicdom.

SOUTHLAND LEGACY #2: SPEAKING OF THE SOUTH—
VOICES OF THE SOUTHERN
EXPERIENCE.

College students down South call it "grit lit." The more serious minded of us refer to it as the literature of the "Southern Renaissance" or the "Southern genre." What everybody is talking about—and has been for decades, now—is the highly acclaimed literary tradition of the twentieth-century Southland.

GRACELAND: HOME SHRINE OF THE KING

As far as the pop culture of the South-land is concerned, Elvis is as good as can-onized. Just pay a visit to the King's home, Graceland (in Memphis), along with over half a million others who arrive each year, to see what we mean.

In a Hollywood version of the southern plantation house pilgrimage, you can join throngs of reverent, die-hard Elvis fans for a tour of the mansion (filled with such arcana as giant stained-glass peacocks and a nine-foot grand piano covered in twenty-four-karat gold) and view his grave ("He was a precious gift from God") in the Meditation Garden. Be sure to take lots of Kleenex. Graceland is for grieving the loss of the King, and there's a lot of weeping and wailing and gnashing of teeth going on by despondent fans. End your mournful moments in the shops across the street from Graceland,

Graceland, home of Elvis Presley.

where you can soothe your aching heart with Elvis memorabilia (don't forget the Love Me Tender hair conditioner).

If you're a true fan of the King's, you've probably already been to Grace-land. If you've got some catching up to do, order your tickets now; you may have to wait a few months to get in.

Short stories, novels, poetry, and plays—some of the best ever written—were made in Dixie, as were their creators. A great many of these writers simply wrote of what they knew best: the southern experience, the good and the not-so-good, as it was then or as they see it today.

Understanding the South and Southerners isn't an easy thing to do, but you can make a lot more sense of the south-ern experience by listening to our voices of experience. We'll even get you started with our Suggested Grit Lit Reading List. Pick yourself a theme and see what some of us have had to say for ourselves.

Coming of Age in the South.

Young folk growing up in a changing South were often used as metaphors for the South's own coming of age. Read: Carson McCullers, *The Heart Is a Lonely Hunter;* Harper Lee, *To Kill a Mockingbird;* Thomas Wolfe, *Look Homeward, Angel;* Alice Walker, *The Color Purple.*

The Decaying South.

Themes of anguish and desolation, moral confusion, and social decay in the Southland. Read: Flannery O'Connor, *A Good Man Is Hard to Find and Other Short Stories;* Tennessee Williams, *A Streetcar Named Desire;* William Faulkner *Absalom, Absalom!*

Decadence, Eccentricity, and Other Controversial Subjects.

A taste of the wilder side of the Southland. Read: Erskine Caldwell, *Tobacco Road;* Tennessee Williams, *Cat on a Hot Tin Roof;* Florence King, *Southern Ladies and Gentlemen.*

Small-town and Rural South.

Recountings and re-creations of days forever gone in Dixie. Read: Eudora Welty, *The Wide Net;* Truman Capote, *Tree of Night;* Ferrol Sams, *Run with the Horseman;* Olive Ann Burns, *Cold Sassy Tree.*

The Glorified Good-Old-Boy Life.

Contemporary southern-fried ruminations by the quasi-Good Ole Boy set. Read: Lewis Grizzard, *Elvis Is Dead and I Don't Feel So Good Myself;* Roy Blount, Jr., *Crackers;* William Price Fox, *Chitlin Strut and Other Madrigals.*

SOUTHLAND LEGACY #3: THERE'S NO HOUSE LIKE THE BIG HOUSE—PLANTATION STYLE DOWN SOUTH.

We could go on till the cows come home about all the impressive architectural accomplishments of the Southland. From the likes of George Washington and Thomas Jefferson (architects of the new American republic) to John Portman (the premier architect of today's New South), the architectural imprints of Southerners are legion and legendary.

But without a doubt, the architecture that's nearest and dearest to our southern hearts is much closer to home, because home is where the heart is in Dixie. Just ask someone who's ever laid eyes on any of the palatial homes of the plantation South. They're deservedly the pride and joy of southern architecture.

This fancier side of southern living was born out of the glory days of farming and trading staple crops (like tobacco, indigo, rice, and cotton) when those few and fortunate folk who thusly accumulated their wealth often situated themselves in equally glorious accommodations.

Our ever-present southern sense of place has seen to it that many of these homes are still proudly standing across the Southland. So although you won't find Tara (which, as all Southerners know, never existed), you can still find plenty of resplendent mansions on view today, any of which would have equally well suited Miss Scarlett and her clan.

Greek Revival plantation homes.

If it's the Old South you're itching to see, you can't do better than a Greek Revival plantation mansion. Once you've seen any of these majestic manor houses, you'll know why Greek Revival style was especially trendy during the early-to-mid nineteenth century among the Deep

Houmas House was the setting of the movie, *Hush Hush, Sweet Charlotte.*

South's wealthiest planters. A sampling of our many stand-outs includes:

- *Dunleith,* Natchez, Mississippi (c. 1856, National Historic Landmark).
- *Gaineswood,* Demopolis, Alabama (1843–1861).
- *Houmas House,* Burnside, Louisiana (1840, National Register of Historic Places).
- *John Thomas Grant House,* Athens, Georgia (1857–1859).
- *Sturdivant Hall,* Selma, Alabama (1853, National Register).

Oakley House. It was here that houseguest John James Audubon painted 32 of his celebrated "Birds of America" works.

"Cottage" Plantation Homes.

Before there was Greek Revival grandeur, there was the less formal, but still distinguished, cottage style of plantation home. In fact, cottage-style plantation houses are more native to Dixie in their design than their grandiose successors. Designed to cope with muggy and buggy coastal climates, these wood-framed homes typically were raised off the ground and featured high ceilings, many tall windows, and expansive open-air verandahs across the front and back. The grandest include:

- *Rosedown*, St. Francisville, Louisiana (1835).
- *Oakley House*, St. Francisville, Louisiana (1799).
- *Fripp Plantation*, Beaufort, South Carolina (c. 1800).

"Traditional-style" Estate Homes.

The founding fathers of the South's plantation and land-owning society often reinterpreted Old World architectural styles (Georgian or Palladian) for their estate homes. Theirs were the homesteads of the *real* Old South—the family seats of those settling colonists who helped found and govern the southern states—and should not be confused, as those who are sticklers for accuracy will point out, with the nouveau riche palaces of first-generation antebellum planters who had only recently made good. So there.

Distinguished examples of these traditional-style ancestral homes include:

- *Berkeley Plantation*, Charles City, Virginia (1726).
- *Westover*, Charles City County, Virginia (1730–1734).
- *Drayton Hall*, Charleston County, South Carolina (1742).
- *Carnton*, Franklin, Tennessee (1826, National Historic Landmark).

Berkeley Plantation, the ancestral home of two U.S. presidents, William Henry Harrison and Benjamin Harrison.

SONS AND DAUGHTERS OF THE SOUTHLAND

The Dixie roll call of giants among men and women is so long it would make you late for your own funeral if you listened to it all. That's because Southerners were making a name for themselves even before the United States had a name of its own (if you think this sounds a little bigheaded, then talk to a Virginian).

Remember, we Southerners are taught early on that we're supposed to amount to something (heaven help you if you're a low-down, good-for-nothing lazy sack of bones; you should know better), so no wonder so many of us have done just that. No wonder the list keeps getting longer every day.

To prove that we're anything but all talk and no action, we're naming names. They belong to the homefolk of today who've made a name for themselves and, in the spirit of fairness, a few whose names are mud.

FAMOUS FACES OF THE SOUTHLAND.

They look as familiar as the back of your hand, but did you know they were born down South?

Claude Akins (Nelson, Georgia)
Kim Basinger (Athens, Georgia)
Warren Beatty (Richmond)
David Brinkley (Wilmington, North Carolina)
Nell Carter (Birmingham)
Fanny Flagg (Fairhope, Alabama)
Henry Gibson (Fairhope, Alabama)
Ava Gardner (Smithfield, North Carolina)
Andy Griffith (Mount Airy, North Carolina)
Bryant Gumble (New Orleans)
Kitty Carlisle Hart (New Orleans)
Tish Hooker (Nashville)
Kate Jackson (Birmingham)
James Earl Jones (Tate County, Mississippi)
DeForrest Kelley (Atlanta)
Dorothy Lamour (New Orleans)
Sondra Locke (Shelbyville, Tennessee)
Shirley MacLaine (Richmond)

Gerald McRaney (Collins, Mississippi)
Mary Ann Mobley (Brandon, Mississippi)
Ben Murphy (Jonesboro, Arkansas)
Patricia Neal (Packard, Kentucky)
Bert Parks (Atlanta)
Burt Reynolds (Waycross, Georgia)
Nipsey Russell (Atlanta)
Dianne Sawyer (Glasgow, Kentucky)
George C. Scott (Wise, Virginia)
Cybill Shepherd (Memphis)
Stella Stevens (Yazoo City, Mississippi)
Jim Varney (Lexington, Kentucky)
Vanna White (Myrtle Beach, South Carolina)
Oprah Winfrey (Kosciuscko, Mississippi)
Joanne Woodward (Thomasville, Georgia)

Do You Know Your Southern Celebrities' Claims to Fame?

1. He's best known as "Bones," the physician of *Star Trek* fame.
2. She made it sexy to be over forty and to have grey hair.
3. Everybody knows him as Earnest, Vern's friend.
4. This former "Laugh-in" star was a country music singer in Robert Altman's film *Nashville*.

(Answers on page 94)

MUSIC MAKERS.

You're sure to know their music, but did you know from whence they came in Dixie?

Alabama: Jim Nabors, the group Alabama, Lionel Ritchie, Hank Williams, Tammy Wynette, and Emmylou Harris.
Arkansas: Glen Campbell, Johnny Cash, and Al Green.
Georgia: Ray Charles, Gladys Knight, Jessye Norman, Little Richard, Jerry Reed, and the bands REM and The B-52's.
Kentucky: Don and Phil Everly, Bill Monroe, and the Judds.

Louisiana: Louis Armstrong, Van Cliburn, Fats Domino, Al Hirt, and Mahalia Jackson.

Mississippi: Jimmy Buffett, Jerry Clower, Bo Diddley, W. C. Handy, B. B. King, Leontyne Price, Charlie Pride, Jimmie Rodgers, Conway Twitty, and Muddy Waters.

North Carolina: Charlie Daniels, Donna Fargo, Roberta Flack, and Randy Travis.

South Carolina: Dizzy Gillespie.

Tennessee: Roy Acuff, Chet Atkins, James Brown, Aretha Franklin, Amy Grant, Loretta Lynn, Dolly Parton, Bessie Smith, and Kitty Wells.

Virginia: Pearl Bailey, the Carter Family, June Carter, Roy Clark, Patsy Cline, Ella Fitzgerald, Wayne Newton, and Kate Smith.

TRAIL BLAZERS AND TRENDSETTERS.

They're some of today's biggest thinkers, and they're from the South. Even if you don't recognize all their names, we bet you'll recognize how they made a name for themselves.

James Earl ("Jimmy") Carter (Plains, Georgia): Former peanut farmer, Georgia governor, and President of the United States. He was most admired for his foreign policy achievements and humanitarian efforts, but his political nemesis was caused by Khomeni and inflation.

Billy Graham (Charlotte, North Carolina): World-famous television evangelist and religious leader; he doesn't need his own cable television network to spread the gospel.

Elizabeth Hanford Dole (Salisbury, North Carolina): Former U.S. secretary of transportation under Reagan, former FTC Commissioner, and wife of Sentor Bob Dole, she's a *magna cum laude* graduate of the iron-hand-in-velvet-glove school for southern ladies.

Alex Haley (Henning, Tennessee): Acclaimed author of block-buster tome *Roots* and Pulitzer Prize winner. In one fell swoop he captivated a nation with the epic history and heritage of black America.

Jim Henson (Greenville, Mississippi): Ingenious creator of ever-popular characters the Muppets, celebrities of television and film.

Charlayne Hunter-Gault (Due West, South Carolina): First black woman student at University of Georgia; now an award-winning (two Emmys and a Peabody) journalist and correspondent for public television's McNeil/Lehrer News-Hour.

Alexander Julian (Chapel Hill, North Carolina): Acclaimed clothing designer for men and women (his Colours line is biggest selling); known for his distinctive tailored stylings using subtle colorations and textures.

Jan Kemp (Griffin, Georgia): The Joan of Arc of academic reform in collegiate football, this prof sued the University of Georgia after she was fired for protesting the academic coddling of star athletes. She won her case and a one million dollar-plus settlement; college athletics will never be the same again.

Charles Kuralt (Wilmington, North Carolina): CBS news correspondent for the Emmy award-winning program. "On the Road," he's the gifted chronicler of American life and culture.

Bob Pittman (Forest Hill, Mississippi): Visionary of cable TV's Music Television at age twenty-seven, he now heads the successful MTV Networks (MTV, Nickelodeon, VH–1),

Answers to "Do You Know Your Southern Celebrities' Claims to Fame" Quiz on page 92.

1. Actor DeForrest Kelley. 2. Tish Hooker, Nashville socialite and Germaine Monteil face model. 3. Actor Jim Varney. 4. Actor Henry Gibson.

Fred Smith (Memphis): Undaunted that his Yale professor considered the idea *C*-grade, he followed his hunch to found the first and largest overnight delivery service, Federal Express.

Issac Tigrett (Memphis): Founder of the trendy and successful Hard Rock Cafe enterprise (called the "Smithsonian of Rock and Roll" by actor Dan Aykroyd).

Ted Turner, III: Controversial media scion (Turner Broadcasting System), brash sports mogul (Atlanta Braves and Hawks), daredevil yachtsman (America's Cup winner, 1977), and self-acknowledged braggadocio.

Andrew Young (New Orleans): Civil Rights leader, Georgia politician, and former U.S. ambassador to the United Nations.

ROGUE'S GALLERY

And then there are our skeletons in the closet, those Southerners whose reputations have gotten a little tarnished amongst the homefolk of Dixie. Some hands-down winners of this generation's Your Name Is Mud award include:

John and Rita Jenrette (South Carolina). This former U.S. senator was caught with his hand in the ABSCAM cookie jar in 1980 to the tune of 50,000 cookies. His siren wife, Rita, didn't exactly paint a picture of clean living to a lot of Southerners, either, when she bared more than her soul for *Playboy* after John's conviction.

Bert Lance (Georgia). Lance has the dubious distinction of being one of the South's most famous has-beens. Exposed for such mischief as check kiting and shady loan making, T. Bertram Lance found himself making many exits, including his role as U.S. budget director and chairman of Walter Mondale's presidential campaign, Georgia's Democratic party, and the Calhoun (Georgia) First National Bank.

Marie ("The Black Widow") Hilley (Alabama). The stuff that mini-series are made of, Marie Hilley slowly poisoned her husband and daughter with arsenic (disguised as vitamin shots) to collect life insurance money. She managed to put hubby away and collect his policy, but an *Anniston Star* reporter unearthed the real dirt and the Black Widow (so named by the defense attorney) was retrieved from her second husband in New Hampshire and ensnared in an Alabama prison.

Donna Rice (South Carolina). Sweet tart who nearly broke a Hart. Her much-headlined liaison in 1987 with presidential candidate Gary Hart prompted him to drop out of the race (for a while, anyway) while the former University of South Carolina cheerleader considered her options for more favorable limelight. So far, there's no evidence that all gold diggers make a lucky strike.

BEST OF SHOW

Jim and Tammy Bakker (no forwarding address). They're not Southerners by birth, but since they were happy to situate their "gospel of prosperity" empire and their Babylonian lifestyle in Dixie, we figure they qualify for the Rogue's Gallery. In a land where enough is considered plenty, it was bad form for Jim and Tammy to flaunt their worldly ways. It was even worse that they funded their pleasures from the offering plate. But where they *really* went astray in the eyes of most Southerners was entertaining the world at the expense of God *and* the Southland, holy subjects indeed to desecrate around these parts.

Chapter Five

Social Studies Southern Style

Every Southerner has a sense of place, but some enjoy a more elevated sense of place than others. These are the Southlanders who, as we like to put it, live high on the hog. They walk in tall cotton. They live off the fat of the land because they're the ones with the prime acreage. They're the ones who belong to southern society, as in the high variety.

Southern Style for these folks is a whole 'nother ball of wax. On top of the privileges granted by being born and bred in Dixie, they possess the perquisites that can only come from being born and bred to the right social station.

Life in the upper reaches of the Southland's social strata comes with its own rules and regulations. Like everything else that has to do with Southern Style, it is steeped in tradition and of our own creation. So if you want to understand what it's like to walk on the high side of life down South, you'd do well to sit tight and read on.

KNOWING YOUR PLACE IN SOUTHLAND SOCIETY

Every Southerner occupies a rung on the ladder of southern society and, as the saying goes, we know our place. Your place is assigned at birth, and you die in the same place you started. No matter what happens in between, Southlanders know you can't change your place in Dixie. Your place is your lifelong social station—the down-South version of AKC registration.

Your place is assigned according to the rules of southern society. The rules are very old. The rules do not change. The rules are what put you in your place and keep you there. The rules are why some people Not-From-Here have used such words as "provincial" and "unfathomable" to describe the southern social order.

The rules are yet another example of why Southerners say to this day, "There are just some things about the South that you can't explain to Yankees." These are the rules:

RULE #1: An approved southern pedigree is what determines your social station in Dixie.

Don't think twice about getting in the southern social register if you don't have a reputable family name from an old southern family. What really counts is who your mama and daddy are and who their mamas and daddies were and how they earned their distinguished family names.

RULE #2: If you come from old southern money and an old southern family, you're really sitting pretty.

We must admit, a lot of folks in the upper reaches of southern society have more in common than a good family name, and that's a good net worth, probably several generation's worth on *both* sides of the family. This is indeed fortunate since a lifestyle suitable to such a place on the social ladder down South takes as much discretionary income as it does proper discretion (more on this shortly). So while a good name is indeed rather to be had than great riches in Dixie, most Southerners in the Order take a liking to having both.

However, if you're of "reduced circumstances" in Dixie (translated: your family lost its wealth during Reconstruction or due to some other unfortunate cause), you haven't lost your place. You'll always have a place in southern society, for as long as your honorable name is intact in the Southland, so also is your good social station—even if you *are* wearing the same ball gown for the third year in a row.

RULE #3: If you don't already have a place in the Order, don't count on getting one.

Your elevated place is inherited and passed on; rarely is it acquired (the notable exception being the possession of an MD degree). This applies even to those who "marry up," since everyone in town will be quite aware of your more humble origins. The moral of this rule is: It's a sight easier to improve your address than your social station in Dixie.

RULE #4: Don't confuse social station with social status in the South.

Merciful heaven, social status is something to be strived for, not born with, or, worse yet, displayed. Social status is a reward for social climbing, a pursuit that may get you the attention of other limelighters but won't move you up one skinny rung as far as your social station in Dixie is concerned.

DO YOU SIT IN HIGH PLACES IN DIXIE?

If you were born with a place on the highest social rungs of all, you belong to the Order of the Old Southern Family, the most desirable pedigree of all to have (or wish you had). A place in the Order means that you come from what we Southerners call an "established southern family" or "a long line of really fine folk."

It means your family has been a part of the southern landscape for many generations and probably had a hand in putting your county on the map way back when. It means

SOUTHERN STYLE #2: THE ORDERLIES
Born to the Order with mint julep cups in their hands.

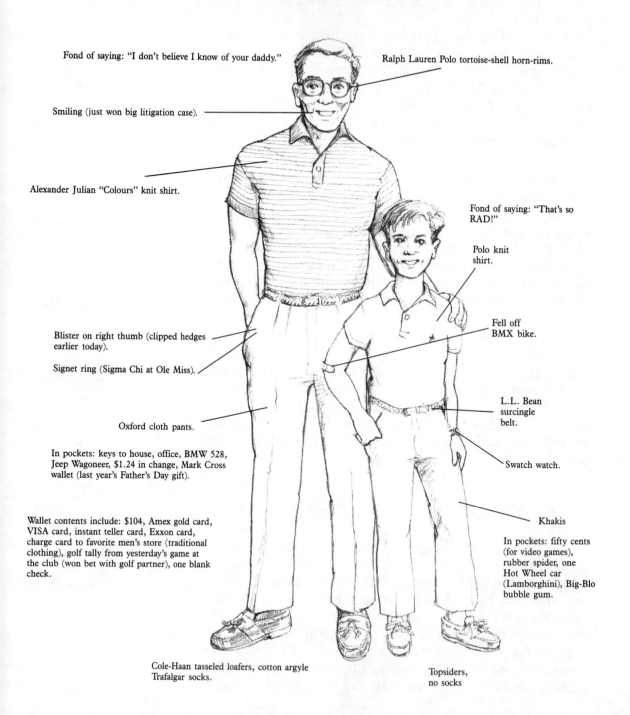

Fond of saying: "I don't believe I know of your daddy."

Ralph Lauren Polo tortoise-shell horn-rims.

Smiling (just won big litigation case).

Alexander Julian "Colours" knit shirt.

Fond of saying: "That's so RAD!"

Polo knit shirt.

Fell off BMX bike.

Blister on right thumb (clipped hedges earlier today).

Signet ring (Sigma Chi at Ole Miss).

L.L. Bean surcingle belt.

Oxford cloth pants.

In pockets: keys to house, office, BMW 528, Jeep Wagoneer, $1.24 in change, Mark Cross wallet (last year's Father's Day gift).

Swatch watch.

Wallet contents include: $104, Amex gold card, VISA card, instant teller card, Exxon card, charge card to favorite men's store (traditional clothing), golf tally from yesterday's game at the club (won bet with golf partner), one blank check.

Khakis

In pockets: fifty cents (for video games), rubber spider, one Hot Wheel car (Lamborghini), Big-Blo bubble gum.

Cole-Haan tasseled loafers, cotton argyle Trafalgar socks.

Topsiders, no socks

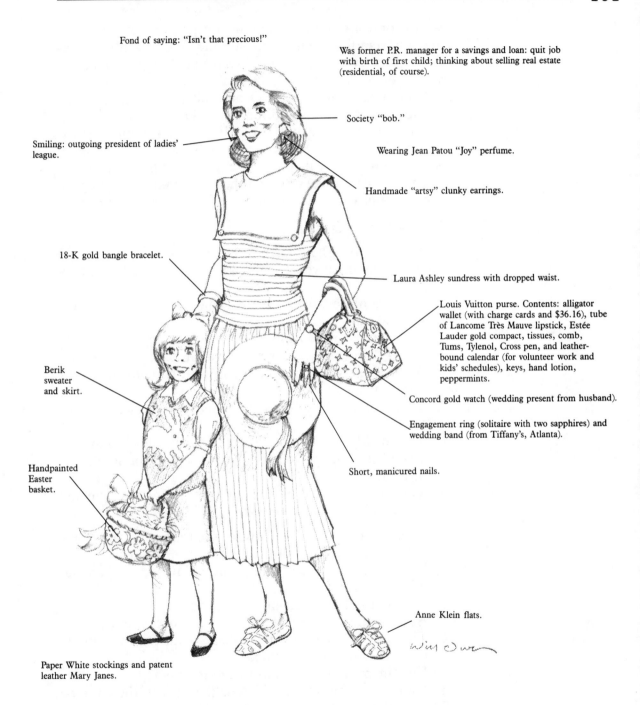

Fond of saying: "Isn't that precious!"

Was former P.R. manager for a savings and loan: quit job with birth of first child; thinking about selling real estate (residential, of course).

Society "bob."

Smiling: outgoing president of ladies' league.

Wearing Jean Patou "Joy" perfume.

Handmade "artsy" clunky earrings.

18-K gold bangle bracelet.

Laura Ashley sundress with dropped waist.

Louis Vuitton purse. Contents: alligator wallet (with charge cards and $36.16), tube of Lancome Très Mauve lipstick, Estée Lauder gold compact, tissues, comb, Tums, Tylenol, Cross pen, and leather-bound calendar (for volunteer work and kids' schedules), keys, hand lotion, peppermints.

Berik sweater and skirt.

Concord gold watch (wedding present from husband).

Engagement ring (solitaire with two sapphires) and wedding band (from Tiffany's, Atlanta).

Handpainted Easter basket.

Short, manicured nails.

Anne Klein flats.

Paper White stockings and patent leather Mary Janes.

your people are some of the most upstanding, outstanding, and longstanding Southerners around. When you're an Orderly, most everybody around your part of the state knows your family—or knows of it—and thinks well of it.

Should you belong to the Order, you already know there's a place permanently saved for you in Dixie society. In fact, you *are* Dixie society, the old-line, good-name variety, which is as high on the ladder as anyone can get down here. Should you wonder if you belong, well, you probably don't. But just in case, take our Qualification Quiz below, to get a good idea of what it takes to have a place in the Order.

QUALIFICATION QUIZ

It's a safe bet that you belong to the Order of the Old Southern Family if you can answer yes to most of the following:
1. Your family has been in the same county for over five generations.
2. Your family owns property in the country.
3. At least one of your ancestors was an officer in the War.
4. At least one street or building in your hometown bears a family name.
5. Your mama was a Junior Leaguer (or the like) in your town.
6. Your daddy is/was a deacon or elder in the church.
7. One of the men in your family was a judge or an elected official.
8. There's a scholarship or endowment in the family name at one of the state colleges.

If you answer yes to all or most of the following, you don't have a piddling chance of belonging to the Order:
1. Your parents moved to town from Michigan when the mill opened in '54.
2. Your house has a satellite dish in the yard.
3. At least one of your ancestors was a Bluecoat in the War.
4. The only street in town that bears your family name is the one with your mailbox.
5. Your mama had to work outside the home.
6. Your daddy rarely ever darkens the door of the church.
7. One of the men in your family served time.
8. It's a family tradition to attend the local technical school.

TOEING THE LINE IN SOUTHERN SOCIETY

As representatives of the Order of Old Southern Families, you have to toe the line very carefully when it comes to carrying off your special kind of Southern Style. You may secretly hanker to spend your Saturday nights at the Talladega Race Track or wish you knew how to make ceramic bookends, but if you walk in tall cotton in Dixie, you know better than to let loose those fantasies, even to your own mother.

Why, that wouldn't become your social station a'tall; you *know* folks would think you'd gone plumb out of your *mind* and your family would surely be shamed to *death* when the rest of the town heard about it, which they most certainly would.

No ma'am, the higher your rung on the social ladder, the more carefully you had better tread. Conformity is one of the essential ground rules of an elevated social station down South. Sticking out like a sore thumb is not. And since the consequences of not toeing the line are losing face or, worst of all, losing place, 99 percent of those in the Order choose to behave themselves as becomes their station.

Don't think, however, that toeing the line is too heavy a burden for these Southerners. Truth is, most folk in Dixie would give their eye teeth to have such a row to hoe. Just consider the sorts of accommodations you'd have to make to suit your station in tall cotton:

TWENTY-FIVE WAYS TO GRACE YOUR PLACE IN SOUTHERN SOCIETY

1. Wear traditional, conservative, and expensive clothes. Men should favor the preppy/Ralph Lauren look; women should be partial to the "grown up little girl" look (Laura Ashley, Belle France, Cullinane, etc.) whenever possible.

2. Live in established, traditional neighborhoods in spacious, traditional-looking residences with classic, traditional interiors. The older the neighborhood and your home's architectural style, the better.

3. Enroll your children in the same private schools that you and your spouse attended.

4. Belong to the country club and perhaps a town club; belong to civic and political organizations. Wives should belong to the Junior League or comparable ladies' auxiliary. Patronize the fine arts or performing arts; be active in your college and Greek alumni organizations.

5. Build a lake house or, better yet, a beach house. Best of all, spruce up the one you inherited from your mother's side of the family. Move the family there each summer (Dad comes to visit on weekends).

6. Have portraits painted of the children (and maybe the dog) when they're young. Have yours and your spouse's done before your fortieth birthdays.

7. Give substantial sums of money to the church building fund.

8. Renovate the family ancestral home (or an old, in-town home) for your own family to live in. Open it for annual home tours.

9. Send your kids to summer camp in the North Carolina mountains for a month.

10. Leave hubby at home and go to New York each fall for a three-day shopping spree and museum circuit with a pal from the hospital auxiliary. Take your daughters along, too, and stay at the Plaza.

11. While the wife is in New York, join your duck-hunting cohorts in Stuttgart, Arkansas, for a fall weekend of men, guns, ducks, dogs, and whiskey.

12. Send your daughter to a good southern girls' school for her first two years in college and then let her transfer to the state university so she can pledge a sorority and find a husband.

13. Take the family skiing in Crested Butte, Montana, each year over Thanksgiving.

14. Introduce your college-age daughter to society with her debut. Spend a small fortune and a year of the family's time for the clothes, the parties, the ball, and the requisite community service work.

15. Invest in southern primitive folk art. Scout the rural areas for the next Mattie Lou O'Kelley or the Reverend

Howard Finster. Invest in prints and sculpture commemorating the War Between the States.

16. Bankroll your college-junior son while he and a classmate backpack across Europe one summer.

17. Spend your fall and winter weekends fox hunting, tending your horses, and hobnobbing with your horsey-set friends.

18. Bankroll your son's and daughter's participation(s) in the courts of Mardi Gras, first as children and later as young adults.

19. Donate an old family heirloom to the area art museum.

20. Open an antique linens store in a renovated storefront building, using a $35,000 "loan" from your husband.

21. Leave the wives at home and take a few of your pals deep-sea fishing on your fifty-foot Bertram for a week each summer.

22. Visit the Holy Land with your spouse on a church-sponsored tour led by the pastor.

23. Invest heavily in the breeding and training of championship bird dogs with hopes of qualifying them for the National Field Trial Competition in Grand Junction, Tennessee.

24. Purchase a limited-partnership interest in a Thoroughbred horse racing syndicate with hopes of having your own Seattle Slew success story.

25. Spend large sums of money and time becoming a two-goal polo player, tending your ponies, and traveling to and from meets with your club.

OLD SOCIETY AND THE THE NEW SOUTH

Who'd have ever thought they'd live to see the day when some of the unwritten laws of old southern society would be regularly bent, even by many of Dixie's most socially astute constituents? Surely great-grandmother Cunningham never expected that what she considered *faux pas* would become *status quo*, but, then again, did great-grandmother Cunningham ever expect life without corsets?

Lordy, Lordy, what *is* the South coming to?

Welcome to the New South. One hundred years after Georgian Henry Grady made his "New South" appeal to Northern financiers, there really is a New South everywhere you look in Dixie. And that includes some of our southernmost social conventions.

For those of you in the Order, this means the advent of the Old Society/New South lifestyle—living in the time-honored manner of old southern society (some things never change), but doing so with a New South twist. Translated, this means respect the old traditions but don't be an old fogey about them, either. Here's how to do it.

1. Let the twain meet—and mix.

Don't be a bit surprised to see old money and new money rubbing elbows at even the swankiest social clubs and functions in Dixie. Let's be pragmatic; it's new money (and there's lots and lots of it being made) that is helping to rev up southern commerce and culture. Those folks may not be from one of our older families, dear, but some of them *are* so *interesting* to talk to, don't you think?

2. Be modest—in a Mercedes.

No longer do you need to eschew the glitz or save for such glittering occasions as merger weddings or debutante balls (when it gets toted out in full tilt). In this day of the New South, it's quite all right to look luxe, even when you're slumming.

So go right ahead and get that $45,000 BMW and wear that $8,500 Piaget watch. The accoutrements of worldly high style no longer automatically label you as flashy trash in Dixie. Just be sure not to act pretentious, though, because not even in this era of the New South can we tolerate folks who are high-falluting.

3. Downhome has gone uptown.

Being cosmopolitan in the metropolitan South has become the preferred mode for many Southerners. In these meccas of the New South, "supper" has become "dinner" and "eating dinner" has become "doing lunch." Parking-lot fundraisers are now referred to as "*al frecso* benefits." Folks sit in sunrooms, not on front porches, and knock on the front door (expected, of course), not on the back door (drop-in, naturally).

In these uptown environs, it's even OK to talk about power and money—who has it and how they got it—since those are the rewards of the urban harvest. What's not OK is for you to forget your genteel upbringing while growing those greenbacks. Lose your manners and you'll lose your "in" with southern society, even in the starry-eyed New South. Some things *never* change in Dixie.

FIVE IMMUTABLE NO-NO'S FOR LADIES OF THE ORDER

Real ladies of the Southern Order know and observe a multitude of exacting social strictures. Some will vary from town to town, but others are universal and unyielding. Here are five of the latter.

A lady of The Order should know better than to:

- Wear white shoes or carry a white purse in public before Easter Sunday or after Labor Day.
- Drink a gin and tonic if it's not summertime.
- Tell a betrothed lady "Congratulations" upon learning of her engagement (proper form is "best wishes" for fiancées, "congratulations" after the wedding).
- Clean her plate.
- Allow herself to be mentioned by the press on occasions other than birth, debut, marriage, and death.

BOWING TO SOCIETY IN THE SOUTHLAND

For most young ladies in Dixie, being crowned beauty queen or homecoming queen would be the utmost honor to receive (looking pretty and pleasing people remains an unyielding aspiration for southern women and girls). But for young ladies whose families constitute the *crème de la crème* of southern society, aspiring to such public spectacle is an unnecessary and, well, rather *undignified* pursuit. Who needs to walk a runway with nineteen other eager hopefuls in the school auditorium or shiver in the middle of a football field during halftime, when they've got something ahead of them that's much more exclusive and carries much more social panache?

Not these gals, because they get to make their debut to society. Out of all the coeds in the city, they are the ones who get to curtsy in the country club or landmark location before an appreciative gallery of the city's finest folk. They get to be feted at dozens of natty luncheons, cocktail parties, and dinners for an entire season. They might even take a year off from college to do it, and they get there without having to perform a "talent" or beam a 100-watt smile. They've got the right pedigree, and that's what matters.

So for these lasses, having such high-rolling social triumphs to anticipate does tend to make public displays of pulchritude and charm seem a shade trifling. Gracious, there's much more at stake here than a full-page picture in a yearbook; we're talking the preservation of a long-established social tradition and, really, the veneration of front-row southern society itself. Now *that's* something to take seriously.

The Lowdown on Coming out down South

Tips for making sense of a southern tradition.

Making the cut.
There are more coming-outs in the Southland than you can shake a long-stemmed rose at. Almost every southern city of appreciable size annually honors the daughters of its most prominent families. But the toniest debutante presentations occur in the larger cities, where the standards for qualification are loftier (sometimes *so* much so that the largest cities often have two or three debutante clubs, one for the Old Money and others for the New Money).

If your family has real social clout in your area, you'll make your debut at a major deb ball whether you hail from a small town or not. If you belong to a *really* heavy-hitting family, you could be presented twice in the same season, either in another city (probably one of your parents' hometowns) or, in some cases, in a statewide or regional presentation (and maybe even a New York City deb ball, if your family is one of Dixie's most top-hat).

Camellia Ball, Mobile, Alabama.

When the admission qualifications get bent.

In this age of the New South, even the firmly fixed admission qualifications can, on rare occasions, get waived. This happens when what we'll call the VIP Clause is invoked, which amounts to including in the debutante lineup the daughter of someone who is not a native of that city (and maybe not even the South) but is very important to the city. Look at it this way. Would *you* snub the daughter of the president of the company that brought millions and millions of dollars to your local economy and its family-owned businesses?

Fun and fund-raising.

In many southern cities, the deb ball doubles as a charity benefit. Proceeds from the gala are donated to a pet cause, and often the debutantes in these clubs spend many hours in volunteer work. But elsewhere in Dixie, deb assemblies forego the higher ideals, preferring to keep the event a purely social ritual.

Pretty is as pretty does?

Outside observers are invariably disappointed to discover that few of a given year's clutch of debutantes are, shall we say, raving beauties. In all fairness, we must admit that some of those faces peering out from the Sunday social page can be a little on the homely side. But lest you forget, these young ladies were not selected on the basis of such an ephemeral qualification as good looks. Nope, it's the family that counts. Not the face.

If you're curious to find out more about debutante phenomena in Dixie, you're probably not going to get too far. The reason for this is very simple: You'd already know all the skinny if you belonged to the right families. You can, however, follow next year's goings-on in your local society column ("Dr. and Mrs. Hubert Crenshaw of Lakeside Manor entertained debutantes CAROLINE WINN and KATHY CLARKE last Sunday with a brunch in the garden gazebo . . ."). And who knows, if you play your cards right, maybe you can finagle yourself an invitation to the presentation and see southern society in one of its finest hours.

NOTEWORTHY DIXIE DEBUTANTE BALLS

*The
Mobile Debutantes of 1986
request the pleasure of your company
at the
thirty-fourth Annual Camellia Ball
on
Thursday, the twenty-seventh of November
at nine o'clock in the evening
Riverview Plaza
Mobile, Alabama*

"Admit one" to southern society.

Atlanta
The Harvest Ball. Friday after Thanksgiving; since 1911. Old-line Atlanta all the way.
The Phoenix Ball. The week before Christmas; since 1964.

Birmingham
The Beaux Arts Ball. Held in February. The Magic City's old-name deb ball.
The Christmas Ball. Held the Saturday before Christmas at the Country Club of Birmingham; since 1907.

Charleston
St. Cecilia Ball. Held in late January; since 1762. One of the most aristocratic presentations anywhere but also the least publicized—intentionally so.

Chattanooga
The Cotton Ball. Held in early August; since 1933. Many Cotton Ball debs are from nearby states. Highlight is a coronation of an honest-to-goodness king and queen.

Columbia, South Carolina
The Assembly Ball. Held the weekend before Christmas; since 1889.

Durham, North Carolina
The Debutante Cotillion and Christmas Ball. Held in late December; since 1955. For young ladies in the Durham and Chapel Hill area. Non-alcoholic.

Greenville, Mississippi
The Delta Debutante Ball. Held in late December; since 1942. For daughters of families in the Mississippi, Arkansas, and Louisiana Delta region.

Jackson, Mississippi
The Debutante Ball. Held the Friday night after Thanksgiving.

Lexington
Bluegrass Charity Ball. Observed in December; since 1937.

Little Rock
The Country Club of Little Rock Debutante Presentation. Held during the Christmas season.

Louisville
The Debutante Ball. Held just before Christmas; since 1931.

Memphis
The Holiday Ball. Held the weekend before Christmas.

Mobile
The Camellia Ball. Held the Saturday after Thanksgiving; since 1953.

Nashville
The Bal d'Hiver. Held in February by Kappa Alpha Theta. Nashville's oldest deb presentation.
The Eve of Janus Ball. Held New Year's Eve; sponsored by Delta Delta Delta.

New Orleans
Le Debut. Held in August.
The Debutante Club Presentation. Held around Thanksgiving.
The Courts of Mardi Gras. Young ladies are honored by the members of various Mardi Gras krewes. Oldest-line daughters usually come out at one of the deb presentations plus "lead" one or two krewe balls.

State of North Carolina

Terpsichorean Ball. Held in Raleigh over the Labor Day weekend. One hundred and twenty-five debs from all over the state represent its most prominent families.

Richmond

Richmond German. Held Christmas week at the Commonwealth Club; since 1832.

SOCIAL MONARCHY IN DIXIE

One of the most superlative social statements made in the Southland occurs each winter in the southern port cities of Mobile and New Orleans, the courts of Mardi Gras. At the heart of Mardi Gras is Deep South social history in the making and remaking year after year after year.

If you belong to the Order of Old Southern Families in these locales, you're well aware that Mardi Gras means much more than mirth, frivolity, and revelry. It represents the annual promenade of the social upper crust (to which you belong) under the auspices of socially elite "mystic societies" (to which you belong). But even more socially significant to you and your peers, the arrival of Mardi Gras also heralds the final act of the annual drama of social clout, made public, no less: the announcement of Mardi Gras royalty, better known as "the Court." In Mobile there's one reigning court for the citywide celebration; in New Orleans there's a court for each krewe. Yes, Virginia, you *can* be a monarch in America.

In these cities, being selected Mardi Gras royalty is *the* social coup for any debutante or bachelor. With the revelation of the court(s), not only does it become clear to the entire city whether your family measures up against society's yardstick, but everybody also learns exactly how your family measures up against the others in the running.

Despite these weighty social implications, the results are far from surprising, since the same families have been jousting in this courtly rivalry for generations. Don't forget: This is a social tradition, not a popularity contest or a beauty pageant. It doesn't matter how gregarious or fetching you are. If you don't have the lineage and a long family

Vintage Mardi Gras costume design, New Orleans.

King and Queen of 1987
Mardi Gras, Mobile, Alabama.

history of supporting the carnival organizations (and extremely deep pockets), you have nary a chance of becoming Mardi Gras royalty, at least not in the big-league mystic societies, which are the only ones that *really* count.

If you do have what it takes, the biggest suspense is not whether you'll be invited to become royalty, but for which year and for which distinction (in New Orleans, for which krewes; in Mobile, for which title—king, queen, knight, lady in waiting, *et al*). After all, this social ritual runs in the families of the Order, which means if you made Court, you're no doubt following in the footsteps of your mama and daddy and their mamas and daddies, and so forth.

We, of
King D'Iberville
Son of Night
God of Mockery and Mirth
Come again to gladden Earth
To fill the hours of this one night
With revelry and wild delight—

And you, my dear,

Miss Tallulah Radcliffe Turner

We designate
As Maid our Court to decorate
With your sweet presence, fair
and gay
And help us drive dull Care away.

Thursday, February 11, 1988

—Mystic krewe proclamation to the young ladies of its court.

PROPRIETY IN DIXIE SOCIETY

Helping others has long been a lifetime avocation for raised-right Southerners. Not only do we consider "showing charity" the godly thing to do (and you know how deep those principles run), it's only natural that we show charitable concern for fellow Southerners. Also, this propensity for giving a hand probably has more than a little to do with the fact that the Southland is pretty much one big extended family. No wonder showing brotherly love comes naturally to folks in Dixie.

In fact, being deficient in the lend-a-helping-hand department is a grievous sin, not only of moral proportions, but of social ones, as well. The unwritten code is: the higher your social station in the Southland, the more you need to work for a good cause. If you're not willing to roll up your sleeves and work like a field hand in the name of a good cause, don't be surprised if your good standing in the ranks of Good Folk slips a few notches. You were blessed enough to have more than enough; how about returning in kind?

Some of the most ardent practitioners of this ethic are the ladies of southern society. Without the endless corps of volunteers that these gentlewomen of the South have assembled and led, life would indeed be very different in Dixie. Name a noble cause—such as community service, education, the arts, preservation, health, and religion—and you can be sure that leagues of southern ladies have wielded considerable effort and yielded considerable results with the fervor of a zealot, the organization of a corporation, and the discipline of the military. You can be sure that their best-laid plans have grandly succeeded, under budget and over goal.

You can be sure they did it with plenty of southern grace and charm and without being undignified, pushy, or otherwise ruffling feathers (except maybe a few of their own). You can count on it because, like most well-bred southern ladies, they're honors graduates of the iron-fist-in-velvet-glove school, a tradition unique to Dixie and as ingrained in our culture as the southern accent. Where else could a lady move mountains and never work up a sweat, much less perspire? Well, it happens regularly all over the Southland.

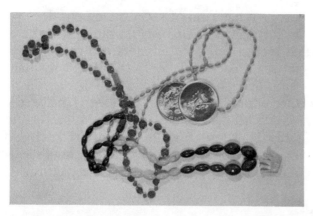

Mardi Gras "throws."

THE JUNIOR LEAGUE: SENIOR SOCIAL STATEMENT

You'll find one in most of the South's larger cities; sometimes two or more. There are about 50 of them in the Southland, including the largest in the world. You'll have to pass a tough social muster to join their genteel ranks, but you'll also have to work off your derriere to remain in their good standing.

Welcome to the Junior League, ladies.

Few other volunteer organizations, if any, carry such social cachet in the Southland as its Leagues. Even in this age of the New South, League membership rosters tend to read like the local social register, and most southern ladies tend to view League membership as an infallible test of social substance. Like joining a soror-ity as a college coed, joining the League is a natural rite of passage for southern ladies in the Order. It comes with the ter-ritory.

Detractors like to classify Leaguers as syrupy-spoken society matrons whose idea of supporting charity is to publish cute cookbooks. In truth, few volunteer organizations in Dixie can compare with the League when it comes to sheer grit, determination, and magnitude of civic service—even if its members *were* born with a silver demitasse spoon in their mouths. And besides, the vast sums of money that those cute cookbooks have ginned up for charity are anything but small potatoes.

USING ACADEMIA TO MAKE THE SOCIAL GRADE

What kind of social statement does your col-lege make for you in Dixie? Say no more than the name of your alma mater, and Southlanders can get an easy fix on your appetite for social *savoir faire*. This is why mamas and daddies who are, shall we say, socially *aware* do not take lightly their child's selection of a college (and vice versa).

Why surely, academics are a consideration for most col-lege-material Southerners. But since we're such *sociable* a folk, you can bet your last goober that a school's social pro-file is going to figure prominently in the picture.

See what sorts of social statements are being made with the following college selection scenarios:

"It will be good for James/Jennifer to expand his/her horizons outside the South."
Translation: My child is going to a Northeastern name school because it's socially prestigious.
Likely choices: Ivy League school, Seven Sisters school. (Note: Many Southlanders still take a rather dim view of shipping kids up North to get educated, even if it *is* the age of the New South.)

"My child is going to a quality southern school with kids from quality southern families like ours."
Translation: My child is going to an exclusive country club school in the South with all her/his prep school pals.
Likely choices: private institutions such as Centre, Davidson, Duke, Hampden-Sydney (all male), Millsaps, University of the South, Vanderbilt, Wake Forest, Washington and Lee. Although a public school, William and Mary otherwise fits into this category.

"My daughter needs a quality education in a refined, close-knit environment."
Translation: Liz is going to an old southern girls' school.
Likely choices: Mary Baldwin, Converse, Hollins, Meredith, Mississippi University for Women, Sophie Newcomb, Queens, Randolph-Macon, St. Mary's, Salem, Agnes Scott, Sweet Briar, Wesleyan.

"My child is going to get a well-rounded education right here in the South." (Also known as, *"What more does Nancy or Mark need to run the family business?"*)
Translation: I'll buy my child a four-year degree and maybe a sorority/fraternity membership, but I won't float the national debt to do it.
Likely choices: In-state universities or colleges.

"Will needs to grow up a little."
Translation: Will's going to a military school where they'll beat his rump if he misbehaves.
Likely choices: The Citadel, Virginia Military Institute.

"My Bobbette excels in social pursuits; academics are not her forte."

Translation: My child is a good kid, but she couldn't make over 900 on the SAT if God took the test for her.

Likely choices: Open-admissions state universities or regional colleges glad to get the tuition.

A final note: Don't think that attending a public university is going to sabotage your social approval quotient in Dixie, no matter how socially prominent your family. On the contrary, it's a popular choice for plenty of youth from the South's old-line peerage. But you do need to adhere to a few critical guidelines if you're serious about passing social muster:

1. Be sure to attend the most prestigious university in the state. It will also probably be the oldest and will probably have a respectable liberal arts program. It will probably *not* be the state ag-tech school.

2. Be sure you pledge a sorority or fraternity, and only one that's well thought of. Till your dying day, you'll be graded on your response to, "You went to Chapel Hill? What sorority (fraternity) were you in?" And to those who care enough to inquire, the only response worse than the name of a crummy sorority or fraternity is, "I wasn't in one."

Foxhunting in Virginia's hunt country.

SOUTHERN STYLE #3: SOUTHERN WASP PRINCE AND PRINCESS
They're climbing the ladder of southern success.

Favorite saying: "Hunker down, you hairy Dawgs!"

Favorite saying: "That child has *no* class."

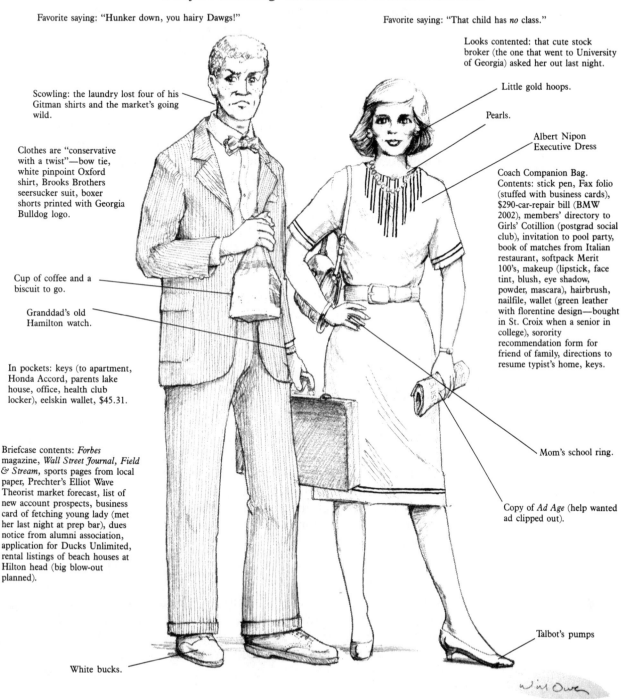

Scowling: the laundry lost four of his Gitman shirts and the market's going wild.

Clothes are "conservative with a twist"—bow tie, white pinpoint Oxford shirt, Brooks Brothers seersucker suit, boxer shorts printed with Georgia Bulldog logo.

Cup of coffee and a biscuit to go.

Granddad's old Hamilton watch.

In pockets: keys (to apartment, Honda Accord, parents lake house, office, health club locker), eelskin wallet, $45.31.

Briefcase contents: *Forbes* magazine, *Wall Street Journal*, *Field & Stream*, sports pages from local paper, Prechter's Elliot Wave Theorist market forecast, list of new account prospects, business card of fetching young lady (met her last night at prep bar), dues notice from alumni association, application for Ducks Unlimited, rental listings of beach houses at Hilton head (big blow-out planned).

White bucks.

Looks contented: that cute stock broker (the one that went to University of Georgia) asked her out last night.

Little gold hoops.

Pearls.

Albert Nipon Executive Dress

Coach Companion Bag. Contents: stick pen, Fax folio (stuffed with business cards), $290-car-repair bill (BMW 2002), members' directory to Girls' Cotillion (postgrad social club), invitation to pool party, book of matches from Italian restaurant, softpack Merit 100's, makeup (lipstick, face tint, blush, eye shadow, powder, mascara), hairbrush, nailfile, wallet (green leather with florentine design—bought in St. Croix when a senior in college), sorority recommendation form for friend of family, directions to resume typist's home, keys.

Mom's school ring.

Copy of *Ad Age* (help wanted ad clipped out).

Talbot's pumps

DYNASTIES: FORTY OF THE WEALTHIEST NAMES IN DIXIE AND HOW THEY CAME TO LIVE SO HIGH ON THE HOG

Don't let that humble I'm-just-a-hard-workin'-southern-boy demeanor fool you. Behind that plainly dressed, courteous facade might be a Southerner so rich he could buy half the state if he wanted to. There are plenty of such Southerners around, whether they subscribe to the traditional southern approach ("Be modest") or find the New South style ("A little flash don't mean trash") more to their liking.

Some of our homefolk roll in so much money that the rest of the nation (and sometimes, the world) has taken notice, including *Forbes* magazine's list of Wealthiest Americans and other such dynastic barometers.

Now that's what's known as living high on the hog—by anybody's standards—and here are forty such southern names who qualify, stock market gyrations notwithstanding.

BILLIONAIRES

Samuel M. Walton, Bentonville, Arkansas.
He's the richest man in the entire United States, and he and his brother got that way by building their hugely successful chain of Wal-Mart Stores (numbering near 1,000). Known for his retailing smarts and unpretentious style, Sam's estimated worth is over eight billion dollars and growing steadily.

Forest E. Mars, Jr., and John F. Mars, McLean and Arlington, Virginia.
Heirs to their dad's candy empire, the sons of Mars continue the family tradition of satisfying sweet teeth the world over. (Forrest Mars, Sr., is retired and lives in Las Vegas.) Dad and sons' worth is placed at more than four billion dollars.

Anne Cox Chambers, Atlanta.

She was ambassador to Belgium during the Carter administration and, with her sister, shares the wealth of media conglomerate Cox Enterprises (built by their dad). The two ladies control a company worth well over three billion dollars.

Wilton R. and Jackson T. Stephens, Little Rock.

These brothers built a massive fortune from investment banking (including stock offerings for Sam Walton) and gas and oil holdings. Both are admired as good old southern boys who've done swell, to the tune of around one billion dollars.

Roger Milliken, Spartanburg, South Carolina.

He's at the helm of a profitable 120-year-old family tradition in textiles. There's added wealth in his extensive stock holdings of a retail store group, a fortune, all told, of about one billion dollars.

$500,000 MILLION TO $1 BILLION

John T. Lupton, Chattanooga, Tennessee.

Coke has been the Real Thing for the Lupton family ever since granddad became a bottler at the turn of the century. The Lupton territory grew like kudzu, eventually including the thirsty (and lucrative) West and Southwest. A few years back, John sold his dynasty back to daddy Coke.

Winthrop P. Rockefeller, Winrock Farm, Arkansas.

He's an heir to the J. D. Rockefeller family fortune, son of a two-time former Arkansas governor, and is involved in banking and charitable causes.

Orville W. Rollins, Atlanta.

Scion of Sunbelt growth investment opportunities, Rollins built his fortune (now publicly traded) in media, pest control, security systems, and oil and gas enterprises.

The Brown Family of Louisville.

For over 100 years, this closely knit family has made its name and money in distilling (Old Forester; later, Jack Daniels). This generation has expanded the family's stock in trade to other libations as well (wines, brandy, coolers, champagne).

The Richardson Family of Greensboro, North Carolina (and elsewhere).

A pharmaceutical success story was born with the concoction of Vicks Vaporub in 1907; so was a family fortune, from this and other medicine cabinet products.

The Gottwald Family of Richmond (and elsewhere).

Savvy business investing (and divesting) in manufacturing (paper, gasoline additives, plastic, metals) and insurance paid off in handsome yields.

John M. Harbert, III, Birmingham.

A self-made millionaire whose fortune was, literally, built through construction ventures. Stock investments help to further fill the Harbert coffers.

Donald J. and Barbara Tyson, Springdale and Fayetteville, Arkansas.

Any way you cut it, theirs is the nation's leading poultry supplier, having laid a golden egg by selling chickens to grocers and restaurants.

The Murphy Family, El Dorado, Arkansas.

Charles, Jr., followed in his father's oil patch footsteps to engineer a lucrative and diversified energy corporation; now he shares the helm with siblings and in-laws.

$250 MILLION TO $500 MILLION

Claude B. Pennington, Baton Rouge.

He made his money through oil and gas (drilling, leases, etc.) and likes to give generously to Louisiana State University.

The Bingham Family, Louisville.

Patriarch Barry Bingham carried on his dad's publishing tradition and later expanded into broadcasting. Highly publicized squabbles amongst his heirs compelled him recently to sell out and divide the ample spoils.

The Belk Family, Charlotte.

This century-old retailing enterprise remains largely in the hands of descendants of founder William Belk. At last count, they held close to 350 stores in Dixie.

The Belz Family, Memphis.

Long-time buyers and developers of real estate in Tennessee and now points elsewhere, they keep things in the family and to themselves.

Robert E. ("Ted") Turner, Roswell, Georgia.

Young Ted erected a fortune from an ailing family billboard business, which became a springboard for even more visible accomplishments: cable television, professional sports teams (Atlanta Braves and Hawks), yachting, and movies. Tune in . . . More to Come.

Alice Francis du Pont Mills, Middleburg, Virginia.
Constance Simons du Pont Darden, Norfolk, Virginia.
Eleanor Francis du Pont Rust, Thomasville, Georgia.

They are members of the extensive and megawealthy du Pont dynasty and heiresses to sizable shares of its investment holdings.

Stephen Van Every and Family, Charlotte.

Their snack food kingdom, which was cultivated from the humble peanut, is anything but small change in its industry.

William A. Fickling, Jr., Macon, Georgia.

He established his wealth through health care: nursing homes, hospitals, medical facilities.

The Close Family, Fort Mill, South Carolina.

They share in the generous wealth woven from Springmaid bed linens and prudent re-investing.

James L. Walton, Bentonville, Arkansas.

With brother Sam, James earned his considerable fortune through their success-story discount store chain.

Frank Batten, Virginia Beach, Virginia.

He parlayed his uncle's newspaper into a publishing and broadcasting empire.

William S. Morris, III, Augusta, Georgia.

He proved that "information is power" *and* money with his profitable newspaper chain and outdoor company.

$100 MILLION TO $250 MILLION

Frederick W. Smith, Memphis.
He staked his family bus-line inheritance on a lofty idea and won, successfully building an overnight air express business and sparking an entirely new industry.

Jesse ("Mack") Robinson, Atlanta.
A financier who banked upon banking and prospered in the process, the former principal investor in Yves St. Laurent's fledgling label furthered his fortune by bankrolling other ventures.

Allen E. Paulson, Savannah.
In 1978 he purchased the Rolls Royce of private jet-crafters, Gulfstream Aerospace. Seven years later, Paulson increased his investment tenfold when he sold it to Chrysler (he's still in charge).

J. B. Hunt, Springdale, Arkansas.
Yet another boy from the Ozarks who struck the mother lode, J. B. made his first strike in the poultry business and a second with truck and trailer transport.

Angelo J. Bruno and family, Birmingham.
Their grocery superstores are where Deep South shoppers go to fill their pantries.

Marion Day Smith, Atlanta.
Her husband built a fortune by building the Day's Inn budget hotel chain.

James F. Harrison, Chattanooga.
He slaked his thirst for fortune with immense holdings in Coca-Cola bottling operations.

Raymond L. Danner, Nashville.
He fattened the family bank accounts by feeding lots of hungry Southerners in his Shoney's restaurants.

Arthur L. Williams, Jr., Monroe, Georgia.
Demonstrating that investing in futures doesn't have to mean speculating on pork bellies, he built a nationally respected insurance empire.

Alvin Copeland, New Orleans.

He wrote a recipe for success by spicing up our favorite stand-by with his Popeye's fried chicken.

Frank D. Hickingbotham, Little Rock.

Proof positive that "Try it, you'll like it" can work, his Country's Best Yogurt franchise chain has consumers and investors licking their lips for more.

William S. Farish III, Versailles, Kentucky.

Heir to the Humble Oil fortune (and so forth), he's a devoted member of the Kentucky horse set (breeding, racing, polo).

Winton M. Blount, Montgomery, Alabama.

Thinking big was his ticket to grand-scale construction projects the world over and even a rehaul of the U.S. postal system.

Leon Levine, Charlotte.

In less than thirty years, Leon Levine amassed big-time money from small-town shoppers with his Family Dollar Stores, now a familiar sight in almost half the United States.

Chapter Six

What's Cooking in Dixie

Seems as of late folks in the rest of the world finally have latched onto something we've known about down South for centuries: the eating's great, and biscuits and red-eye gravy are just the start of our vast repertoire of culinary classics. Any doubting Thomases need only to conduct a Southland taste test or brush up on their trend watching to see the light. Don't even *try* to count all the southern cookbooks Yankee publishers have issued recently.

We don't go halfway with food around here. Why should we, since we're blessed with what noted southern food expert Camille Glenn calls "an embarrassment of riches"? Our motherland is the mother lode. With her abundant bounty on land and water and a plentitude of cultures, we were destined to make food an all-consuming passion in Dixie. And we have doubtless obliged.

Times may change, but our gastronomic legacies are permanent landmarks on the southern landscape. They're too good to pass up or, God forbid, forget.

Dig in and help yourself!

CLASSIC SOUTHERN-STYLE CUISINE

There's far more to our proud, prolific foodlore than our famous southern home cooking, but it's those traditional southern-style meals that have come to be synonymous with the Southland. Like the way we talk and behave ourselves, our best-known way with food has a singular style of its own, the classic Southern Style, to be precise.

The classic Southern Style of cooking is a gastronomic lesson in our Dixie heritage. Old World food fare, New World bounty (like corn, turkeys, possum), and foods from Africa (such as watermelons, okra, and benne or sesame seed), the West Indies, and the Southern Hemisphere were stirred into our culinary stock pot by resourceful southern cooks. They shaped a cuisine that became—and remains—a legend among those who know what good food is.

Whether grand-scale or routine, the classic Southern Style of cooking is an unforgettable feast of the freshest, the finest, and the most honest ingredients faithfully prepared according to treasured methods. There's no doubt that fast food, frozen entrees, and calorie counting have made their marks upon the supper table in today's Dixie. Even so, most of us Southerners still try our darnedest to make time and room for meals the way God meant them to be: our way, of course. Some things down South are sacred, you know.

Any Southlander will unequivocally declare that you haven't lived until you've had a genuine home-cooked, southern-style meal. It's true. But if you don't yet belong to the land of the living, there's still hope. Just read on.

BASIC TRUTHS ABOUT HOME COOKING SOUTHERN STYLE

Tastes great because the ingredients come straight from the garden or barnyard.

Using techno-grown and processed provisions just won't get you to the same gastronomic nirvana. After all, real southern cooking is real country cooking, originally made by and for Southlanders whose foodstuffs were as close as the backyard and barnyard (and the pantry and the smokehouse). Even though few of us have chickens or pigs behind the house any longer, finding fresh foodstuffs is not a hopeless cause as long as you grow your own vegetables (or know where to find them) and know where to look for wild game (in the woods or your deer-hunting neighbor's freezer).

Takes a long time to prepare and cook.

You don't just "whip up" a genuine southern-style meal. The original versions were days in the making and if you're aiming to replicate one of them, clear your calendar. That country ham took about a year to cure, overnight to soak, and a few more hours to glaze (or slice and fry). That barbecue has to roast in an open pit at least twelve hours, with lots of basting. Those vegetables have to be picked, cleaned, prepared, and slow-cooked. Those sweets and desserts don't come in a box; neither do those cat-head biscuits. And don't forget the condiments you "put up" over a couple of weeks last summer to round out your meal.

Sticks to your bones.

Nobody has ever claimed that southern-style cooking would make good spa food. Remember, it was originally made to keep folks' engines running steady over a hard day's work out of doors. For a meal high in protein and carbohydrates, help yourself to some southern cooking. So for a meal that's lowfat, low salt, or low sugar, you'd better look elsewhere, like maybe California.

Not every meal we eat down South these days is a genuine whole-hog version of yesteryear; seems the New South lifestyle often precludes a steady diet of our classic downhome cooking. But often enough, we find ourselves celebrating our culinary heritage with a proper Old South meal at home, especially a Sunday dinner (that means lunch) and sometimes a country breakfast.

The whole family attends. So do relatives and lucky friends. Everybody leaves fat and happy, and glad to be a Southerner.

"COMPANY'S COMING" SUNDAY DINNER
A mighty respectable rendition of the old-time Sunday spread.

*Recipes to follow

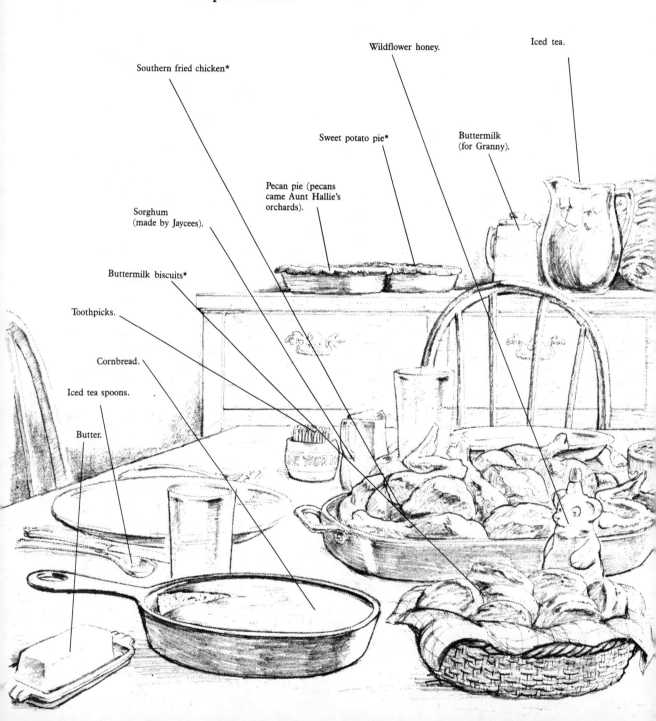

Wildflower honey.

Iced tea.

Southern fried chicken*

Sweet potato pie*

Buttermilk
(for Granny).

Pecan pie (pecans
came Aunt Hallie's
orchards).

Sorghum
(made by Jaycees).

Buttermilk biscuits*

Toothpicks.

Cornbread.

Iced tea spoons.

Butter.

Green beans, butter beans, turnip greens, and field
peas (all homegrown and slow-cooked with salt meat).

Fried okra
(pod of the Gods).

Vintage tablecloth and
cloth napkins (from
grandmother's trousseau).

Pepper sauce
(made by pastor's wife).

Fresh sliced tomatoes on old pressed glass
saucer ("free with box top of Crystal Oats").

Peanut butter and
jelly sandwich (for
William Jr.).

White rice.

"Damask Rose"
sterling silver
flatware by
Oneida (Mama's).

Pan gravy
(made from fried
chicken drippings).

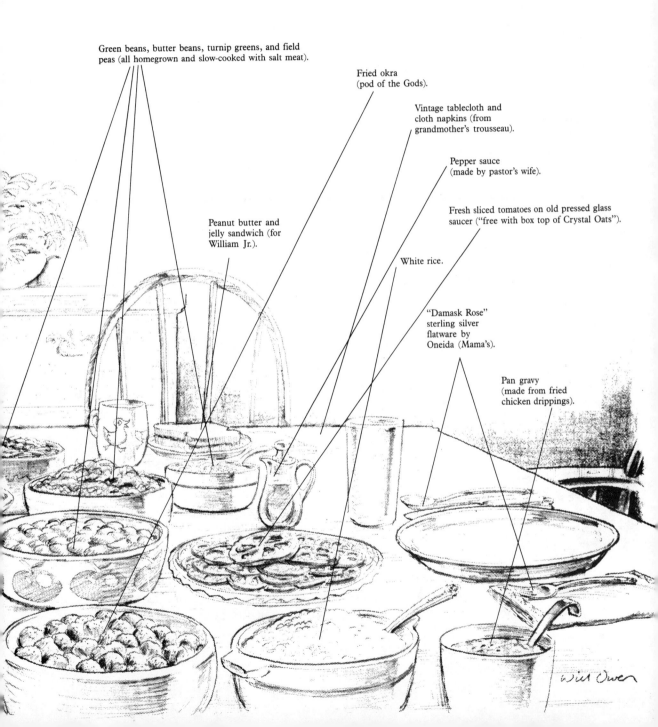

WISH UPON A BONE

Every bona fide fried chicken dinner in Dixie concludes with the wishbone ritual: two diners face off, each holding one "leg" of the bare wishbone (held thumbs up). Each makes a wish. Both then pull the bone until it snaps in two. Legend holds that whoever ends up with the shortest piece will have his wish come true. A favorite ritual for kids down South.

Southern Fried Chicken

Whether you buy whole chickens and cut them up yourself or choose special cuts (breasts, thighs), select the leanest, smallest bird(s) you can find. (There are no more "barnyard" chickens to be fried the same day they are killed, but just remember that young and lean is better than old and fat, and do the best you can.) Soak the pieces in lightly salted cold water for an hour or more to extract the blood. Drain and pat dry, then rub with salt and pepper. In a deep, heavy black skillet, melt enough shortening to reach a depth of ½ inch or so and add 3 or 4 tablespoons of bacon grease to it. Put a cup or more of flour and ½ teaspoon each of salt and pepper in a paper sack and shake each piece of chicken individually in the sack until it is well coated. Then lay the pieces gently into the medium-hot grease (sizzling but not smoking). Don't crowd the pieces. When golden brown and crispy-looking on one side, turn with tongs and cook to the same state on the other side. Depending on the size of the chicken and the heat of the grease, the total cooking time should be 20 to 30 minutes. An uncovered skillet will make drier, crispier chicken. When done, lay the pieces out on absorbent paper to soak up excess grease.

—*Southern Food*, by John Egerton, © 1987 by John Egerton. Reprinted by permission of Alfred A. Knopf, Inc.

Southern Buttermilk Biscuits
2 cups all-purpose flour, plus more as needed
¼ teaspoon baking soda
1 tablespoon baking powder
1 teaspoon salt
6 tablespoons lard or solid vegetable shortening
¾ cup buttermilk

1. Sift the dry ingredients into a roomy bowl. Cut in the shortening with a pastry blender or a fork until the mixture has the texture of coarse meal. Add the buttermilk and mix with your hand, lightly but thoroughly. Add a little more flour if the dough is too sticky. Knead for 1 minute. Wrap in wax paper or foil and refrigerate until well chilled, at least 20 minutes.

2. Preheat the oven to 450°F.

3. Roll the dough out ½ inch thick on a lightly floured surface or pastry cloth. (Always roll from the center out for tender, crisp biscuits.) Cut the dough into the desired size biscuits.

4. Place the biscuits on a dark baking sheet and bake until golden brown, 10 to 12 minutes.

Makes 25 to 30 biscuits.
  —*The Heritage of Southern Cooking* by Camille Glenn.

Sweet Potato Pie

3 large sweet potatoes   ½ teaspoon nutmeg
2 tablespoons butter   1 egg
½ cup sugar   2 egg whites
½ teaspoon cinnamon   4 teaspoons sugar

Boil potatoes until soft. Peel and mash well with 2 tablespoons butter. Add sugar, cinnamon, nutmeg, and egg, well beaten. Fill cooked pastry shell and cover with meringue made of beaten egg whites and 4 teaspoons of sugar. Brown in medium oven. Serves 6.

  —*Charleston Receipts.*

COUNTRY BREAKFAST SOUTHERN STYLE

Tradition holds that you don't skimp on breakfast down South. Lots of Southlanders to this day eat a substantial breakfast, including a hearty serving of meat (even fried chicken). Here's an old favorite, good for breakfast or a lazy weekend brunch.

MENU
Sliced country ham*
Smoked sausage
Red-eye gravy
Grits
Old Virginia Spoonbread**
Fried and scrambled eggs
Sliced tomatoes
Biscuits
Buckwheat pancakes
Fried apples
Fig jam** and cane syrup
Coffee

*Not just any old ham will do. You want real, honest-to-goodness cured country ham, which you should slice and fry.
**Recipes follow

Old Virginia Spoonbread

4 cups milk
1 cup yellow corn meal
1½ tablespoons salt
½ cup water

4 egg yolks, beaten
4 egg whites
⅛ teaspoon cream of tartar

Scald milk. Mix salt and corn meal with water and stir into milk. Cook until thickened. Remove from heat. Add a small amount of hot corn meal to egg yolks, then stir yolks into hot corn meal.

Add cream of tartar to egg whites. Whip until stiff but moist. Fold whites into corn meal and pour into a 2 qt. casserole greased pan. Bake at 350° until light brown and a knife inserted in center comes out clean. Serves 6.

—from *Virginia Seasons.*

Fig Jam

6 quarts boiling water
6 quarts fresh figs
Sugar

1 quart water
8 slices lemon

Pour boiling water over figs; let stand 15 minutes. Drain and thoroughly rinse in cold water. Pat dry; remove stems. Crush and measure figs; place in a large Dutch oven. Add ½ cup sugar for each cup of crushed figs. Add 1 quart water. Bring to a rapid boil; reduce heat, and simmer, uncovered, 3 hours or until thickened, stirring occasionally.

Ladle jam into hot sterilized jars, leaving ¼-inch headspace; add a slice of lemon to each jar. Cover at once with metal lids, and screw on bands. Process in a boiling-water bath 10 minutes. Yield: 8½ pints.

—from *Southern Living* Magazine.

RITUALS WITH VICTUALS:
TABLE ETIQUETTE DOWN SOUTH

Opening Comments
- Always say the blessing before you begin the meal.
- Keep your elbows off the table.
- Use a napkin, not your sleeve or the back of your hand, to wipe your mouth.

TABLE-TOP HOW-TO

Serving savoir-faire (two-methods).

1. Pass to the right. When you're passed a serving dish, hold it so your neighbor on the left can help him or herself. Then pass to your neighbor on the right so he/she can do the same for you. Also known as "boarding house style," this is the most formal and orderly method and is always used when several people come to dinner or supper.

2. Serve others from the bowl or platter closest to you as they hand you their plates from across the table. This is a more informal (and haphazard) method, but works fine if there aren't too many people at the table.

Do's and don'ts for doctoring up your food.

1. *Do* put butter, salt, and pepper or red-eye gravy on your grits. *Do not* sprinkle sugar or pour syrup on them.

2. *Do* sprinkle pepper sauce on your greens.

3. *Do* ladle pot-likker on your cornbread, meat, or vegetables.

4. *Do* pour cane syrup or sorghum on vegetables or breads, if your heart so desires.

FROM HAND TO MOUTH

Southern twists to handling your food.

When to use your fingers at mealtime:

1. When eating fried chicken (be sure to frequently lick your fingers).
2. When eating bacon.
3. When using your bread as "push bread" (to coax your food onto your fork) or to "sop up" tasty liquids (gravy, pot likker, and so forth) from your plate.
4. When crumbling cornbread into your glass of buttermilk.

Utensil utilization.

1. Hold your fork in your right hand. Rest your knife across the top rim of the plate. Do not use the European style of fork-in-left, knife-in-right unless you wish to put on airs of well-travelled sophistication.
2. To cut your meat, switch the fork from your right hand to your left and put the knife in your now-empty right hand. Hold the fork, tines down, and pierce the meat. Cut with the knife and replace it across the plate rim. Switch the fork back to your right hand, tines up. Eat and enjoy.

CONCLUDING COMMENTS

- A southern lady should always eat with dainty bites and leave some of her food uneaten. It is *most* unladylike to exhibit a voracious appetite, even if this is indeed the case.
- Except in the most sophisticated of restaurants, you can use a toothpick in Dixie after a meal. Just don't conduct an overly enthusiastic search-and-destroy mission.
- It is incontrovertibly bad manners to emit a burp or belch while at the table. If you enjoyed the meal, tell the host or hostess in a more refined way. If you didn't enjoy the meal, keep your lips buttoned.

FIVE FAVORITE SOUTHERN PIES

Pecan
Chess
Sweet Potato
Black Bottom
Peach

WHAT EVERY GOOD SOUTHERN COOK KEEPS HANDY

If you're going to cook southern-style meals, your efforts will be sorely lacking if you don't have our standard pantry staples on hand. Every southern cook worth her or his salt pork uses them and uses them often. Here's what to put on your shopping list:

STORE BOUGHT:

White grits
Corn meal: white and yellow
Winter-wheat flour (the secret to our light biscuits and cakes)
Syrups: cane, sorghum
Lard
Fatback/salt pork
Tabasco sauce
Cast iron cookware (for deep-fat frying and for baking cornbread)
Biscuit cutter
Paper sacks (for flour-coating chicken to be fried)
Bourbon whiskey

PUT UP:

Preserves and jams: peach, fig, pear
Jellies: dewberry, blackberry, scuppernong, quince, pepper
Butters: apple or peach
Spiced peaches
Relishes: hot pepper, tomato, Vidalia onion, chow-chow
Pickles: watermelon rind, bread and butter, squash, okra
Beans: green (pole/snap/string), butter (lima)
Field peas (crowder/cow/black-eyed/lady)
Pepper sauce
Sourwood honey
Pecans
Muscadine or scuppernong wine

TAKING IT TO THE LIMIT: MORE THAN MERELY DOWNHOME

For many of us, the mere sight of them is enough to last a lifetime, but others of us were raised to appreciate what we'll classify as the backwoods delicacies of the Southland: poke sallet, chitterlings, possum, and the like. Time was, southern folks who had to make do did just that with this sort of food fare. Nowadays, it's more a matter of taste (and pride) than pure necessity, as anyone who's ever attended the Cosby Ramp Festival in Cosby, Tennessee, or the Chitlin Strut in Salley, South Carolina, for example, can confirm.

If you have an adventuresome appetite and care to sample such of our original foods, don't look for them in the high-rent districts. City folk don't eat them (or own up to it). Instead, find yourself a country cousin or a food festival to dish you up what you've been missing all these years. It'll be a treat you won't be likely to forget.

Poke sallet: a bitter green that grows wild around the South and is slow-cooked like turnip greens.

Ramp: Appalachian delicacy (also known as wild leek) with the pungency of an onion, garlic, or leek. Served raw, fried, boiled, or scrambled with eggs.

Chitterlings (chitlins): pig intestines that are turned inside out, braided, boiled, and then fried. Not for the faint-hearted.

Cracklings: crispy leftovers from the rendering of pork fat during hog slaughtering. Cracklings make a tasty addition to cornbread.

Pigs feet, hog jowls: the former are often pickled in brine for later consumption.

Cooter: turtle. Boil the cooter in the shell and use the meat for soups, stews, or casseroles.

Possum: opossum. Best when baked.

Frog legs: served batter fried.

BEYOND GRITS AND GREENS:

FIVE-STAR SOUTHERN CUISINES

Now that you know that the Classic Southern Style of cooking is the end-all and be-all for the hearts, minds, and stomachs of the Southland, you need to know something else. There's more to southern food than our famous home-style meals, God bless them. We've got plenty more up our culinary sleeves: regional cuisines like Cajun and Creole, coastal fare (a la Carolina Low Country and Gulf Coast), specialties such as barbeque, catfish, Brunswick Stew, and Kentucky Burgoo, plus scores of original Southland delights.

If all this sounds like idle boasting to you, then it's for sure you haven't had the privilege of eating these classics. To know them is to passionately love them, and to crave more. All are worth a trip from anywhere, so make your travel plans now.

FIVE-STAR SOUTHERN CUISINES

Creole and Cajun.
Credit Louisiana's cornucopia of cultures (French, Spanish, Anglo-Saxon, African, Caribbean, and more) and its fertile land and waterways for these two legendary edible legacies. Think of New Orleans's famed Creole cuisine as the more cosmopolitan of the pair and of Cajun cooking as its spicier, bayou-country cousin (the latter recently glorified by Cajun chef Paul Prudhomme). Both maintain a distinct allegiance to traditional French cookery, but their ingredients (most importantly, seafood), seasonings, and style are pure native Louisiana. We can thank Louisiana for such contributions as:

Gumbo	Jambalaya
Crawfish Etouffée	Crawfish Bisque
Oysters Bienville	Oysters Rockefeller
Red Beans and Rice	Blackened Redfish

Shrimp Creole   Shrimp Remoulade
Trout Amandine   Pompano en Papillote
Chicory Coffee   Beignets
Po Boy Sandwiches   Bread Pudding

NOT-SO-SECRET KEY INGREDIENTS TO LOUISIANA COOKING

Filé powder. Made from ground sassafras leaves, filé powder is a thickening and flavoring agent. Often used in making gumbo.

Okra. If you don't swear by filé powder, then the pod of the gods is the power and glory of your gumbos.

Crab boil. These spices are added to the water in which crabs, crawfish, and shrimp are boiled. Louisianans have been loyal to Zartarain's brand of ready-made crab boil for nearly a century.

Cayenne peppers. This is the ultimate way to spice up your Cajun cooking, particularly soups and stews. If you're brave, omit the olive and make a K-Paul-style Cajun martini with a cayenne pepper instead.

Tabasco Sauce. This stand-by adds fiery zest to all sorts of foods.

Crawfish. These small freshwater crustaceans are distant relatives of the lobster. Their tail meat is a key ingredient in many Louisiana recipes and also is a favorite when served fresh-boiled, like shrimp.

Cane syrup. Extracted and boiled sugarcane juice, it often is added to Louisiana recipes.

Andouille. Cajun-made smoked sausage is used as seasoning meat for recipes like jambalaya. The original article was made from hog entrails.

Tasso. Another Cajun-made seasoning meat, tasso is made from pork, also known as Cajun ham.

CUISINES OF THE ATLANTIC AND GULF COASTS.

Of less celebrity than Louisiana cookery, but worthy of equal admiration, are the traditional cuisines of the coastal south. Around these parts, the foodways and foodlore are firmly embedded elements of style. What with some of the South's oldest cities (especially Mobile and Charleston) on the coastlines, the cultures of French and Spanish settlers often in evidence, the fruits of the sea (oysters, crab, shrimp, and salt-water fish) in fresh and plentiful supply, and the essence of Old South flavoring in it all, it's small wonder that generations of coastal Southerners have savored and handed down such favorites as these:

She-crab soup (South Carolina and Georgia)
Baked red snapper (Gulf and South Atlantic coasts)
Fried crab claws (Alabama)
Baked shad (Carolinas and Georgia)
Deviled Crab (Gulf and Atlantic coasts)
West Indies Salad (Alabama)
Crab Norfolk (Virginia)
Shrimp Pie (South Carolina)
Red Drum Stew and Pine Bark Stew (Atlantic coast)
Smoked Mullet (North Carolina and Virginia)

Wild Game.
Hunting used to be the primary means of putting food on the table in Dixie. Nowadays, it's mainly an opportunity for good old boys to stomp around in the woods or flyways with their buddies and whoop it up. Not that they don't take hunting seriously, however. It may be more sport than necessity for this generation, but you won't find a rank amateur in any group of southern hunters.

Quite naturally, our southern prowess on the hunt is matched by our southern savvy in the kitchen. If it moves, not only do we know how to kill it, we know how to make a meal out of it that's some kind of good. Skim a few southern cookbooks, and you'll see more than sufficient evidence:

Roast Wild Duck: stuffed with apple and potato dressing, basted with sherry and served with wild rice.

Squirrel: fried, in casserole, or in stew (once a standard ingredient in Brunswick stews and Kentucky burgoos).

Venison Steak: broiled and served with a hot wine sauce and grits and gravy.

Raccoon: roasted with sweet potatoes, chopped vegetables, and seasonings and served in its own pan gravy.

Dove and Oyster Pie: doves stuffed and layered with oysters and baked with seasonings in pastry.

Quail: sauteed in butter and baked with a sherry or wine baste.

FIVE-STAR SPECIALTIES OF THE SOUTH

To indulge in all the creative cookery the South has to offer, you'll have to do a little traveling. Many of our finest treats aren't found everywhere in Dixie. More than a few of them are local or regional phenomena whose renown far eclipses their availability. But without exception, they're worth going out of your way for and they're definitely worth the wait.

Barbecue.

Of all the delights of the Southern diet, barbecue is the most passionately debated method of preparing meat. Since it goes without saying that a southern meal isn't genuine or respectable unless there's meat on the plate, and since barbecueing dates back to the early days of our settlements, a discussion about barbecue should never be considered mere speculation.

Bona fide southern barbecue demands three things: pork shoulder or ribs, an outdoor cooking pit, and a sauce with which to baste the meat. While this sounds simple, what makes barbecue such a mysterious and controversial topic is the multiplicity of methods employed to make and serve it. Therein also lies its pleasures.

VARIATIONS ON THE BARBECUE THEME

This is a simple introduction to what has become a complicated subject. There's food for debate in it all.

What to cook.

Traditionalists prefer pork shoulder or a slab of pork ribs. Others opt for beef brisket or even lamb (which traditionalists consider pure hogwash).

How to cook it.

About the only thing barbecueists agree upon is that slow cooking is essential, up to twelve hours for pork shoulder. Up for controversy: the coals (hickory wood versus charcoal), the basting sauce (vinegar sauce versus tomato and vinegar sauce versus mustard sauce or other secret ingredients) and when to/not baste.

How to serve it.

First, there's the issue of the meat. Some serve it sliced, others serve it chopped, and yet others serve it pulled in pieces from the shoulder (you may have a choice in the matter at some barbecues). Furthermore, there's a question of whether outside meat (dark meat) or inside meat (white meat) is best. Next, there's the debate whether to serve it on buns or bread (two slices of white) or alongside the latter. Then, there's the matter of whether to add a final ladle of sauce, to provide it on the side, or not at all.

Lest all this sounds confusing, know that the final result is definitely worth the effort. It takes only one finger-licking feast of expertly made barbecue to convince you, at which time you'll think you've died and gone to heaven.

Lucky Southerners who live in the "southern barbecue belt" (which winds through parts of Alabama, Arkansas, Georgia, South Carolina, North Carolina, Kentucky, and Tennessee) get to taste the glories of barbecue whenever the spirit moves them. Around these neighborhoods, the brethren frequently can be found making a quick pilgrimage to their barbecue stand of choice or congregating in the name of civic or religious causes with a barbecue fund-raiser or festival. Two of the most gargantuan barbecue festivals occur annually in the rival barbecue capitals of Memphis, Tennessee, and Owensboro, Kentucky.

If you live too far from the holy land of barbecue for regular worship, fear not. You now can have southern-style barbecue air-expressed to your home and can even buy it in your grocer's frozen food case (see the "Dixie Hall of Fame" later in this chapter). Either should suffice until your next journey to your favorite stop on the barbecue belt.

Country Stews: Brunswick Stew and Kentucky Burgoo.

The bounty of the South is readily apparent in these two similar renderings of a native meat-and-vegetable stew. Often served as an accompaniment to barbecue, they're equally bound to provoke debate. Predictably, no one agrees about where the first was concocted (Georgia, North Carolina, or Virginia), about the proper way to make them (the squirrel-versus-chicken debate is a twentieth-century twist to an already variable list of ingredients), and which recipe is the best.

One thing is for certain, however; no one ever went hungry after downing a round of either. With half the garden, barnyard, and wildwoods represented in their contents and a consistency so thick you can eat them with a fork, our country stews are edible proof that we Southerners don't take good food lightly.

Catfish.

Put all of those notions of nasty scavenger fish out of your mind and pop a morsel of pond-raised catfish in your mouth instead. The lowly catfish ain't what she used to be. Today she's the darling of diners everywhere—not just the South—to the tune of 220 *million* pounds a year. Even a fast food chicken chain is now selling fried catfish in its 1,600 outlets.

Give thanks to southern ingenuity for using aquaculture to put one of our favorite foods in the spotlight, within easy reach. Primarily grown in the Mississippi Delta region (Belzoni, Mississippi, is the "Catfish Capital of the World") and fed a pampered diet of corn, soybeans, and nutrients, you need only taste a southern-bred catfish to see what the fuss is all about.

The most fitting way to go about this is to pay a visit to a down-South catfish house in the country. Don't expect frills; folks in these establishments prefer to stick to the basics (which they do commendably). This includes corn-meal-battered, deep-fried catfish and plump hush puppies, with accompaniments of cole slaw, fresh onion slices, pitchers of iced tea, and friendly southern-style service.

THE VIDALIA ONION: TRÈS CHIC TREAT

Move over, Georgia peach. There's another lip-smacking celebrity in town, the sweet Vidalia onion. It's in such demand that peach sales are the pits, by comparison. A sweet peach is rarely in limited supply; a genuine sweet Vidalia onion always is.

Like Smithfield hams, these onions come from one place and one place only: Vidalia, Georgia. The soil around Vidalia is almost devoid of sulfur (the culprit behind a typical onion's searing bite). Ergo, a Vidalia onion is a mild and sweet delight to eat, even right out of your hand.

Nowhere else on the face of the earth is such an onion found. So for a few months each summer, when the Vidalia is in season, plain folk and connoisseurs alike clamor for a supply of Vidalias and then retreat to their kitchens to devise yet another recipe for the pearly delight. We heartily recommend you do the same. If your grocer doesn't stock them, have a grower ship them (see "Earthy Delights," page 154).

HOW-TO BOOKS FOR COOKING UP YOUR OWN SOUTHERN SPECIALTIES

Ready to try your hand with some southern cooking of your own? Well, we're more than happy to share our recipes with you and, quite naturally, a little commentary as well. You can't go wrong with these cookbook standouts:

The Heritage of Southern Cooking, by Camille Glenn, published by Workman Publishing Co.

Southern Food, by John Egerton, published by Alfred A. Knopf.

Bill Neal's Southern Cooking, by Bill Neal, published by the University of North Carolina Press.

Craig Claiborne's Southern Cooking, by Craig Claiborne, published by Times Books.

Grace Hartley's Southern Cookbook, by Grace Hartley, published by Doubleday & Co.

Miss Mary's Down-home Cooking, by Diana Dalsass, published by New American Library.

White Trash Cooking, by Ernest Mickler, published by the Jargon Society and Ten Speed Press.

Chef Paul Prudhomme's Louisiana Kitchen, by Paul Prudhomme, published by William Morrow and Company, Inc.

The New Orleans Cookbook, by Rima and Richard Collin, published by Alfred A. Knopf.

Gracious Entertaining, Southern Style, by Daisy King, published by Rutledge Hill Press.

The Southern Junior League Cookbook, published by David McKay Company.

Charleston Receipts, published by the Junior League of Charleston, South Carolina.

Recipe Jubilee!, published by the Junior League of Mobile, Alabama.

River Road Recipes, published by the Junior League of Baton Rouge, Louisiana.

Kentucky Hospitality, published by the Kentucky Federation of Women's Clubs, Louisville, Kentucky.

SOUTHERN STYLE #4: COUNTRY FOLK
They're walking away winners at the county fair.

Gimme cap.

Motherly hairdo (goes to Jeanette's Cut'N Curl every Friday).

JC Penney chambray snapfront workshirt.

Her prizewinning pickles, in Ball canning jar, with a personalized label: "From the Kitchen of Doreen Walker."

Gruen watch with bracelet band.

Certificate for Best of Show for his Brahman bull (fifth year he's won).

Vinyl Ambassador Bag (bought by mail-order).

Rattlesnake belt (killed it last year while hunting turkey).

Lee jeans.

Dress made from Simplicity pattern #9876, poly/cotton no-iron blend.

Timex watch with Speidel Twistoflex band.

In pockets: Swiss army pocket knife, RED MAN chew (a plug in his mouth, too), keys to Chevrolet pickup, house, and gates to various cow pastures, hand-tooled leather wallet (with his name on it), handkerchief.

From Kinney's.

Redwing work boots.

Will Owen

DIXIE HALL OF FOOD FAME

Not only has southern foodlore established a name for itself, it boasts quite a few names that have become household words. These are the food and drink products that regularly grace many a Southerner's palate and pantry (and many a non-Southerner's, too). They're so much a part of life down here that we'd be losing the flavor of the Southland were they to disappear.

Fortunately, that's not likely, since nobody's expecting our appetite for these stars of southern foodlore to wane anytime soon. It's precisely because of their esteemed status that they belong to the prestigious Dixie Hall of Food Fame, our Who's Who of favorite and famous foods from the Southland.

DIXIE HALL OF FOOD FAMERS AND THEIR HOMETOWN

Goo-Goo Clusters (Nashville)
Moon Pies [Deluxe Double Decker] (Chattanooga)
Elmer's Gold Brick candy bars (New Orleans)
King Leo Peppermint Sticks (Nashville)
Claxton Fruitcakes (Claxton, Georgia)
Golden Flake Cheese Curls ["Good as Gold"] (Birmingham)
Lance Nabs (Charlotte, North Carolina)
Slim Jim Beef Jerkys (Raleigh, North Carolina)
Tom's Peanuts (Columbus, Georgia)
Planters' Peanuts (Suffolk, Virginia)
Kentucky Fried Chicken (Corbin, Kentucky)
Popeye's Fried Chicken (New Orleans)
Coca-Cola [Classic] (Atlanta)
Royal Crown [RC] Cola (Columbus, Georgia)
Barq's Root Beer (Biloxi, Mississippi)
Jax Beer (New Orleans)
Dixie Beer (New Orleans)
Community Coffee (Baton Rouge, Louisiana)

Luzianne Coffee (New Orleans)
Maxwell House Coffee (Nashville)
White Lily Flour and Corn Meal Mix (Knoxville, Tennessee)
Martha White's Jim Dandy Grits ["Real old-South flavor"] (Nashville)
Duncan Hines Cake Mixes (Bowling Green, Kentucky)
Dixie Crystals Sugar (Savannah)
Blue Plate Mayonnaise (New Orleans)
Bama Preserves and Jellies (Birmingham)
White House Apple Juice (Winchester, Virginia)
The Allen's Popeye Spinach (Siloam Springs, Arkansas)
Tabasco Sauce (Avery Island, Louisiana)
Bryan's Pork Sausage (West Point, Mississippi)
Zatarain's Crab Boil (New Orleans)

DIXIE HALL OF FAME TRIVIA TEST

How much do you know about Dixie food that's done us proud? Take this test and see:

1. Name the ingredients in a Goo-Goo Cluster *Supreme*.
2. Name the Dixie-made product that's been an announced sponsor of Grand Ole Opry broadcasts for over forty years.
3. What major soft drink, originally concocted in New Bern, North Carolina, was first named "Brad's Drink"?
4. Which U.S. president is said to have proclaimed the coffee of Nashville's Maxwell House hotel as "Good to the last drop"?

(Answers on page 152.)

. . . *And the Up to Your Ears in Peas Award* unanimously goes to Allen Canning Company of Siloam Springs, Arkansas, which sells its black-eyed peas under *five* different labels: The Allens, Allens Homefolks, Kitch-n-Kraft, Allens Sunshine, and Allens East Texas Fair. Should these five not fully satisfy your pea-pickin' quota, they offer yet three more varieties of peas from which to choose.

HOW TO BRING A TASTE OF THE SOUTH TO YOUR HOUSE

No matter where you live, the good taste of the Southland is within easy reach. Thanks to mail order, no one need ever again be deprived of some of life's brightest moments. Count your blessings.

DELECTIBLES

Byrd's Benne Wafers, Benne Candy, and more.
Byrd's "crisp, sweet, wafer-thin cookies" are a confectionary legend whose appeal comes from benne (sesame) seeds. The entire line of goodies is especially popular treats for gift giving. Write: Byrd Cookie Company, Post Office Box 13086, Savannah, GA 31406.

Moravian Sugar Crisps Cookies.
Cookie aficionados throughout the United States concur. Evva Travis's crisp and "Flavor-Full" sugar cookies deserve all the superlative praise they receive. Made from an old family recipe, each cookie is rolled, cut, and packaged by hand. Other varieties offered, too. Write: Moravian Sugar Crisp Company, Inc., Route 2, Box 431, Clemmons, NC 27012.

Goo-Goo Clusters and King Leo Stick Candy.
Southerners get hooked on these candies early in life, so much so that the Standard Candy Company regularly ships them to yearning natives at addresses far and wide. The Goo-Goo Cluster is "Tennessee's unofficial Official Candy Bar since 1912." Write: Standard Candy Company, Inc., Att'n: Mail Order Department, 715 Massman Drive, Nashville, TN 37210.

Gethsemani Farms Fruitcakes.
Gourmet columns regularly provide accolades to the bourbon-laced, fruit-packed fruitcakes made by the Trappist Monks at the Abbey of Gethsemani. So do consumers. Gethsemani Farms' volume of business is so large they have their own zip code. Cheese also available. Write: Gethsemani Farms, Trappist, KY 40051.

Pepper Patch Tennessee Tipsy Fruitcake.

As the name implies, theirs is a spirited fruitcake, with a liberal lacing of Jack Daniels Tennessee Whiskey. More high spirits (sherry and triple-sec) come in the Pepper Patch's Williamsburg Orange Wine Cake. Both "made from scratch." Write: Pepper Patch, 1250 Old Hillsboro Road, Franklin, TN 37064.

CONDIMENTS

Conner Farms.

The famous Vidalia onion is the star of Beverly Conner Cole's condiment collanade, which makes regular appearances on dinner tables all over. Her award-winning handiwork includes her famous Vidalia onion pickles, relish, mustard, salad dressings, and more. Write: Conner Farms, Inc., Post Office Box 1566, Dalton, GA 30722.

Pepper Patch.

A showcase of inspired southern condiments, the entire Pepper Patch line is handmade, all-natural, and very intriguing. With such products as Jezebel's Sauce, Spring Onion Jelly, Apple Relish, and Sweet Potato Butter, biscuits and crackers will never be the same again. Write to address above.

Southern Touch Muscadine products.

Muscadine jams and jellies have been a staple in southern pantries for generations, but they're hard to find if you don't put them up yourself. Unless, that is, you know about Southern Touch, which makes jellies, jams, preserves, juices, and syrups in both the red and white varieties of the muscadine berry. Write: Southeastern Specialty Foods Corporation, 2212 B Street, Meridian, MS 39301 (or call 1/800-233-1736).

ANSWERS TO "DIXIE HALL OF FAME TRIVIA TEST" ON PAGE 150.

1. Chocolate, marshmallow, caramel, and pecans. 2. Martha White Flour. 3. Pepsi-Cola. 4. President Theodore Roosevelt.

The Mayhaw Tree products.

Not everybody gets to savor the makings of the tart red Mayhaw berry, because the wild Mayhaw trees grow only in the swamps and bogs of southwest Georgia. The harvest is gathered by hand and scooped out of the water with fish-nets. The results well justify the arduous means: jelly, wine jelly, syrup, ham sauce, and salad dressing, all made with the precious Mayhaw. Write: The Mayhaw Tree, Inc., Post Office Box 144, Colquitt, GA 31737.

COUNTRY HAMS, SAUSAGE, AND BACON

As with barbecue, just about every Southerner has a distinct preference for how country ham should be made. Find your liking among these purveyors.

Kettle Smoke House.
Their method of preparation is native to the Arkansas Ozarks: sugar curing and cold smoking with hickory and fruitwood chips and herbs. Other smoked meats offered by the Kettle Smoke House include bacon, turkey, chicken, and sausage. Write: Kettle Smoke House, 3607 South Thompson, Highway 71 South, Springdale, AR 72764.

Edwards & Sons Virginia Hams.
Three generations of Edwards have been tending the family business, with extraordinary results. Edwards hams have been winning awards and kudos for just about as long as they've been dry curing and hickory smoking hams. Smoked link sausage and bacon are also available. Write: H. Wallace Edwards & Sons, Inc., Highway 31, Box 25, Surry, VA 23883.

The Smithfield Collection.
From the city whose name is synonymous with ham comes an offering of hams that are dry cured and smoked with oak, hickory, and apple woods. Hickory-smoked turkey is featured also, as is an array of complements for the meal, including James River Brunswick Stew and Beef Barbecue. Write: The Smithfield Collection, Post Office Box 487, Smithfield, VA 23430.

Mayo Sausage Company.
Since 1932 the Mayo family has been pleasing Tennesseans with their dry-cured, hickory-smoked pork sausage and similarly prepared hams and bacon. Their products are

so good that several companies depend upon the Mayos to make their own branded sausage for them. Write: Mayo Sausage Company, 7120 Charlotte Pike, Nashville, TN 37209.

BARBECUE

If you can't make your own or lay your hands on somebody else's, don't give up yet. Say grace instead! Two of barbecue's most heralded names will send their best right to your door.

Maurice's Flying Pig Gourmet Barbecue.

South Carolina's king of barbecue will ship his famous pit-cooked pork barbecue (chopped or ribs), sauce, and more anywhere in the United States, even Alaska and Hawaii. Call 1/800-MAURICE.

Charlie Vergos' Rendezvous Ribs.

Rib fans who know about this hallowed barbecue haven will be gratified to learn that Charlie Vergos will air express five orders of ribs, seasoning, and sauce at your command. Call 1/800-524-5554 and dial "BBCUE" after the tone, Tuesday through Friday.

EARTHY DELIGHTS

Vidalia Onions.

These delicacies may be mail ordered from any number of shippers. Two of the larger growers are *Vidalia Sweets*, Post Office Box 426, Vidalia, GA 30474 (1/800-537-7009), and *Southern Cross Farms*, Post Office Box 627, Vidalia, GA 30474 (1/800-833-0009).
Note: Genuine Vidalia onions are shipped during the months of May, June, and July.

Pecans.

Pecan growers abound in the South, especially the Deep South. Two popular sources are: *Sherard Plantation Pecans*, Post Office Box 75, Sherard, MS 38669 and *Priester's Pecans*, Fort Deposit, AL 36032.

Peanuts.

Who would dare dispute that goobers are a quintessentially southern food? Fans from anywhere can get their fill from *Virginia Diner Peanuts,* a frequent food writers' choice, Post Office Box 310, Wakefield, VA 23888 (1/800-642-NUTS); or *A & B Milling Company, Inc.,* Box 327, Enfield, NC 27823 (1/800-843-0105).

LOUISIANA FARE

K-Paul's.

Everything you need to produce an authentic Louisiana meal (with the accent on Cajun) is available from the enterprising Paul Prudhomme. Meats, spices, recipes, wares, videos, and folklore aplenty. Write: K-Paul's Louisiana Kitchen, Post Office Box 70034, New Orleans, LA 70034 (1/800-4KPAULS).

Bon Mélange.

The mystery has been taken out of Creole cooking with Bon Mélange pre-mixed foods. Mixes and makings for traditional Creole sauces, soups, and breads, all developed by a New Orleans native. Write: Bon Mélange Inc., 301 East Second Street, Pass Christian, MS 39571.

SOUTHERN SAMPLERS

More Southern specialties to choose from than you can shake a stick at.

Callaway Gardens.

Their Speckled Heart Grits, which include bits of the corn kernel heart, are commendable examples of great grits. They are sold by mail in combination with a slab of their pepper-coated bacon. Other Southern food products, including condiments, are also available. Write: Callaway Gardens Country Store, Pine Mountain, GA 31822.

Early's Honey Stand.

In addition to their own sorghum, clover honey, and condiments, the Early family sells stone-ground grits, corn meal, seasoned flour, biscuit mix, and the like. That's not all. Early's has been doing a deservedly big business with their smoked hams, bacons, and sausage for over sixty years. Write: Early's Honey Stand, Post Office Box K, Spring Hill, TN 37174.

FOOD AND THE SOUTHERN EXPERIENCE

We admit it. We Southerners are emotionally attached to food. We love and adore fixing it, eating it, and talking about it. Since food has long been a focus of the southern experience, this is naturally so.

Food is part of our heritage of being close to the land. We have hunted food and have cultivated it to survive and also to profit (many of us still do). Food means family, too. As always, that sacred institution in Dixie still regularly convenes around—what else—food.

What's more, eating food can be a religious experience for a great many of us Southlanders. Our church-going brethren regularly break bread together in holy communion (widely known down here as the "Lord's Supper"). The same goes for their more social-minded gastronomic church get-togethers, dinners on the grounds and covered-dish suppers. One feast at these gargantuan events and you'll know why even those who've never got religion have been known to get it in a hurry under such circumstances.

Our love for food goes still further, also having inspired an appetizing route to fund raising. Guess who pioneered the sale of regional cookbooks to raise money for good causes? Southern ladies, of course. What better way to round up willing donations than an all-day barbecue cook-off, fish fry, or bake sale?

For just plain fun, we can count on food to get us there. Lord only knows how many ways we celebrate food down

here in Dixie. If it grows and is edible, we probably commemorate it, from the backyard watermelon repast to the
county-wide food festival. Southerners everywhere know
how to have fun with food; it's as natural as saying grace
over supper. And if there's not an opportunity at hand to do
just that, we'd as soon make one up than do without.

FUN WITH FOOD IN DIXIE: FESTIVALS

To see firsthand how we make our food fun,
you need to join in the goings-on at one of our many food
festivals. There's always plenty of the featured food available, but you also can count on uninterrupted entertainment. Usually there is a themed parade (which can get
pretty imaginative), a pageant to present the festival queen
(if not an entire royal family), downhome music, and lots of
contests (which can also get pretty inventive). Some festivals last a day, and others go on for weeks at a time; but all
are guaranteed to be a genuine slice of life, Southern Style.

Here's a fair sampling of how to have fun with food in
Dixie (for more information, contact local chambers of
commerce):

April

World Catfish Festival, Belzoni, Mississippi. The capital of
   pond-raised catfish commemorates the state's premier ex-
   port.

World Grits Festival, St. George, South Carolina.

World's Biggest Fish Fry, Paris, Tennessee. Over eight tons of
   fresh Tennessee River catfish are fried up for this event.

May

Vidalia Onion Festival, Vidalia, Georgia.

International Bar-B-Q Festival, Owensboro, Kentucky.
   Claimed to be the barbecue capital of the world, over
   40,000 fans join the annual feast, which features mutton.

International Barbecue Cooking Contest, Memphis, Tennessee. Memphis claims to be the pork barbecue capital of the world. The over 100,000 fans attending annually are, no doubt, practicing believers.

Cosby Ramp Festival, Cosby, Tennessee. In celebration of the "sweetest tasting, vilest smelling plant that grows."

June

Pink Tomato Festival, Warren, Arkansas. Celebrate the June harvest of tomatoes picked in the pink of their prime.

Poke Sallet Festival, Harlan, Kentucky. In honor of the wild-growing green.

Wanchese Seafood Festival and Blessing of the Fleet, Outer Banks, North Carolina.

July

South Carolina Peach Festival, Gaffney South Carolina.

Grand Bay Watermelon Festival, Grand Bay, Alabama. Claims to be the world's largest celebration of watermelon.

August

Watermelon Festival, Hope, Arkansas. Hope doesn't claim to have the world's largest watermelon celebration, merely the world's largest watermelons.

Strange Seafood Festival, Beaufort, North Carolina. Your chance to sample many exotica of the sea, thanks to the North Carolina Maritime Museum.

September

International Banana Festival, Fulton, Kentucky and South Fulton, Tennessee. These river towns used to be the nation's largest distribution stop for banana shipments. The festival features a one-ton banana pudding.

National Pecan Festival, Albany, Georgia.

Collard Festival, Ayden, North Carolina. If you don't win the Collard Queen competition, you can always try your hand at the collard-eating contest.

Sugar Cane Festival, New Iberia, Louisiana.

Sorghum Sopping Days, Waldo, Alabama. Sop all the sorghum you crave; homemade biscuits are at the ready.

Bayou Food Festival, Lafayette, Louisiana. Submerge yourself in a plethora of Cajun specialties for a mere pittance. Part of the annual Festival Acadiens.

October

Okra Strut, Irmo, South Carolina. The Pod of the Gods is feted in fine fashion. Don't miss the Shoot-out at the OKra Corral, Irmo's celebrity okra-eating contest.

Arkansas Rice Festival, Weiner, Arkansas.

National Peanut Festival, Dothan, Alabama. Its two and one-half mile parade is capped off with a cement mixer that spews peanuts to cheering onlookers.

National Pumpkin Festival, Spring Hope, North Carolina.

Big Pig Jig Barbeque Cookoff, Vienna, Georgia. Festivities include a five-K "hog jog," a hog-calling competition, and a greased pig contest.

Kentucky Apple Festival, Paintsville, Kentucky.

Yambilee, Opelousas, Louisiana. A big (200,000 festival-goers) celebration, yam-packed with events.

Trigg County Country Ham Festival and Fair, Cadiz, Kentucky. These folks are long renowned for their country hams. Includes the world's largest country ham biscuit.

National Shrimp Festival, Gulf Shores, Alabama.

Andouille Festival, LaPlace, Louisiana.

November

Chitlin Strut, Salley, South Carolina. All you care to eat of those famous fried entrails (over 20,000 pounds to choose from).

Swine Time Festival, Climax, Georgia. As often said, feel free to make a pig of yourself here. There's even a best-dressed pig contest.

FAVORITE FOODFESTS

Some foods are more favorite than others, as these popular festivals attest.

Watermelons are by far the South's most celebrated food, with summertime watermelon festivals in eight of ten states (only North Carolina and Kentucky don't so honor the watermelon).

Apples are almost as favored as watermelon, with fall apple festivals annually scheduled in seven southern states (the abstaining Gulf states of Louisiana, Mississippi, and Alabama aren't blessed with much apple-growing terrain).

Peanut festivals are another annual rite of fall in Alabama, Georgia, North Carolina, South Carolina, and Virginia.

HOW TO EAT A WATERMELON SOUTHERN STYLE

SELECTION TIPS

Best Method.
Go to your garden and select a perfectly ripe *Citrullus Vulgaris*. If neither you nor your invited guests grow your own watermelons, then beg, plead, or cajole one from a neighbor or family member who does.

Next Best Method.
If you come up empty handed, head for the neighborhood produce truck or farmers' market for your watermelon.

Last Ditch Method.
Should still none of the above options pan out, you will have to settle for a

melon from the grocery store (in most cases, this will still be better than no melon at all). However, if you buy a store-bought melon, do not attempt to pass off your melon as home grown. Few Southerners will fall for such a ruse.

PREPARATION TIPS

Where to Eat.

A genuine watermelon repast must be conducted out-of-doors, in the yard or on the porch. Of course it will be as hot as the blue blazes outside, and humid, too, but this is as it should be. Situate everybody in a shady spot in lawn chairs, swings, and picnic tables.

What to Wear.

Be sure to keep the whole affair down-home and relaxed. Bare feet encouraged. No dress-up allowed, since this can get pretty sloppy.

Who Participates.

Your family, friends, and neighbors must be in attendance. Children and pets

All-method Thump Test.

To select a truly ripe and juicy melon, employ the Thump Test. A watermelon that is ready to enjoy will sound full and deep in tone when you give it a hard thump with your finger.

should chase about while grownups swat at gnats and catch up on the latest developments (that is, gossip). Invite the preacher and his wife, if you've a mind to.

Making Ready.

Set out the watermelon(s), salt shaker, and plenty of napkins on a table. Designate an adult to cut the watermelon with a long butcher knife when everyone's ready to eat.

To cut, slice the melon in half vertically. Cut these halves like a loaf of bread, into slices about three inches thick. Cut these rounds in half.

How to Eat the Thing

1. Resist any urges to use a knife and fork. Not only are they unwieldly to use on a slice of seed-riddled watermelon, utensils give an aura of pretension to what is otherwise a very playful occasion. Rest assured, you don't need anything but your hands and your mouth to eat all the watermelon your heart desires and enjoy every bite.

2. Take a slice in both hands and eat it like a big cookie. Slurp, smack, lick, and savor the sweet, red meat.

3. If the juice dribbles down your chin, don't worry. Just wipe it off with the back of your hand.

4. When you encounter watermelon seeds, for heaven's sake, do not eat them. Merely spit them out on the ground and be done with them, unless you wish to

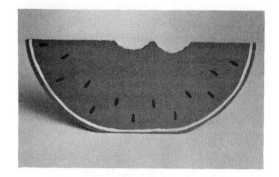

compete in a watermelon seed-spitting contest with fellow eaters. (This little game is self-explanatory. Have fun.)

5. Once you have consumed every morsel of the red flesh, toss the rind in a pile with other rinds (use them for compost). Go back for another piece and have at it again.

How City Folk Eat Watermelon

Directions.

1. In your kitchen, cut open a ripe watermelon. Scoop out the red flesh with a melon baller and place the balls in a mixing bowl. Avoid all seeds.

2. After you have scooped out oodles of little red balls, toss them with freshly made poppyseed dressing. Cover and refrigerate.

3. Throw the rind and seeds in the trash compactor.

4. Serve the watermelon at brunch in cute glass bowls or in individual crystal goblets. Garnish with sprig of mint, if desired. Also makes a delightful dessert for an outdoor picnic (symphony in the park, Shakespeare under the stars, and so forth).

Chapter Seven

In God We Trust in Dixie

Verily, verily, until ye have seen the light about religion down South, ye cannot completely understand Southern Style. Yea, it would be easier for a camel to go through the eye of a needle.

Everywhere you turn in Dixie, you can see the legacy of our religious heritage in action. It runs deep and wide in the southern culture and psyche. You won't need a divine revelation to discover that our approach to religion is one-of-a-kind. Like just about everything else down South, we do religion *our* way and in a *big* way.

You can't escape religion down South. You couldn't if you tried. To put it in the terms of common Bible Belt wisdom, "You can't run from God" when you live around these parts. The upshot of all this is that if you care to truly fathom Southern Style, we advise you to factor in the kinds of godly considerations we'll be pointing out in this chapter.

We know you'll find them illuminating.

YOU GOTTA HAVE RELIGION

While folks in other cultures may find it sufficient to *practice* their religion, in the Southland you've got to *have* religion.

The vast majority of Southerners know what it means to have religion. Many got religion at an early age. Some got religion, but then lost it. Still others lost their religion, but later recovered it. And some are still holding out.

Having religion is the southern way of saying you've gone whole hog for Jesus. It means you have been saved (also known as having "found the Lord"). To have been saved supplies you with a sort of holy insurance policy against spending forever in hell. (Details available for How to Be Saved, Southern Style, at most Protestant churches and all Fundamentalist ones.)

Once you have your own policy, you no longer have to worry about the dismal prospects of eternal damnation and hellfire. You've been saved from that. Instead, you can look forward to a happy and heavenly ever after, because now you've got religion. As for life on this earth, those who have been saved must live like loyal followers of Jesus (see below) and persuade those who don't have religion to get it right away.

FUNDAMENTALLY SPEAKING . . .

A great many Southerners who have religion (have been saved) consider themselves "Fundamentalists." A Fundamentalist is a very conservative kind of Protestant who very carefully lives by the Book (the Good Book, that is), especially the New Testament, *to the letter.* You could very well say that the Good Book is the Fundamentalists' ultimate handbook to life. Word for word.

The standard Fundamentalist approach to religion is all the way or nothing. You can't relegate it to an hour's worship on Sunday mornings. You have to *live* it, literally by the rules of the Book, twenty-four hours a day. This is known as "practicing what you preach."

Even for Fundamentalists, how exactly to live by the Book to the letter depends upon who's reading it. This explains the proliferation of denominations of Fundamentalist faiths, such as Baptists, Methodists, Assemblies of God, Churches of God, Holiness, Pentecostals, and so forth. This also explains why there are at least fifteen kinds of Baptists, almost as many kinds of Pentecostals, and about ten kinds of Methodists. Clearly, for Fundamentalists, having religion varies six ways to Sunday and back again.

HOW THOSE WHO HAVE RELIGION

TOE THE LINE

Do's:
- Praying and reading the Bible daily
- Living a Godly life (setting a Christian example)
- Sharing the gospel
- Obeying the Ten Commandments
- Attending Sunday school and church services faithfully, on Sunday and during the week
- Tithing
- Teaching a Bible class
- Being on a church committee
- Being a deacon/elder/lay reader
- Singing in the choir or assisting in the kids' nursery during church services
- Having the pastor and wife over at least once a year
- Giving to special church fund drives (building, missionary)
- Helping the less fortunate

Don'ts:
- Acting un-Christian
- Disobeying the Ten Commandments
- Neglecting your church responsibilities
- Changing church denominations
- Cussing
- Behaving rudely
- Being selfish or unforgiving
- Messing around if you're married
- Messing around if you're unmarried
- Engaging in ungodly pastimes (gambling, drinking, drugs, smoking, dancing, etc.) or consorting with those who do
- Dressing immodestly

Hardcore Don'ts
Reading secular books (especially trashy novels, books about evolution, or similar "humanistic" topics), playing cards, attending the movies, listening to secular music, or wearing "worldly," that is, suggestive or trendy clothing.

BIG REASONS FOR TAKING RELIGION
SO SERIOUSLY IN DIXIE

You are probably of the opinion that we Southlanders tend to take our religion very seriously. You are right, brothers and sisters. Religion, Southern Style, is no laughing matter around here. Whatever your religious persuasion (and if you're a Southerner, you've probably been earnestly persuaded to have religion our way), it's advisable to treat the subject like the sacred southern institution it is.

Unless you are prepared to engage in a heated and protracted argument, it is also advisable to do the following should the subject of religion down South come up in your presence. Don't make jokes about it, don't disparage it, and don't toss out provocative statements (for instance, "Creationism is an obsolete concept"). If you do, be prepared to miss supper. Theological debates have been known to run for decades down South, and there is little reason to believe that yours will be exempt.

Consider the reasons why.

1. Big consequences.

Remember, the stakes aren't just high, according to those of us who have religion. They're high heaven, and eternal. With the surety of everlasting hell as the alternative, this puts having religion and spreading it in the realm of the utmost, the ultimate, and the urgent for its believers.

2. Big image.

H. L. Mencken, man of letters, didn't dub our region the "Bible Belt" on a whim. The shoe fit earlier this century, it fit a hundred years earlier, and it still fits today. Everybody knows it, too, because we've never tried to hide it. On the contrary. The South's You-Gotta-Have-Religion philosophy has been proclaimed to all four corners of the earth. This stance has become part and parcel of the southern identity, which means that impugning our prevalent forms of faith is tantamount to impugning Dixie.

3. Big impact.

Those do's and don'ts of religion our way have wielded considerable influence on the shaping of Southern Style. How else could we have developed our trademark propriety and deportment than from a legacy of Sunday school lessons and church sermons? Those essential southern virtues such as humility, kindness, and good manners do not occur in nature, even in home soil.

4. Big numbers.

By sheer size alone, the Southland's body of believers is a force to be reckoned with. There are *millions* of folks who have religion down South. Our two largest denominations, Southern Baptists and United Methodists, together have about twenty-five million members, the majority of whom live in Dixie. Add in the dozens of other denominations and sects who more or less share the same theological hymnbook, and you are looking at numbers that count for the goodly portion of Southlanders. Period.

The Seven Deadly Sins in Dixie
Secularism
Not attending church regularly
Not tithing
Disparaging the Motherland
Hubris
Bad manners
Indiscretion with your moral lapses

TIPS FOR HYPOCRITES

You know who you are. Once upon a time, you had religion but let it lapse. Not that you're against having religion in principle (few Southerners take such a stand), it's just that you're content with small doses of it on an occasional basis.

Problem is, that's not enough for those around here who have religion. This means two things: (1) You've become classified as a "backslider," "fence-straddler," or "hypocrite"; (2) Unless you wish to remain in an abysmal state of grace with your more exemplary family, friends, and relations, you're going to have to make some concessions. Like the Chinese, sometimes it's important for Southerners to save face. When it comes to religion down South, this is always the case.

So here are a few tried-and-true tips for hypocrites:

1. Occasionally attend church.

Holy day services like Easter and Christmas are popular choices, but you will want to avoid attending Sunday school or other small groups where your feet might get held to the fire for your lax behavior. This is known as the "better than nothing" technique. While in church do these things:

- Sit among the back rows of the congregation.
- Put one dollar in the offering plate when it passes and smile beatifically.
- Refrain from sleeping during the sermon. Instead, look attentively at the preacher while thinking about what you'll do when church is over.
- Be sure to exit through the front door to shake the preacher's hand. Tell him how much you enjoyed the sermon.

2. Leave a large Bible out on the coffee table.

Give it a place of honor in your living room, right next to your favorite magazines and the *Ideals* keepsake books. This gives the impression that you have your priorities right.

3. Indulge in your chosen vices on the sly.

If you are found out, stay calm. Admit your human frailty and act contrite until the lapses of another backslider become the focus of attention (which will eventually occur). Be extra discreet upon resuming your indulgences. You're under the watchful eyes of your concerned brethren and sisters.

THE RISE AND SWELL OF THE BIBLE BELT

Believe it or not, the South hasn't always been as intent upon walking in the footsteps of Jesus as you might think. Fact is, the Southland itself didn't truly get religion in the southern sense of the word until the mid-1700s. This was because few rural settlers owned Bibles (or could read them), much less had churches to attend. It took a religious movement called the Great Awakening sweeping across Dixie to instigate our conversion. Under the impassioned exhortations of traveling evangelists, circuit riders, and farmer-preachers (often at large gatherings known as "revivals" and "camp meetings"), thousands of slumbering sinners in the South were aroused and saved from the clutches of the devil.

On the whole, Southerners took to the Great Awakening like a duck on a June bug. In contrast to their rather staid and disciplined rural life, our forebears carried on aplenty in revivals and camp meetings. Historical accounts vouch that these events reached a pitch of unbridled emotional and physical spectacle that most Southerners would today find out of hand. But for about 100 years, such spells of fervor were the accepted demonstrations of one's conversion from sin. Folks from the backwoods, uptown, and in-between became equally inspired to publicly get religion and be filled with the Spirit of the Lord, often with astonishing results.

Early camp meeting scene.

Bodily Exercises: Letting the Spirit Move During the Great Awakening

Falling—collapsing in a dead faint.
Jerking ("taking the jerks")—convulsive head twitching.
Speaking in Tongues—spontaneous speaking in languages unknown to the talker.
Rolling
Running
Barking
Laughing
Trances
Visions

Let-loose worship of this magnitude is, by and large, out of vogue these days down South as most Southerners prefer to keep their expressions of religion within current boundaries of good taste. Although some religious gatherings are prone to get somewhat unrestrained at times, they're fairly orthodox compared with the goings-on of revivalism. But if you seek, you can still find the holy-rolling venues of old-time, stoked-up, get-down religious fervor, a slice of southern history neither gone nor forgotten.

CANE RIDGE: THE SOUTH'S GRANDEST CAMP MEETING

Over 20,000 Southerners came from hundreds of miles around to Cane Ridge in Bourbon County, Kentucky, in early August, 1801. Camping in tents, covered wagons, sheds, and clearings, they came to participate in a marathon of religious rallying: non-stop sermonizing, hymn singing, praying, river baptisms, marching processions, and unrestrained outpourings of spiritual fervor.

The Cane Ridge camp meeting could rightly be described as a religious extravaganza. Preachers and circuit riders addressed the camp "tabernacles," vehemently stoking the fires of repentance and zeal among the attending throngs. Issuing impassioned, vivid oratory about the terrifying torments of hell and the heavenly rewards of salvation, these sons of thunder led their worshipers to frenzied crescendos of spiritual ecstasy.

Overcome with emotion and religious conviction, members of the audiences would shriek and shout, weep, wail and mourn, and often succumb to the uncontrollable paroxysms of religious exercises (it's well documented that over 3,000 at Cane Ridge "fell"). History also tells us that some of those in attendance were also overcome with passions that were something other than godly, resulting from sharing close quarters and a let-your-guard-down abandon. This prompted several critics of the day to observe that more souls were conceived than saved at Cane Ridge.

Camp meetings like Cane Ridge weren't confined to the Southland but were most numerous inside it. To this day you can find camp meetings (usually in early autumn) in Dixie. These versions are generally more reserved than those of the Cane Ridge era. You can expect that the preaching and singing and testifying will get pretty enthusiastic, but the more sensational dimensions of yesteryear are usually the province of isolated and backwoods assemblies.

MAKING A JOYFUL NOISE IN DIXIE

We Southerners take our religion seriously, but being an expressive lot, we're frequently disposed to do so with a smile on our faces, a song on our lips, and often a host of expressions that are anything but staid. In other words, let it be known that keeping a stiff upper lip rarely has its place in the worship service down South (this includes funerals).

For us, freedom of expression demonstrably goes hand in hand with freedom of religion, and we have been known to take full advantage of these rights when the spirit moves us. Since this happens on a wholesale basis around here, we have amassed boundless ways to evidence our uplifted states.

However, how to praise the Lord, Southern Style, isn't quite the simple matter you might expect. About the only generalization you can make is, the less orthodox the service, the more folks will participate and express themselves. Following that, what constitutes making a joyful noise unto the Lord in Dixie is about as open to interpretation as the Holy Scriptures and can be equally as controversial from one sanctuary to the next.

But don't let this little wrinkle deter you from paying a visit to a church service down South. As any Southlander who has religion will assert, you can't afford to miss it. Instead, read the rest of what we have to say, then try it yourself next Sunday.

Above all else, once you've settled in a pew, *go with the flow.* Even if your intentions are less than ethereal, we swear on the Good Book that you'll find it a glorifying experience, Southern Style.

MAKING HEAVENLY MUSIC ON EARTH

The presence of music in church services is by no means original to the Southland, but the way we have long gone about singing our heavenly praises most certainly is. Ever since the fires of revivalism blazed during the Great Awakening, Southerners have been pulling out all the stops to praise the Lord in song.

In fact, much of our region's remarkable musical tradition was cradled within the walls of southern churches. Considering how much time Southerners have spent in church and considering the source of inspiration, this is perfectly understandable.

A few grave verses of a somber hymn or two would never do for most southern congregations. What these folk yearn for are the spirit-stirring anthems, harmonizing hymns, and toe-tapping choruses of Old Time Religion

And the more, the better. Because not only does the music provide a sanctioned outlet for releasing spiritual zeal, the experienced know well that even if you can't count on the sermon to move you, the music assuredly will. No need for proselytizing; there's a way to say it in song that almost always strikes a responsive chord.

LONG-LIVED BIBLE BELT HYMNS

Praise and adoration

"All Hail the Power of Jesus' Name"

"Glorious Things of Thee Are Spoken"

"Come, Thou Long-Expected Jesus"

"Rejoice, Ye Pure in Heart"

"Crown Him with Many Crowns"

"Holy, Holy, Holy"

"Come, Thou Almighty King"

"O For a Thousand Tongues to Sing"

Faith

"Love Divine, All Loves Excelling"

"What a Friend We Have in Jesus"

"We're Marching to Zion"

"How Firm a Foundation"

"The Unclouded Day"

"The Solid Rock"

"Have Faith in God"

"Standing on the Promises"

Repentance, Unworthiness

"When I Survey The Wondrous Cross"

"Alas, and Did My Savior Bleed"

"Jesus, Lover of My Soul"

"There Is a Fountain"

"I Am Thine, O Lord"

"Savior, Like a Shepherd Lead Us"

Salvation

"Softly and Tenderly"

"Wherever He Leads, I'll Go"

"His Way with Thee"

"I Surrender All"

"Jesus Is Calling"

"Trust and Obey"

"Nothing But the Blood"

Favorite Old-Time Religion Songs

"The Old Rugged Cross"

"Sweeter Than the Day Before"

"Rescue the Perishing"

"Shall We Gather at the River"

"Amazing Grace"

"Bringing in the Sheaves"

"Send the Light"

"Sweet By and By"

"Rock of Ages"

"When They Ring Them Golden Bells"

Most dreaded hymn

"Just As I Am" (all six verses)

SHOWING MUSICAL SAVVY IN THE CHURCH SERVICE

Use these tips to enhance your worship wherewithal.

1. *Sing from the heart.* Make a joyful noise, even if you're tone deaf. Whether you can carry a tune is beside the point, so open up and sing like there's no tomorrow.

2. *Harmonize if you can.* Four-part singing is a favorite. Sounds pretty, too.

3. *Watch the song leader.* If you don't, you can never be sure when to stand or remain seated, skip a verse, or sing the Amen at the end.

4. *Demonstrate your enthusiasm.* Feel free to pat your foot or nod your head to the music. Some congregations clap to the music; others even sing responses on cue.

5. *Don't be overwhelmed by lots of bells and whistles.* Prepare yourself for something beyond a pipe organ should you attend a large evangelical church. Expect similarly large musical statements like eighty-member choirs, ten-piece orchestras, guitars, percussion, spotlights, and full amplification.

6. *Be especially reverent during the closing hymn (the "invitation").* This is the chance for those who don't have religion to get it, so keep as quiet as a church mouse.

. . . . But once the church service is over, don't think that the music has been silenced. One of the most rousing experiences in religious musicdom is a down-South hymnfest or gospel musicfest, enraptured choruses on earth the likes of which you've probably never heard before. Folks come from all around to appreciate or participate in these church-wide, city-wide, or state-wide musical convocations.

Sunday morning across the Southland, rain or shine.

SHAPED NOTE MUSIC: DEEP SOUTH MUSICAL TRADITION

Echoes of our pioneer past regularly and melodically recur across the Deep South with the haunting strains of shaped note music. With its distinctive musical style, Elizabethan origins, and its poetic, narrative lyrics, shaped note music is a moving example of southern folk music.

The debt of this sonorous legacy is owed to South Carolina native Benjamin Franklin White, the first to assemble a collection of shaped note hymns. His songbook *Sacred Harp*, put harmonizing song within the reaches of rural and frontier Southerners during the mid-1800s. The key was a simplified system of musical instruction that employed four musical syllables (fa, sol, la, mi), each of which was depicted with a shaped note (triangle, circle, square, and diamond). With no instrumental accompaniment needed, shaped note singing soon became a popular southern phenomenon, both in and out of churches.

Because of its unusual style, shaped note music has an unusual sound by tra-

ditional standards, one that's been likened to the eerie, minor-key effect of bagpipes. The lyrics are from the heart, often spinning out mournful sentiments of the common man (despair, fear, death) and religious themes (afterlife).

Shaped note singing still flourishes in today's Southland. Conventions of Sacred Harp and Christian Harmony enthusiasts often meet, and singing schools continue to instruct this unique, intriguing musical legacy.

. . . *And the Eat-Your-Pious-Words Award* goes to the hymnal revision committee of the United Methodist Church, who in 1986 raised the dander of thousands of disgruntled Wesleyans by recommending the removal of the old standard, "Onward Christian Soldiers," from a forthcoming edition. Their rationale: the hymn's "unrelenting use of military images."

After a flood of indignant protests, the committee relented and decided to keep the misunderstood hymn, conceding that the lyrics referred not to overzealous militarism, but to the perpetual struggle between good and evil.

Emoting: Exponential Religious Expression

In many church services down South, all that joyous singing may not be sufficient to express your religious convictions. Maybe you feel impelled to deliver a resounding Amen! after a particularly inspiring performance by the choir or upon hearing a particularly inspiring sermon by the preacher. Or you may feel that you need to say a few things yourself about the matter by "testifying," or "giving testimony," to the congregation. Or perhaps you even feel led to react spontaneously and uninhibitedly as the spirit moves you, letting your body talk and your mouth speak whether or not you know what you're doing or saying, all in the name of the Lord.

Should this be the case for you, then you've come to the right part of the country to do it. You can find ample company, whatever the extent of your urgings, because emoting comes with the religious territory down South. To us, it's a (super)natural extension of our innately expressive southern temperament. But do keep your navigational skills sharpened. Every congregation has its own firm persuasion regarding whether to emote and how to go about it properly.

For many, emoting is limited to an occasional and fairly conventional "Amen, Brother" (or perhaps a composed "Praise the Lord!"). For others, emoting is an authenticating dimension of their religious experience, a rite of passage of sorts into spiritual adulthood. These folk, known as Pentecostals or "Charismatics," call this "getting filled with the Holy Spirit," which manifests itself in all sorts of ways (most widely known are their dramatic "gifts," such as "speaking in tongues" and healing).

Then there are the Southlanders on the fringe whose idea of emoting eclipses the prevailing notions of modern worship. For them, exhibits of their faith include—at the least—the physical exercises of revivalism and—at the utmost—close-to-the-edge encounters with snakes and poisons.

No doubt, depending upon your persuasion, emoting can be either an uplifting or disturbing experience. This is why, before you decide to darken the door of a church down

South, you had better determine its emotive protocol. Unless you look before you leap into this arena, you may well find yourself the proverbial fish out of water. Should that be true, you may well also find your reception to be something less than warm hearted, open armed, or open minded.

BIBLE BELT LEXICON

The lingo of down-South religion:

Amen corner: group of church brethren who sit in the front of the congregation and loudly issue amens and other praise words. The more they like what the preacher says, the more the amens.

Backslider: someone who once had religion but gave in to sin and lost it. Often describes one considered a repeat offender.

Bible thumper: slang for a dogmatic and proselytizing Fundamentalist.

Fundamentalists: Protestants who define five basic doctrines considered fundamental to their theology, including viewing the Bible as inerrant and therefore to be taken at its literal word, the Virgin Birth, bodily resurrection, substitutionary atonement, and second coming of Jesus.

Glossolalia: speaking in tongues; viewed by Pentecostalists and charismatics as a gift of the Holy Spirit. Few of those who speak in tongues understand what they are saying but, blessedly, others receive the gift of interpretation.

Holy Roller: slang for an extremely zealous or fanatical Bible thumper. Also refers to extremists who actually roll about during moments of frenzied worship.

Mourner's bench: in old-time religion meetings, gathering place for worshipers to "pray out" the devil and "pray through" the Holy Spirit. Site of much weeping and wailing and gnashing of teeth, also of hosannas and hallelujahs.

Pentecostals: Fundamentalists who believe that one must repeatedly experience the "second blessing" of the Holy

Spirit (glossolalia, healing, visions, and so forth) in order to authenticate their faith.

Revival: specially held series of church services with emphasis upon soul saving. It often features a visiting evangelist.

Second Coming: describes the anticipated return to earth by Jesus Christ. What everyone who has religion looks forward to.

Tent meeting: a twentieth-century version of an old-time camp meeting. It usually is conducted in a temporary shelter by a traveling evangelist.

Testify: to stand before a group of worshipers and proclaim one's religious convictions or concerns.

Tithing: process of pledging and giving 10 percent of one's income (that's gross income, mind you) to church or religious causes.

Vacation Bible School: summertime church camp for school-aged kids. Five or more weekday mornings of Sunday school, revival, and play school, combined.

Witnessing: process by which those who have religion tell those who don't have it why they need it and how to get it.

WHEN RELIGION GOES UPTOWN IN DIXIE

As we Southerners are fond of saying, there's a church on every street corner down South. Why, we've got so many churches around here that sometimes they even outnumber the service stations. And although this may seem a trifle exaggerated to those Not-From-Here, those who have seen it for themselves know it's pretty close to God's truth.

Our plentitude of churches is but one of many things about Dixie religion we take for granted. Like—to offer a monumental example—the southern mega-church. A mega-church is one of those gargantuan Fundamentalist churches in southern cities that often surpass small colleges in attendance, facilities, operating budgets, and endow-

ments. You will find at least one mega-church in every sizable southern city these days (and others yearning to be one).

But don't confuse a mega-church with a big church or a
"First church." Every southern town has at least two of
those (First Baptist, First Methodist, First Presbyterian,
and so forth), but these Firsts may be second or even last
when compared to a mega-church. In fact, *nothing* com-
pares to a southern mega-church, which is a stunning example of our whole-hog approach to religion in the Bible Belt.

That is why folks who don't know better could well mistake one of these massive complexes of gracious buildings
and spacious grounds for a large corporation or private
school. They wouldn't be far from the truth. A southern
mega-church is these and more—lots more—because
there's something for everyone at a mega-church. Seven
days a week. Which is exactly the point.

If you belong to a mega-church (head counts usually
range between 2,500–6,000), you and your fellow church-
goers could choose from extras like the following:

1. Attend Sunday services and Bible classes in impressive-
   looking and comfortable quarters with hordes of other
   members. Don't let the television cameras in the sanctuary distract you; that's just the weekly broadcast in production.
2. Sing in one of the several choirs or choral groups or play
   in the orchestra. Attend weekly rehearsals and join them
   for "tours" to perform at churches in distant locations.
3. Work out regularly at the fitness center in the "Family
   Life" facility. (You might want to swim some laps, play
   basketball, or bowl a few lines.) You can take the kids
   there for bowling or for their interchurch team basketball games.
4. Enroll your children in the church's accredited school.
   Have them participate in its extracurricular activities,
   such as drama, debate, gymnastics, and soccer.
5. Attend intensive Bible study sessions taught by renowned visiting Bible scholars and theologians.
6. Help host statewide denominational association meetings.
7. Chaperone the annual teen tour to the Holy Land.
8. Patiently explain yet again to your country cousins that
   your mega-church is *not* a religious country club in dis-
   guise.

Type of Church	Clues and Cues
	Minister
Staid/Orthodox (Presbyterian, Episcopal)	• Is composed, dignified. • Usually well educated (private university and divinity school). • Rarely gets emotional during sermon. • Wears vestments; looks distinguished.
Fundamentalist (Baptist, Methodist)	• Is composed but informal and friendly. • Probably went to seminary. • Will get emotional during delivery of sermon. May shout, wave arms and Bible, beat pulpit for emphasis. • Prefers to wear three-piece suits in muted colors (may remove jacket during throes of sermon).
Pentecostal (Church of God, Assemblies of God, Holiness)	• Informal, intense and expressive. • Possibly went to seminary. • Can get very emotional during service. Gestures freely and dramatically. Will shout, beat pulpit, strut amongst congregation. May preach for hours. • Will probably "lay on hands" for healing and other gifts of the Spirit. • Often preaches in shirt-sleeves. Looks undistinguished, intentionally.
Extremists/Holy Rollers	• Neither sophisticated nor erudite but doesn't pretend to be. • Employs fanatical style: prolonged and histrionic oratory, no holds barred. • Conducts congregation to pitches of frenzy. • Directs "acts of faith" (snake handling, strychnine ingestion, etc.) of congregation.

EXPECT IN A CHURCH SERVICE IN DIXIE

Congregation	Other
• Same. • Uses Bible in pew rack. • Except for responses and hymns, keeps mouth shut. • Distinguished folk, fairly cosmopolitan.	• Baptizes infants with a sprinkle of holy water. • Refer to the Eucharist as Holy Communion. • Urban, suburban, and sometimes small-town. • Doesn't oppose a nip or two of libations.
• Same. • Brings own Bible to church. • Usually reserved, but can be responsive. May issue spontaneous amen or clap after stirring music. May weep during closing hymn. May profess or testify if invited by preacher. • Just plain folk. Conservative in appearance and attitudes.	• Baptizes adults with a dip in a pool of water. • Refers to the Eucharist as The Lord's Supper. • Found anywhere and everywhere down South. • Vehemently opposes a nip of any quantity.
• Informal, expectant and expressive. • Brings own Bible to church. • Can get very emotional during service: may wave arms and moan, pray aloud softly, speak in tongues, clap. May say amens and other praise words spontaneously. • May help "lay on hands." • Very plain folk. Ultra-conservative in appearance and attitudes.	• Baptizes adults (dunks or anoints). • Refers to the Eucharist as The Lord's Supper. • Suburban, small-town, rural. • Vehemently opposes a nip of any quantity.
• Same. • May not own a Bible or be able to read one. • Employs wide-open means of expression, no holds barred: physical exercises *en extremis*, chanting, shaking, shouting, rolling, wailing. • Demonstrates religious faith by performing death-defying acts (sometimes they work, sometimes they don't).	• No other generalizations possible, except that they are scattered across the backwoods of Dixie.

TUNING IN TO JESUS DOWN SOUTH

Not only is there a church on every street corner in Dixie, there are a half dozen in every home, all as close as our television dials. And dial we do down South, scores of us tuning in channels of blessings at all hours of the day.

Praise be to Pray-TV, from which these blessings flow. Home of the "video vicars" and their praise-and-pray corps (plus local legions of faithful armchair soldiers), Pray-TV is the next best thing to Baby Jesus Himself to a great many of us Southerners. With our Pray-TV, we need not fast for forty days and nights, much less forty seconds, for an infusion of gospel inspiration between church services (often delivered, no less, with a southern accent, Praise the Lord!). Nor do we lack for pep talks, advice, entertainment, pathos, or even real-life drama. We just need to turn on our televisions.

Here in the heartland of Pray-TV, finding Jesus on the airwaves is old hat for us Southerners. We've been tuning in for a helping of gospel or gospel music for generations, first on radio and later on television. Some very familiar examples include old-time religion radio stations, broadcasts of "First church" Sunday services (radio and television), and native son Billy Graham's "Hour of Decision."

Now there's Pray-TV in the line-up, which has put having religion in a new and different light, to say the very least. Quite naturally, our Bible Belt is homeplace to several of Pray-TV's most illustrious evangelists and empires:

Mother Angelica. From a start with Pat Robertson, this Birmingham-based Franciscan nun sends out inspirational broadcasts daily from her Eternal Word TV Network.

Jerry Falwell. He broadcasts fundamentalist services from his 21,000-member Thomas Road Baptist Church in Lynchburg, Virginia, which is also home to his Liberty University. Falwell founded the Moral Majority (later a part of his Liberty Federation) and was temporary chairman of the PTL Club in 1987.

Jimmy Swaggart. His Jimmy Swaggart Ministries, including the Jimmy Swaggart Bible College, is located in Baton Rouge, Louisiana. He has two syndicated Pray-TV programs: "Jimmy Swaggart"; and "A Study in the Word." He's known for his fulminating evangelistic, old-time religion style, and lately for failing to live up to his own ideals.

PTL Club. Under the leadership of Jim and Tammy Faye Bakker, PTL preached its feel-good "name it and claim it" pop gospel of prosperity. Famous for its Heritage USA Park and its tumultuous and ungodly state of affairs in 1987, the reorganized PTL is headquartered in Charlotte and struggling to regain its religious luster.

Pat Robertson. Presidential aspirations aside, this founding father of the Pray-TV format established The 700 Club, the Christian Broadcasting Network, and CBN University (of which he is chancellor), all based in Virginia Beach, Virginia.

JIM AND TAMMY BAKKER: CARPETBAGGERS RUN AMUCK

Wouldn't you know it, they weren't even From-Here. But like Sherman, they left a scarred swath of destruction and ill will behind them, all for a cause that not even most Bible Belters can justify.

What it all boils down to is that Jim and Tammy got too tangled up in their own underwear, felled at their own hand. One does, however, have to begrudge them credit for marketing smarts, wrapping earthly aspirations in a tantalizing "name it and claim it," feel-good gospel of prosperity. It worked. Folks flocked to learn how they could have it all with Jesus and go first class, too. Praise the Lord!

But lo, this did not sit well with those who could not find this modern gospel in their Bibles. These people were not in the least bit happy to have the duo propounding a "happiness is a warm puppy kennel" religion as a substitute for good, old, tried-and-true fundamentalism. Soon, all was not well in the holy land, down South.

Then an epic commotion broke loose in 1987. Jimmy had sinned, big-time! A flap to beat all ensued. Jim and Tammy

184

retreated. Everybody else in Pray-TV joined the fray, trading accusations and jabs in the name of Jesus. The Bible Belt was nearly torn asunder. The rest of the world forsook "Dallas" and "Dynasty" to watch the unholy wars rage.

Meanwhile, like Imelda and Ferdinand, the deposed couple held intermittent press conferences and searched for a new home and new horizons.

To be continued . . .

TURNED OFF AND TUNED OUT IN DIXIE

Even though our Southland is home to a host of Pray-TV evangelists, don't take it on blind faith that the entire Southland is taking these fellows' words as the holy Word. Lord, no. Far from it. Many of us wouldn't give you two cents for Pray-TV—much less *to* Pray-TV—and those who consider themselves naysayers include a sizable portion of those who have religion.

But it figures, the subject being religion, that Pray-TV would become the target of some of the most unholy debates around, even were it not for some unholy aspects of its own. After all, this is the Bible Belt, land where having religion and respecting it are issues of grave consequences in both the here and hereafter and where finding theological agreement is about as likely as finding the Holy Grail. So when the subject of Pray-TV comes up, it won't be long before you'll hear Southerners square off about these points of contention:

1. Pray-TV is actually Pay-TV.

Pray-TV can't fill your cup for long unless you do the same for it. If you join its loyal followers, be prepared to pay a price, usually sweetened with merchandise, boosterism ("Become a Heavenly Walk partner!"), and telethon pledge drives with dramatic pleas ("If we don't raise $10 million by Friday, this ministry will cease!").

2. Pray-TV is McReligion.

With its slick, variety show/telethon format, Pray-TV often amounts to little more than religious fast food (some prefer to call it junk food). In other words, a steady diet of Pray-TV may be easy to get and may go down easy, but it's better suited as a religious snack, not a square meal.

3. Holier-than-thou holy wars.

Things can get mighty unholy in the world of Pray-TV, what with backbiting and backstabbing amongst its competing contingents, questionable financial practices, and even behind-our-back moral turpitude. This understandably worries many followers who would prefer that the Bible Belt be a guiding light, not the laughing stock.

SOUTHERN STYLE #5: TELEVISION EVANGELIST AND WIFE
He's got a hotline to heaven. She's his heavenly helpmate.

Signet ring with inset diamonds in cross design.

Silently reviewing words of her upcoming solo.

Wearing makeup from her line of Heavenly Walk Beauty Products (sold at home shows by Club members).

St. John knit dress.

18-K gold bracelet.

Her latest book, *Pray Your Way to Heavenly Beauty* (available in bookstores: video to come soon). Folded inside book is day's agenda: tape television show, meet with book publicist, ladies' association luncheon, club fundraising drive strategy meeting with club officers, press conference, session with interior designer to refurbish studio reception areas, college fundraising dinner with husband.

Plain gold wedding band.

In his coat pocket: brochure for his latest Bible instruction video ($39.95 to Club members), day's schedule—taping of show, speaking engagement at businessmen's luncheon, press conference (introducing line of Bible character toys), afternoon meeting with state politicos, fundraising dinner for his Heavenly Walk College.

Custom-made three-piece suit from Paul Stuart.

Silk foulard tie and pocket square.

18-K gold Heavenly Walk Club logo pin.

Special limited edition leatherette Bible—available to dedicated supporters of The Heavenly Walk Club ($150 plus postage and handling).

Rolex Datejust watch with diamond Bezel (gift from wealthy trustee).

In his pants pockets: money clip with $140 in bills, no change (sound of jingles would be declasse); sterling silver key ring with club logo; keys to Jaguar XJ12 (gift of wealthy board member), five-bedroom home ("nothing special"), and office.

Bruno Magli pumps.

Bally dress loafers.

PRAY-TV TRIVIA TEST

1. In which southern state did televangelist Earnest ("Healll!") Angley grow up?
2. What is Tammy Faye Bakker's complete name?
3. With what publisher was Jerry Falwell involved in a libel suit?
4. Who is Pat Robertson's ever-present sidekick and co-host?
5. Match these wives with their televangelist husbands: Dede, Macel, Frances.

(Answers on page 187.)

HOW POLITICS AND RELIGION MIX IN DIXIE

Naturally, there's no such thing as the separation of church and state in the Southland. How could something like that conceivably happen in a region so aptly known as the Bible Belt? It couldn't, and it hasn't. Why, all hell could just as easily freeze over.

It should come as no surprise to learn that this connection between church and state leads, by and large, in one direction only, from church to state. When as many constituents have religion as does the South, there's not much latitude for it to be any other way. True, the Madolyn O'Hares of the world have had it their way on momentous occasions, but they're just whistling Dixie when you get right down to it. If the Bible Belters don't approve, you might as well kiss a cause good bye.

This is why our Southland is known for steadfastly resisting things like these:

- *Repeal of Blue Laws,* which mandate the closure of most establishments on Sundays.
- *Repeal of local liquor options,* with which counties determine by vote whether liquor can be sold/served within their limits (many remain "dry" to this day).
- *Legalization of gambling* (bingo included).

- *Use of textbooks with themes of secular humanism,* which includes those scientific theories (for instance, evolution) and social attitudes (for instance, careers for women) that are believed to contradict biblical teachings.

However, some standards of what's approvable and what's not have relaxed considerably for many Southlanders who have religion. As a result, recreation in the South these days may include playing the racetrack as easily as playing the piano, and resting on the Sabbath can include heavy-duty shopping in the mall or a liquid lunch at the corner fern bar after church.

If all this is beginning to sound more than a little contradictory to you, then you see the rub that's making more than a few Southerners a little hot around the collar. These pasttimes may no longer invoke guilt for some or the ire of the law, but their legalization has provoked the wrath (or the staunch and vocal disapproval) of many others who've got religion.

It is best to conclude from all this that as far as toeing the line in Dixie is concerned: (1) The line is getting moved around; and (2) What constitutes having religion today is up in the air, however you look at it. But one thing that will remain forever immutable is the balance of power between church and state in the Southland, no matter what the predominant biblical theology. Take that for gospel.

ANSWERS TO "PRAY-TV TRIVIA TEST" ON PAGE 186.

1. North Carolina. 2. Tamara Faye Lavalley Bakker. 3. Larry Flynt, publisher of Hustler *magazine. 4. Ben Kinchlow. 5. Dede Robertson, Macel Falwell, Frances Swaggart.*

Chapter Eight

Good Old Boys Are Good Sports

Seems like we Southerners are happiest when we're out of doors. Put us outside in the backyard, beside the creek, tending the vegetable garden, or on the deer stand in the north forty and you'll find yourself some kind of happy Southerners. Happiness turns to ecstasy if we're outdoors *and* barefoot. Now that's true bliss.

In fact, not having a little dirt under our fingernails or on the soles of our feet—at least on occasion— is the exception for most Southerners (Goodness, child, do you mean to say you don't even grow tomatoes?). That's because we Southerners belong to the land. It's our heritage, which means that almost all of us are country folk at heart, even the most effete residents of our New South Gothams.

This also means that once a genuine Southerner goes outside, it's down South all the way. The universal Good Old Boy (or Gal) in us will emerge, as right as rain and just as welcome.

Not surprisingly then, we have yet to run short of entertaining reasons to get out of doors. What nature has not already generously provided, we have ingeniously invented, a bonanza of pursuits of happiness outdoors—sports, Southern Style.

THE GOD'S TRUTH ABOUT SPORTS DOWN SOUTH

Sports is major league material in Dixie. It's *big* stuff. Sports is part of the Holy Southern Trinity, along with religion and food. There is no life down South without sports. It's that simple. And that important.

This is why you must understand our attachment to sports if you have any hope of understanding us. Dismiss it as inconsequential, and you won't have a prayer of figuring us out. To us:

- *Sports is tradition.* It means we can follow in our forebears' footsteps, true to down-South style, whether it be firing a rifle or a football.
- *Sports is the good earth.* It reunites us with mother nature and our motherland. You know what that means.
- *Sports is down to earth.* Like we are.
- *Sports is a common denominator.* It's something we can all share, despite other differences.
- *Sports is fun.* And we're always a threat for a good time around here.

To top it all off, we behold our unwavering dedication to sports as a divine calling down South, a legacy ordained by God. Many in Dixie believe that on the eighth day of creation, God created sports and it was good.

This revelation will help to explain something else significant to the subject. Southerners do not think of sports in terms of recreation. Recreation is for people who think in terms of "leisure time activities," which is only a small step away from "pastimes" and, worse yet, "hobbies." This may be fine for old folks or the housebound, but it just won't do for any self-respecting Southlander. Sports, southern-style, demands whole-hog body-and-soul dedication. One does not dabble in sports around here, even if one cannot participate.

CORE SPORTS OF DIXIE

Not just any old sport will do in Dixie. We definitely have our druthers about what makes for a real southern sport. No matter that the New South has arrived, endowing us with more cosmopolitan concepts in sporting. The core sports come first. Anything else, including the newcomers, are add-ons. They come later.

These are the Core Sports of Dixie:

- Football.
- Football.
- Football.
- Basketball.
- Baseball.
- Hunting.
- Fishing.

FOOTBALL: THE OTHER RELIGION IN DIXIE

Let's get specific. Next to Jesus, the South loves football most. Like the good Lord, football occupies a very special place in Southerners' hearts. Like religion, football is something all Southlanders learn about from an early age and live with till death. Likewise, football can inspire us to behave in ways not otherwise sanctioned in modern society. Utter an unkind word about either religion or football, and folks around here are liable to brand you a heretic.

Yep, Bubba, football reigns supreme in Dixie. Sure, we love basketball and we're mighty fond of baseball, but if we were forced to make a choice, there's no doubt about the outcome. The Southland is football land, with more fans and teams per capita than any other place in America. Come fall, anything except the bare necessities—other sports included—takes a back seat to football.

Exalted above all else is college football. Like Elvis and fried chicken, college football is a sacrosanct southern institution. Don't ask us to imagine life down South without college football. We'd rather give up Santa Claus.

So believe us when we tell you that *nothing* can compare to the hog-wild football fanaticism that saturates the Southland each autumn and the sheer madness that erupts each weekend in our college towns. There's nothing else like it. Perhaps the closest thing to it might be the gung-ho gospel fervor of a freshly-converted backslider, but even we would not mislead you that such burning religious zeal can be so persistently sustained.

Just why is it that many Southerners would consider performing compromising acts to get 50-yard-line tickets to the Alabama–Auburn game? Why would otherwise sensible individuals happily remit usurious fees for the privilege of leasing a parking space near a college stadium? Why do some southern parents pray to be blessed with a football champion the way others pray to be blessed with the Messiah?

Lots of people Not-From-Here think they know why, but usually they're hopelessly misled. As a student of Southern Style, you ought to know the difference, and we're going to explain it to you next.

WHY SOUTHERNERS ARE SO DADGUM CRAZY ABOUT FOOTBALL

All right, sports fans, let's get it straight once and for all why so many Southerners are such die-hard, dyed-in-the-wool college footballs fans. Here's the real lowdown, separating the fiction (some pretty creative stuff!) from the genuine facts.

FICTION

The "Forget, Hell!" theory.

This notion (obviously not formulated on home turf) holds that we Southerners have built our football powerhouses and passions to exact revenge upon those damn Yankees. Obviously not formulated on reason, it fails to consider a few key facts, including the paucity of opportunities for bloodletting that a typical conference schedule avails. This means that we'd be making a pitifully long run for a short slide or, in most cases, no slide a'tall. Also ignored is the fact that we have more than aplenty intra-Southland rivalries of our own to tend to with great enthusiasm, and neither the ethnic composition of our teams nor our fans suggests that an overwhelming urge for revenge threatens to burst loose anytime in the next millenium. So to those who offer this disingenuous position, we reply not "Forget, hell," but "Who's *really* carrying a grudge?"

The Military Metaphors theory.

This is a tangential corollary to the "Forget, Hell!" notion. True, team sports in general often possess martial characteristics (plans of attack, infantry, cavalry, and artillery), but unless you are firmly convinced that Southerners are avid warmongers, this Johnny Reb-in-helmet-and-pads theory peters out in a hurry.

The Ticket Out of Dodge theory.

Be careful with this one, or you're liable to rile up more than a few Southerners because this notion is a foul corruption of a respected and age-old southern value: *Make something of yourself.* Fact is, few of our boys have sweated bullets for most of their young lives just to hitch an all-expense-paid ride out of Dixie. On the contrary, they're just doing what their mamas and daddies raised them to do. Besides, those who make it to stardom are usually the most vociferous defenders of the Southland and have been known to sponsor a few converts along the way.

The Misplaced Priorities theory.

Elitist detractors like to observe disdainfully that the South is a region with far more gumption than education and far more interest in winning championships than four-year degrees. *Au contraire*, you guys. We'll be the first to agree that we often spare no expense for our college football teams. But as every sensible southern college administrator knows, those game receipts and television rights are far more generous than the tax base in most of their states will ever be, and they'd be nuts to bite the hand that feeds them well.

FACT

It's democratic, it's all-American, and it's southern to boot.

Having the Right Stuff in this case doesn't require wealth or genius. This playing field's wide open to any Good Old Boy who's got grit and talent enough to hold his own in the trenches (not unlike becoming a country music star, you might say). Fandom knows no barriers, either, since all fans are really just Good Old Boys or Gals at heart, gathering to watch a bunch of southern folk heroes tussling it out on the gridiron.

It's a great chance to party—all fall, all over Dixie.

College football season down South packs in all the revelry and excess of Mardi Gras for a three-month marathon (plus maybe a bowl game) without the prospects of Lenten penance—all within driving distance, too. Lest you've forgotten, we Southlanders are socializers *extraordinaire*. So what better opportunity for

us to eat, drink, and be merry, nonstop? This is *football* and you're in Dixie, by golly, and what grander excuse to party could anyone ask for?

We get to let it all hang out.

Attending a college football game down South gives us special dispensation to cross the otherwise hard line of good deportment and decorum. Commonly known as "getting fired up" or "showing team spirit," this explains why many of us choose to look like complete fools, dressed in get-ups that have no other place in the civilized world. It's also good enough reason for us to behave like fools, too, hollering for all we're worth, waving our arms and jumping around like holy rollers, and similarly flaunting with the limits of good taste.

We can talk to God in public.

During the course of a game, college football fans down South frequently and openly talk with God on a first name

basis, employing a broad repertoire of invocations to suit the action downfield. Making a plea for divine intervention in public is never more commonplace than during the crucial moments of a game, when multitudes of Southerners can be heard alternately beseeching "Holy #♀★&! God almighty! or "O Lord, have mercy on us *now*, let that young'un in the endzone catch the ball!"

Men are men and women aren't.

Here's one boys' club that will never have to worry about admitting women, because not even a sturdy country gal from Dixie has enough brawn to make the cut for this form of hardball. This suits most of us fine and dandy, since women look better in cheerleading uniforms, anyway.

We just happen to be right good at it.

Must be all that good southern cooking and clean living in God's country, because

we sure know how to grow some strapping big boys. Topped off with a generous helping of southern work ethic and pride, building formidable football teams is just one of those things we're cut out to do.

FOR THE RECORD:
NCAA CHAMPIONSHIP FOOTBALL TEAMS
FROM THE SOUTHLAND
(Division I)

Proof positive we take our football seriously.
1981 Clemson
1980 Georgia
1979 Alabama
1978 Alabama (AP Poll)
1973 Alabama (UPI Poll)
1965 Alabama (AP Poll)
1964 Alabama
1961 Alabama
1958 LSU
1957 Auburn (AP Poll)
1951 Tennessee

SOUTHERN STYLE #6: COLLEGE FOOTBALL FANS
They're pumped up and ready for a rout.

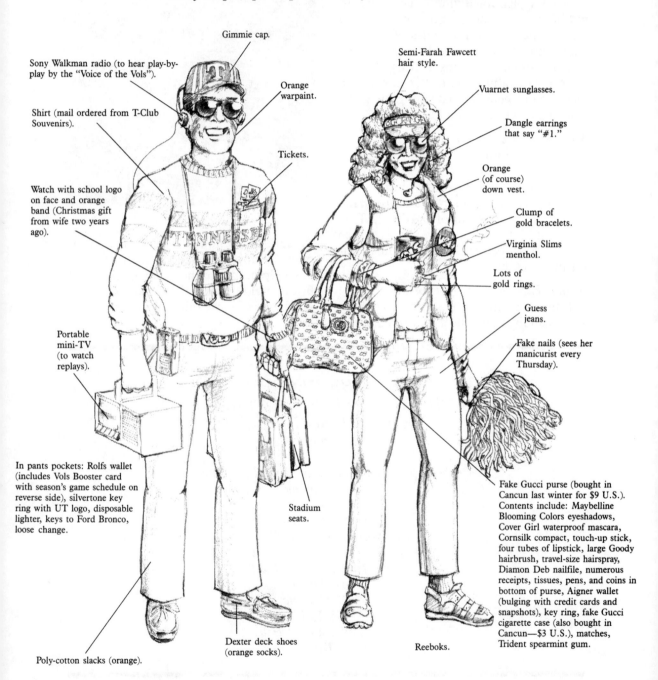

Gimmie cap.

Sony Walkman radio (to hear play-by-play by the "Voice of the Vols").

Shirt (mail ordered from T-Club Souvenirs).

Watch with school logo on face and orange band (Christmas gift from wife two years ago).

Portable mini-TV (to watch replays).

In pants pockets: Rolfs wallet (includes Vols Booster card with season's game schedule on reverse side), silvertone key ring with UT logo, disposable lighter, keys to Ford Bronco, loose change.

Poly-cotton slacks (orange).

Dexter deck shoes (orange socks).

Orange warpaint.

Tickets.

Stadium seats.

Semi-Farah Fawcett hair style.

Vuarnet sunglasses.

Dangle earrings that say "#1."

Orange (of course) down vest.

Clump of gold bracelets.

Virginia Slims menthol.

Lots of gold rings.

Guess jeans.

Fake nails (sees her manicurist every Thursday).

Fake Gucci purse (bought in Cancun last winter for $9 U.S.). Contents include: Maybelline Blooming Colors eyeshadows, Cover Girl waterproof mascara, Cornsilk compact, touch-up stick, four tubes of lipstick, large Goody hairbrush, travel-size hairspray, Diamon Deb nailfile, numerous receipts, tissues, pens, and coins in bottom of purse, Aigner wallet (bulging with credit cards and snapshots), key ring, fake Gucci cigarette case (also bought in Cancun—$3 U.S.), matches, Trident spearmint gum.

Reeboks.

A WEEK IN THE LIFE OF A TYPICAL FAN.

Down in Dixie, the game's the thing. All week long.

Sunday. Reads every word of the newspaper's Sunday sports section. Watches team's postgame show on afternoon television and the sports report on the local evening news.

Daily. Follows the scouting reports in the newspaper and on television. Analyzes prior game, top-ranked teams, conference teams, and upcoming game's opponent with fellow sports fans at the office.

Monday. Spends majority of day discussing game with pals at office. If team lost, argues how statistics prove it really won despite scoring fewer points. Late afternoon, tunes in radio for AP and UPI poll results. Makes plans for next game: who's going along, who's driving, when to leave.

Tuesday. Reads new issue of *Sports Illustrated.* Glances through other sportsrags at newsstand.

Wednesday. Spends lunch at desk reading this week's batch of tip sheets. PM: plays weekly flag football game (intracity league).

Thursday. PM: Attends son's Pop Warner football game.

Friday. Places bet with football pool at office and elsewhere. May depart midday for tomorrow's game if owns motor home, or will attend local high school matchup that night.

Saturday. Rises early; scans newspaper for high school scores and any last minute news about college teams. Dresses in team colors (runs the gamut from tokenism to full dress uniform) and packs picnic (fried chicken, bloody marys, and beer, of course). Heads off to game with spouse and friends in "fan van" (conversion van in team colors), Jeep Cherokee, or the like (team mascot emblazoned on spare tire cover, rear window, and front tag). Arrives in college town, which is crawling with similarly attired fans in similarly decorated cars and trucks.

Cheers spontaneously on street and is greeted with equally enthusiastic responses by nearby fans. Eats tailgate lunch (may even bring barbecue grill). Tours sections of campus if time permits. Enters stadium at least an hour before game time to: (1) see team walk the field and (2) get worked up into a frenzy by kickoff time. Goes wild at opening kickoff and for four quarters thereafter. Returns home on same day in sassy spirits or sore as hell.

SOUTHERN FRIED FOOTBALL

Some of the more noteworthy claims to fame of schools here in football country.

BEST TEAMS

The first measure is a zero in the loss column.

Alabama, 1961. Outscored ten regular season opponents 287–22 and then beat Arkansas in the Sugar Bowl 10–3. All-SEC quarterback Pat Trammell led the offense while linebacker Lee Roy Jordan led the defense.

LSU, 1958. Led by the famous "Chinese Bandits" on defense and Heisman Trophy winner Billy Cannon on offense, Paul Dietzel's best team at LSU went 11–0, outscoring the opposition 285–53.

Georgia Tech, 1952. Bobby Dodd's best team had eight All-SEC players and went 12–0 to win the national championship. Running back Leon Hardeman led the offense, and the Morris brothers, George and Larry, led the defense.

Honorable Mention: Clemson, 1981 (12–0); Alabama, 1979 (12–0); Auburn, 1957 (10–0); Tennessee, 1938 (11–0); Georgia, 1946 (10–0); Ole Miss 1959 (10–1).

LOUDEST FANS

Where attendance is not measured in numbers, but in decibels.

LSU. Nobody can yell like a Cajun who has had all day to get ready for the game.

Clemson. What would you expect from 75,000 people who had the nerve to wear orange overalls?

Honorable Mention: Georgia, South Carolina, Tennessee.

TOUGH TICKETS

Scalpers' delights, if the scalpers can get a ticket.

Clemson–South Carolina. In the state of South Carolina, losing these is grounds for justifiable homicide.

Auburn–Alabama. A few of these spread around in the right places will get you elected governor.

Georgia–Florida. In the divorce courts of Georgia and Florida, they decide on the custody of these before the children.

FIGHT SONGS

The most frequent amount of times they are played in a single game.

"Rocky Top" (Tennessee). 6,454. Would be more if the band didn't have to stop to play the national anthem.

"Glory, Glory to Old Georgia." 3,951. State law says it must be played once for every ounce of Jack Daniels consumed.

"Dixie" (Ole Miss). 1,334. Would be more if the Rebels could score.

Honorable Mention: "Ramblin' Wreck" (Georgia Tech); "Hold That Tiger" (Clemson).

BEST BAND

No classical stuff allowed.

Virginia. Because of its often controversial skits, the "Scatter Band" is an equal-opportunity offender.

LSU. The first three notes of "Hold That Tiger" will make the hair stand up on a dead man's neck.

Tennessee. Would be No. 1 if it knew anything other than "Rocky Top."

Honorable Mention: Alabama, Clemson.

BEST GAMES

Of great plays, goal line stands, and days stars were born.

LSU 7, Ole Miss 3, Halloween night, 1959. Voted the "game of the decade" by the SEC, LSU was ranked No. 1 and Ole Miss No. 2. Billy Cannon's 89-yard punt return with ten minutes left put the Tigers ahead. Ole Miss drove close to the LSU goal but was stopped on fourth and one.

Notre Dame 24, Alabama 23, Sugar Bowl, 1974. The lead changed hands six times as Notre Dame prevailed to win the national championship. After a 69-yard punt by Alabama's Greg Gantt, Notre Dame was backed up to its one-yard line with a one point lead. But the Irish gambled and won as quarterback Tom Clements hit tight end Robin Weber on the 38 to secure the victory.

Alabama 33, Ole Miss 32, Oct. 4, 1969. Quarterback Archie Manning of Ole Miss set the all-time SEC record for total offense in a single game, but it wasn't enough as Alabama and Scott Hunter won by a point. Manning had 436 yards passing and 104 yards rushing.

Honorable Mention: Georgia Tech 7, Alabama 6, 1962; Georgia–Florida (any year); North Carolina 34, North Carolina State 33, 1972; Clemson 10, North Carolina 8, 1961; Georgia 28, Georgia Tech 24, 1971.

—"Southern Fried Football" © 1986 by *The Atlanta Journal-Constitution.* Reprinted with permission.

TOUCHDOWN TRADITIONS

Match the post-touchdown spirit with its school.

1. Mascot does pushups equal to total game score.
2. Fans used to ring cowbells before visiting coach Bear Bryant had his say.
3. Fans clap politely, if at all.
4. Fires a cannon.

A. North Carolina   B. Virginia Tech   C. Duke
D. Clemson   E. Mississippi State   F. North Carolina State
(Answers on page 202.)

JAN KEMP: ACADEMIC JOAN OF ARC

Some of the most exemplary practitioners anywhere of southern hospitality have to be our football powerhouse universities. They are more than happy to supply athletes with the facilities, amenities, and services that the rest of their student bodies (and most of the free world) only dream of having, and in the spirit of our foremost football tradition, most Southerners see these perks as a fair enough trade for a winning season.

But in 1982, one lady decided to put her foot down on the unspoken perquisite of college athletics, handing passing grades to failing athletes. Jan Kemp, Professor of Remedial Studies at the University of Georgia, was demoted for her contrariness. She complained and was fired.

But Jan Kemp held her ground. She sued, and the state of Georgia was thrown into a tizzy. To many, Kemp became Public Enemy Number One, but in the bitter end she was vindicated. Defying the university's athletics-first attitude, an outraged jury awarded her $1.1 million and her former job. The university lost its president and Kemp lost her husband, but precedence of sheepskins over pigskins in academia was reaffirmed.

Pro Football: Riddle of the Southland

Strange but lamentably true, our awesome reputation for playing ferocious football becomes a laughable one when our professional teams take the field. That the hapless Atlanta Falcons and New Orleans Saints have piddled around with this holy sport of Dixie for decades has been a big bug in the craw of Southerners everywhere. You must admit, twenty years without a championship is a long time for any fan to keep the faith, even down here in Football Country.

There is a way out of this quandary, however, and it's certainly worth a try: Put the local football factories to work and put genuinely *southern* teams in uniform, 100 percent homegrown only, nobody else allowed.

Atlanta Falcons

New Orleans Saints

Why not? Our boys are born and bred to play football to *win*. To win for mama and daddy, for their hometown, for their alma mater, and for the Southland. Lose a game and not only have these fellows tarnished their reputations, they've let everyone down for miles around. And Bubba Ray knows better than to do *that*.

Fans, too, would have plenty more motivation, what with all those home boys grueling it out on the gridiron. Like college football, they'd really have something to cheer about. Now that's a far more inspiring proposition than watching players from God-knows-where flubbing up and getting paid handsomely to do it.

Answers to "Touchdown Traditions" on page 201.
1. D; 2. E; 3. A, C, F; 4. B.

ALL HEPPED UP FOR HOOPS IN DIXIE

Not every college in Dixie succumbs to total football madness each fall, if the truth be told. At some schools around the Southland, football season is a mere waiting game for more promising activity.

A football match-up for these Southlanders makes for a pleasant fall afternoon's outing, but it is hardly cause for them to work up a sweat. Those in attendance are more aptly described as polite spectators—rowdy fans they are not. Traffic jams? No problem here, unless the tailgate parties get out of hand.

But just hold on. There's a good reason why these paragons of restraint choose to behave so. They are saving themselves for basketball. And for good reason: They live in the reigning kingdoms of southern basketball, where the roundball tradition runs every bit as deep and proud and successful as football at any pigskin university elsewhere. Come the opening tip-off, brace yourself, because all the frenzy of the biggest southern football schools will erupt in equally full force on the courts.

Basketball bravado like this is nowhere more entrenched than in North Carolina and Kentucky, whose college teams wield wicked clout without fail in conference and NCAA play. Their records and reputations say it all. Thanks to them, basketball in Dixie is on a roll, arguably as bigtime as football.

This sort of mighty ball is played elsewhere in the Southland, too, at all NCAA Division levels, by male and female teams. (Every roundball fan knows about the formidable prowess of the SEC's lady basketballers.) These days basketball is no longer the stepchild sport of Dixie. It does us proud and, with the kind of court and crowd action under muster, no wonder.

NCAA Championship Basketball Teams From the South

(Division I)

Men's	Women's
1986 Louisville	1987 Tennessee
1983 North Carolina State	1985 Old Dominion
1982 North Carolina	1982 Louisiana Tech
1980 Louisville	
1978 Kentucky	
1974 North Carolina State	
1958 Kentucky	
1957 North Carolina	
1951 Kentucky	
1949 Kentucky	
1948 Kentucky	

DIXIE SPORTS HALL OF FAME

Given our divinely assigned passion for sports down South, you might expect that we accord our sports heroes nothing less than sainthood. You'd be right. Those who become all-time sports legends receive as much honor and deference around here as Saint Paul himself, and maybe even more.

Those most blessed among men and women from the Southland include:

Muhammad Ali (Kentucky). Three-time heavyweight boxing champion.
Hank Aaron (Alabama). Baseball slugger and Hall of Famer.
Evelyn Ashford (Louisiana). Olympic medalist and world champion sprinter.
Paul ("Bear") Bryant (Arkansas). Invincible football coach.

Tracy Caulkins (Tennessee). Olympic swimming gold medalist.
Steve Cauthen (Kentucky). Thoroughbred racing jockey.

Paul ("Bear") Bryant on the sideline.

Ty Cobb (Georgia). Baseball slugger and Hall of Famer.

Howard Cosell (North Carolina). Controversial sports commentator.

Dizzy Dean (Arkansas). Baseball pitcher and sportscaster.

Bobby Jones (Georgia). Golfing great and Grand Slam victor.

Joe Louis (Alabama). Twelve-year heavyweight boxing champion.

Jesse Owens.

Joe Louis.

Willie Mays (Alabama). Baseball slugger and twice MVP.

Willie McCovey (Alabama). Home run star, MVP, and Hall of Famer.

Jesse Owens (Alabama). First black Olympic track and field gold medalist.

Leroy ("Satchel") Paige (Alabama). Legendary baseball pitcher in Negro leagues and 1971 Hall of Famer.

Walter Payton (Mississippi). All-time NFL leader in yards rushing.

Richard Petty (North Carolina). NASCAR trailblazer and seven-time champion.

Eddie Robinson (Mississippi). Winningest college football coach ever.

Jackie Robinson (Georgia). Baseball MVP; first black to play in majors.

Wilma Rudolph (Tennessee). Olympic medalist and record-setting sprinter.

Fran Tarkenton (Virginia). NFL career record breaker.

Wyomia Tyus (Georgia). Holds world records and Olympic medals in women's track.

Wilma Rudolph (second from left).

GOOD OLD BOYS AND GUNS IN DIXIE

You can bet your last can of snuff that autumn is the hands-down favorite time of year for males throughout the Southland. Come fall, they get to conduct two of the most most high and holy rituals of Good Old Boydom. Not only do they get to glory in the rough and tough thrills of football, they get to become headhunters in their own right, which they do *en masse*. With fall comes hunting season in Dixie; like Christmas, it's well worth waiting for the rest of the year.

Hunting is one of those things that comes with the territory down South, like bourbon whiskey. Do not try to envision the Southland *sans* hunting. That is a hopeless cause. Imagine instead, each fall and winter, hundreds of thousands of southern males clad in camouflage and crouched on tree stands or in duck blinds in the southern outback. Also imagine thousands of trucks and three-wheelers scattered like buckshot over southern backwood roads, the muddy sentinels of two-footed, tobacco-chewing predators.

Duck hunting in eastern Arkansas.

This annually comes to pass down South because hunting is a core curriculum subject for southern menfolk. If you are a Southerner and you are male, then you know how to hunt. Chances are good that you handle your gun with the same skill and nonchalance as you would a toothpick, and just about as often.

Of course you do, because as a thin-eared boy you learned how to use a long gun, just like your daddy (who probably taught you) and your ancestors who settled the southern frontiers and fought in wars. Hunting is your privilege and reward for having the good fortune and sense to call Dixie home. If for no other reason, you would hunt because tradition mandates it.

This is not the only reason most men of the South go hunting every chance they get and love every minute of it. Another factor accounts for why southern men crave hunting like women and will spend more time, energy, and money than you can imagine in getting their satisfaction.

Just remember the magic words and you'll have the answer: Good Old Boyism. Hunting goes with Good Old Boys like a hound dog and ticks, like fatback and turnip greens. Hunting is Good Old Boyism incarnate, its hallowed province and last sacred bastion. At no other time or place can the art of being a Good Old Boy be more expertly practiced than when hunting. Never mind the New South or sex role confusion; there's always hunting camp.

When a man goes hunting in Dixie, life is automatically converted from the complicated to the simple, operating under one social code ("I'm just a downhome country boy from Dixieland"), one dress code, and two goals ("shoot that sucker" and "pass the bottle"). Under these circumstances, being a Good Old Boy is plenty good enough, which is precisely the point.

Remember, everybody down South knows it is only right that a southern man be a genuine Good Old Boy at heart. He can be wealthy and urbane, and he can be president; but he should always be a Good Old Boy first and foremost. Hunting is one of the finest ways there is to revel in this southernmost state of grace.

Dixie Varmints
Always in season

Possum	Squirrel
Coon	Cooter (turtle)
Armadillo	Rabbit

A (GOOD OLD) BOY AND HIS DOG

Good Old Boys have fixed notions about dogs. The bottom line for these fellows is, a dog isn't good for much if it isn't good for hunting. But a hunting dog is an able and honored animal. It will help you track deer and chase rabbits and other critters. It will tree coons for you. It will flush quail and retrieve ducks. With all this and giving you unconditional love, too, a good hunting dog is a thing of joy forever.

A good hunting dog can also be a thing of one-up-manship. Even midst the camaraderie of Good Old Boy-dom, there lingers the subtle scent of status, and its presence is most detectable around hunting dogs. Do you want to impress any serious hunter? Do you wish to make the final statement about dedicated huntsmanship?

Then do not bother with fancy trappings, like ultra-expensive guns, newfangled gear, or similar badges of conspicuous consumption (you're just a downhome Good Old Boy, not a peckerhead, remember?). Invest instead in a pedigreed bird dog, preferably a pointer, one with a bloodline as long as your arm and a name to match. This is all you need to do to say it all: This Good Old Boy don't mess around. He is *serious* about his hunting.

If—still yet—you should also wish to have the final word, too, then send your bird dog to school with a world-class trainer. Put it on the championship trail, where your canine can show its stuff in rigorous tests of bird work before the critical eyes of field trials judges. As for yourself, you now can grandly consort with other "shooting gentlemen" (mostly Good Old Boys with impressive pedigrees themselves) whose labors have elevated the lot of hunting dogs to the classy status of Thoroughbreds.

Most Favorite Name For A Dog In Dixie

Beau
(as in General Beauregard)

FAST CARS AND REDNECKS

Though they reign sovereign down South, we wouldn't go so far as to declare that the core sports are an exclusively Dixie phenomenon. We're well aware that people outside the Southland do indeed play football, roundball, and baseball and that they know how to hunt and fish, (although certainly not with the finesse and flair of a Southlander).

However, there is a sport that is pure home-grown Dixie. It's a genuinely Southern-made, big-bucks, big-name sport, and it's a hair-raising, hell-raising one, at that: stock car racing, better known as NASCAR (National Association for Stock Car Auto Racing).

Stock car racing got its start as the reckless sport of Dixie's daredevil piney woods boys. Spurred on by whiskey, beer, and bets, they'd show off their get-up-and-gumption in souped-up family cars on backwoods stretches of sand or red clay. There wasn't much money in it, but there were plenty of revved-up thrills on the tracks and off, what with the Saturday night drinking and brawling by spectators and drivers alike.

This sort of entertainment suited everybody of redneck persuasion just fine. After all, this was *their* sport (everybody else had the presence of mind to stay away), and it fast became a ribald weekend ritual across the southern outback.

Somewhere along the stretch, the sport's founding father, Bill France, Sr., decided a little organization was in order and founded NASCAR to sanction races and give the boys a championship. Their four-wheel dueling legitimized, it wasn't long before corporate sponsors upped the ante and the media decided to recognize the South's favorite warm weather spectator sport, redneck or not.

So in the space of about forty years, backwoods dirt road bravado has given way to big-budget, celebrity chariot races that routinely attract 50,000 or more rowdy fans. It's still as southern redneck as the day is long (only one Yankee has ever been a NASCAR champion), but it has become plumb respectable under the auspices of NASCAR. Why, these days even folks from well-heeled neighborhoods will venture to the speedways for the big races.

You can still find the Saturday night crash-and-bash races in full swing, however. As long as we have rednecks and motorized transport, some of us will be outrunning others of us for the sheer guts and glory of it, whether in cars, on tractors, motorcycles, bog-mobiles, or God knows what other kind of saddle on wheels. It's the red-blooded, redneck thing to do.

NASCAR'S WINNINGEST NAMES

Five of those in the league of all-time champions.

Richard Petty (Randleman, NC). Reclusive, seven-time NASCAR champion. Known as "King Richard," "Richard the Great." Son of NASCAR trailblazer Lee Petty and father of NASCAR contender Kyle Petty.

Cale Yarborough (Timmonsville, South Carolina). Three-time NASCAR champ and one of the biggest money makers ever on the circuit.

SOUTHERN STYLE #7: THE REDNECKS
They're everything you've heard about and then some.

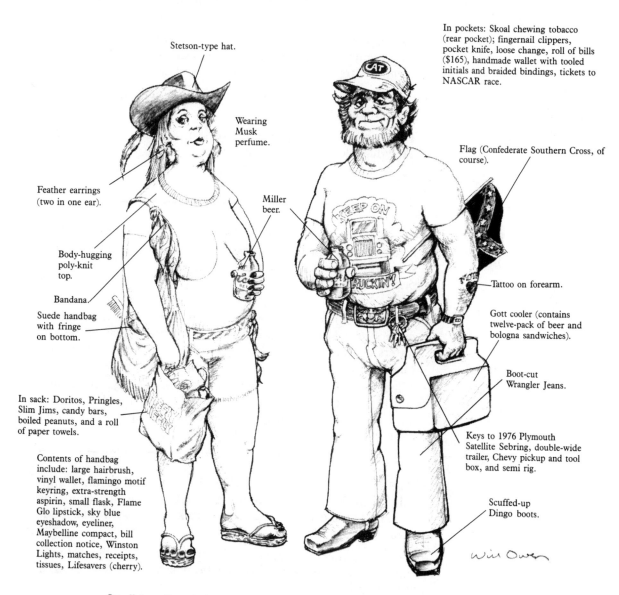

Stetson-type hat.

In pockets: Skoal chewing tobacco (rear pocket); fingernail clippers, pocket knife, loose change, roll of bills ($165), handmade wallet with tooled initials and braided bindings, tickets to NASCAR race.

Wearing Musk perfume.

Flag (Confederate Southern Cross, of course).

Feather earrings (two in one ear).

Miller beer.

Body-hugging poly-knit top.

Tattoo on forearm.

Bandana.

Suede handbag with fringe on bottom.

Gott cooler (contains twelve-pack of beer and bologna sandwiches).

In sack: Doritos, Pringles, Slim Jims, candy bars, boiled peanuts, and a roll of paper towels.

Boot-cut Wrangler Jeans.

Contents of handbag include: large hairbrush, vinyl wallet, flamingo motif keyring, extra-strength aspirin, small flask, Flame Glo lipstick, sky blue eyeshadow, eyeliner, Maybelline compact, bill collection notice, Winston Lights, matches, receipts, tissues, Lifesavers (cherry).

Keys to 1976 Plymouth Satellite Sebring, double-wide trailer, Chevy pickup and tool box, and semi rig.

Scuffed-up Dingo boots.

Cut-off shorts (formerly Gloria Vanderbilt jeans).

CORE SPORTS

Orderlies

- They keep up with college football and will attend a few games a year. Couples are heavily into tailgating parties with cute food.

- He keeps up with basketball and baseball; he will attend decisive games (often with office buddies, using tickets from a client or supplier). She probably doesn't care to go.

- He goes on hunting and/or fishing expeditions several times a year, often to exotic places.

- Their children may play on core sports teams at school, but likely have less *mainstream* sporting interests.

Good Old Boys and Gals

- Are dedicated followers of college football and basketball. Will listen to all games of pet teams; will attend all those within striking distance (probably have season's tickets) and raise plenty of cain while there. Religiously watch pro football on TV.

- If not watching a game, he is liable to be in camouflage or waders in the Dixie backwoods or backwaters (maybe the salt waters), toting a gun (or bow) or rod 'n reel. Enjoys organized turkey shoots, coon hunts, and fishing tournaments.

- Their sons play core team sports from an early age (daughters will likely play hard-core softball or basketball). Everybody takes it *extremely* seriously. It may be juvenile sport, but it *ain't* child's play.

Rednecks

- Are mildly interested in football or basketball (county high school, probably), but love to watch televised games as means to hang out and put away a twelve pack or two with their buddies in their trailer.

- If not watching a game, he will be up to his ears in camo, hunting whatever's in season (or maybe what's not); may be at a fishing hole.

- Redneck kids *may* play team core sports, but they're more disposed to the free-wheeling pursuits (see next column).

CLASS FAVORITES

- They play tennis regularly (she plays ladies' doubles once a week at the club; he plays there Saturdays). They play golf on occasion (they love to go to Pinehurst, et al, too). He may play polo during the spring and summer; they may fox hunt during the fall and winter.

- The kids will play soccer, rugby, lacrosse, and similar prep sports; may be on swim or gymnastics teams (if they need a personal coach, so much the better). Young adult Orderlies will play pool and throw darts when slumming it.

- Everybody knows how to sail and how to water ski (this is, after all, the South). Families go snow skiing out West during the holidays.

- They are likely ardent fans of NASCAR and will make a race annually.

- Country cousins love a good rodeo.

- Other favorites (when core sports are not in session):
  Water skiing
  Motocross, etc
  Tractor pulls
  Skeet shooting
  Bowling (in leagues)
  Tennis (in leagues)
  Snow-skiing in North Carolina

- Loves the down 'n dirty sports like a Good Old Boy loves football. Favorites include:
  Wrestling (male and female)
  Tractor pulls, bogging, etc.
  NASCAR
  Drag racing
  Motocross
  Racing anything motorized and on wheels
  Chicken fights
  Pit bull fights

- Loves to raise hell on a lake in a cheap ski boat.

- Plays a wicked game of pool.

Darrell Waltrip (Franklin, Tennessee). Has won three NASCAR cups and top dollars on the circuit.

Dale Earnhardt (Kannapolis, North Carolina). Also a three-time champ and top money maker.

David Pearson (Spartanburg, South Carolina). Three-time NASCAR winner and dad of NASCAR newcomer Larry Pearson.

PLAYING BY THE RULES DOWN SOUTH

"Know thy core sports" is a cardinal rule in Dixie. Knowing your core sports assures everybody that you're a good old Southerner because you're keeping up with our national interests. You *care* about the important things, which is a statement that a punctilious Southlander really can't afford not to make, regardless of his or her social station.

There is life in Dixie beyond the core sports, however. There is, indeed: high life, low life, and more than a few strata in between where, socially speaking, some Good Old Boys (and Gals) are created more equal than others. Even for the sacred rites of southern sportsdom, it seems another cardinal rule down South often prevails: "Know thy place."

Just what happened to all those Good Old Boys and Gals united for a common cause in Dixieland sports? Well, it depends. You see, some of us Southerners are Good Old Boys only *some* of the time (quasi-Good Old Boys), those times generally being when the core sports have commenced. Others of us, however, are Good Old Boys *all* of the time, because God made us that way, core sports or tiddlywinks notwithstanding. There *is* a difference.

This means that, once beyond the core sports, sporting for the masses down South becomes sporting for the classes, and that makes it a whole new shootin' match, folks. So much of the time many of our Good Old Boys don't get within a country mile of one another, not even for sports.

Some rules *never* get broken down south.

Chapter Nine

Where to Go for a Good Time in Dixie

By now it should be pretty clear: There's lots to do in Dixie. No doubt this is because we happen to be downright resourceful when it comes to entertaining ourselves (and anybody else within earshot). Besides diversions like pilgrimages, social whirls, foodfests, and sporting events, we have lots more to do around these parts, ranging from the downhome to the uptown and points in between.

If you're aiming for good times in Dixie, then look no farther. Here's a sampling of ideas to get you started.

Where to Go for a Good Time in

ALABAMA

Events for the Asking

JANUARY
Senior Bowl All-star Football Classic, Mobile.

FEBRUARY
National Amateur Free-for-All Shooting Dog Championship, Union Springs.
Mardi Gras (occurs some years in March), Mobile.

MARCH
Azalea Trail and Festival, Mobile.
Southeastern Livestock Exposition and World Championship Rodeo, Montgomery.
Rattlesnake Rodeo, Opp.

APRIL
Square Dance Jubilee, Birmingham.
Indian Dance Festival and Pioneer Fair, Childersburg.
Decorator's Show House, Birmingham.

MAY
Winston 500 NASCAR Stock Car Race, Talladega.
Sacred Harp Singing, Huntsville.
Southern Appalachian Dulcimer Festival, Helena.
Rhododendron Festival, Mentone.

JUNE
Helen Keller Festival, Tuscumbia.
Blessing of the Fleet, Bayou La Batre.
Hank Williams Memorial Celebration, Mount Olive West Community.
America's Junior Miss Pageant, Mobile.

JULY
Alabama Deep Sea Fishing Rodeo, Dauphin Island.
World Championship Domino Tournament, Andalusia.
Dixie Cup Annual Regatta, Guntersville.
Talladega 500 NASCAR Stock Car Race, Talladega.

AUGUST
State Fiddle Championship and Folk Arts Festival, Oxford.
PGA Championship, Birmingham.
W. C. Handy Music Festival, Florence.

SEPTEMBER
Dulcimer Festival, Meridianville.
Mule Day, Winfield.
Racking Horse World Celebration, Decatur.

OCTOBER
Tennessee Valley Old Time Fiddler's Festival, Athens.
Covered Bridge Festival, Oneonta.
Alabama Tale-Telling Festival, Selma.
State Fair, Birmingham.

NOVEMBER
Southern Wildfowl Festival, Decatur.
Poarch Band of Creek Indians Thanksgiving Pow Wow, Atmore.
Championship Charity Horse Show, Montgomery.

DECEMBER
Blue-Gray All-Star Football Classic, Montgomery.
Festival of Trees, Birmingham.

NOT ✦ TO ✦ BE ✦ MISSED
An eclectic selection of things to do in Alabama

1. Honor a legend in country music with a visit to Hank William's gravesite in Montgomery.

2. Take a covered bridge trek across Blount County and examine four of the nation's most impressive examples of covered bridges.

3. Enter the Space Age at the U.S. Space Academy in Huntsville. Experience first-hand astronaut training, shuttle mission simulations, and flight crew assignments, and explore the museum of space travel at the NASA Space and Rocket Center.

4. See 150 million years' worth of geologic history exposed in the side of Red Mountain in Birmingham. Study the Red Mountain Museum's intriguing collection of fossils and view the sun's surface through its spectrohelioscope.

U.S. Space Academy.

5. Pay your respects to prized coonhounds at the Key Underwood Coon Dog Memorial Graveyard near Tuscumbia.

6. Watch classical and contemporary performances by an acclaimed repertory company at the Alabama Shakespeare Festival in Montgomery. Attend pre-show and post-show discussions to expand your theatrical erudition.

7. Explore the pentagonal brick forts that formerly protected opposite ends of Mobile Bay—Forts Morgan and Gaines—and review their critical roles during the War Between the States.

8. Go fishing for lunkers at the big bass capital of the world, Lake Eufaula.

9. Visit two important cradles of history within a two-block area in Montgomery: the first White House of the Confederacy, where President Jefferson Davis resided, and Dexter Avenue King Memorial Baptist Church, where, less than a century later, the Reverend Martin Luther King, Jr.,

presided over the civil rights movement.

10. Get back in the saddle again with a trip to the American Cowboy Heroes Museum in Boaz. Recollect the days of silverscreen buckaroos, trusty horses, scrappy heroines, and heroic shoot-em-ups. See the famous faces of the wild west serials and watch Saturday reruns of television "horse operas."

11. Surround yourself with breathtaking blooming color with a late March/early April trip to Bellingrath Gardens and Home near Mobile. Witness the beauty of 200,000 azaleas in vivid bloom in the sixty-five-acre garden of this famous estate.

12. Step into the distinguished domiciles of antebellum and Victorian Huntsville during its annual April Pilgrimage. While you're in the neighborhood, walk the Twickenham Historic District for outstanding examples of nineteenth-century architecture.

13. Tour the eerie and beautiful onyx caves of DeSoto Caverns near Childersburg. Take your sleeping bag and camp out in the caverns.

[For the full lowdown on Alabama, straight from the horse's mouth, contact: Alabama Bureau of Tourism and Travel, 532 South Perry Street, Montgomery, 36104.]

Fort Morgan.

ALABAMA CLOSE-UP: *Wintzell's Oyster House*

You can get it fancier, but you won't get it any fresher or more honest-to-goodness than the Gulf Coast seafood served at Wintzell's Oyster House in Mobile. Chances are you won't find anybody else's surroundings nearly as entertaining, either, because every available square inch of the bustling place is covered with the sardonic wit and wisdom ("When a Little Shot Gets Half Shot—He Thinks He Is a Big Shot") of its late founder, J. Oliver Wintzell. Every oyster lover worth his Tabasco knows about Wintzell's ("Oysters fried, stewed, and nude"), and so does most everybody else who is partial to good Gulf Coast seafood. The wisecracks and the fair prices make it all the more worth your while.

Outside Wintzell's Oyster House.

Where to Go for a Good Time in

ARKANSAS

Events for the Asking

JANUARY
King Cotton Holiday Classic Basketball Tournament, Pine Bluff.
Toys Designed by Artists Exhibition, Little Rock.

FEBRUARY
National Walleye Contest, Greers Ferry Lake.

MARCH
Jonquil Festival, Washington.
Yell County Wildlife Federation Bird Dog Field Trial, Dardanelle.

APRIL
Open Fiddle Contest and Spring Music Festival, Eureka Springs.
Ozark Folk Festival and Craft Guild Show, Mountain View.
Ozark Scottish Festival and Highland Games, Batesville.
Spring Trail Rides, Booneville.

MAY
Home Tours, Batesville, Helena, Little Rock.
Armadillo Festival, Hamburg.
Back-in-the Hills Antiques Show and Heritage Crafts Fair, War Eagle.
Riverfest, Little Rock.

JUNE
Diamond Festival, Murfreesboro.
String Band and Fiddle Contest, Salem.
Lum and Abner Sunday, Pine Ridge.
Antique Auto Show and Swap Meet, Morrilton.

JULY
Rodeo of the Ozarks, Springdale.

Old-Timers Parade, Ozark.
Independence Day Horseshoe Tournament, Lake Chicot State Park.

AUGUST
Greers Ferry Lake Water Festival, Heber Springs.
Sundown to Sunup Gospel Sing, Springdale.
Muzzleloaders Fall Shoot, Mountain View.

SEPTEMBER
Pioneer Days, Berryville.
State Fair and Livestock Show, Little Rock.
Grand Prairie Festival of the Arts, Stuttgart.
State Fiddlers' Championship, Mountain View.

OCTOBER
National Wild Turkey Calling Contest and Turkey Trot Festival, Yellville.
Apple Festival, Lincoln.
King Biscuit Blues Festival, Helena.
Ozark Arts and Crafts Fair, War Eagle.

NOVEMBER
National Bluegrass Fiddlers Championship, Mountain View.
World's Championship Duck-Calling Contest and Wings over the Prairie Festival, Stuttgart.

DECEMBER
Home Tours, North Little Rock, Heber Springs, Eureka Springs, Helena.
Re-enactment of the Battle of Prairie Grove, Prairie Grove Battlefield State Park.

NOT ✦ TO ✦ BE ✦ MISSED
An eclectic selection of things to do in Arkansas

1. See history and prosperity preserved in Little Rock's Quapaw Quarter, the original city site and heart of its antebellum and Victorian heritage. Don't miss the prized Arkansas Territorial Restoration (fourteen significant structures) or the Old State House (Doric architecture at its grandest).

2. Visit Eureka Springs, Bethlehem of Bible Belt folklore. See the seven-story-tall Christ of the Ozarks statue and a dramatic performance of the great Passion Play. Tour the Christ Only Art Gallery, the Bible Museum, Inspirational Wood Carving Gallery, and the fifty-acre new Holy Land to complete your uplifting outing.

The Clayton House in the Belle Grove district of Ft. Smith.

The Christ of the Ozarks.

3. Hike the mountainside trails of White Rock Mountain in the Ozark National Forest for spectacular bluff vantages and secluded wilderness settings. Extend your trek on the neighboring Ozark Highlands Trail.

4. Go West with a trip to Fort Smith and nearby Van Buren, pioneer outposts and stopping-off points to and from the western frontier. See where the Wild West, the Old South, and Indian cultures converged and the landmarks and legacies are preserved in their honor. In Fort Smith, tour Fort Smith National Historic Site (where Hanging Judge Isaac C. Parker restored law and order), the Old Fort Museum, and Belle Grove Historic District; in Van Buren don't miss Historic Old Main Street (a handsome ten-block area), the Frisco Depot, and the Fairview Cemetery.

5. Round up the family and saddle up for a dude ranch vacation in the Ozarks.

6. Get a taste of Arkansas's century-old wine heritage in Wiederkehr Village near Clarksville, where you can tour and sample the fruits of its four wineries.

7. Challenge the state records for rainbow trout with a float trip down the famed White River, trout fishermen's paradise, starting near Bull Shoals Lake. Head south to Heber Springs and the Little Red River for more prime lunker casting.

8. Pay a visit to the homeplace of Ozark homespun, the Ozark Folk Center near Mountain View. Browse the authentic crafts and skills of Arkansas's mountain culture; enjoy spirited performances of music, dance, and narratives of Ozark history.

The Ozark Folk Center.

9. Dig for diamonds and semiprecious stones at the Crater of Diamonds State Park near Murfreesboro. Once you're in the park you can keep all you find, and quite a few keepers (over 65,000) have been unearthed there.

10. Canoe between soaring limestone bluffs overlooking the Buffalo National River. Tackle its white water sections or leisurely float on calmer stretches; over 125 miles to choose from.

11. Don your waders and set your sights on the finest duck hunting anywhere, with a November visit to the Mississippi flyway around Stuttgart. Do it in style with a helping hand from one of several area hunting clubs whose acreage lies beneath the prime skies of migrating quarry and whose hospitality is southern all the way.

[To get the full lowdown on Arkansas, straight from the horse's mouth, contact: Arkansas Department of Parks and Tourism, One Capitol Mall, Little Rock, 72201.]

Buffalo National River.

ARKANSAS CLOSE-UP: *Hot Springs National Park*

Even before statehood, Arkansas was known far and wide for the thermal waters that gushed from natural springs in its Ouachita Mountains. By the early 1800s, Hot Springs had become akin to a nineteenth-century Golden Door Spa; its elegant bathhouses and hotels were patronized by the wealthy and famous. Like these well-heeled visitors, the Indians, and even Hernando De Soto before them, folks today flock to Hot Springs National Park to relish the beneficial (and, some swear, medicinal) properties of the ever-flowing springs, warmed deep underground by near-molten rock. Like almost all popular tourist attractions, Hot Springs is not exempt from campy commercialism (an alligator farm and wax museum beckon, for instance), but the park itself continues to fascinate and refresh its guests. So take a tour of yesteryear's ornate structures on Bathhouse Row and then partake of the relaxing warm waters in the park's special facilities.

Bathhouse Row at Hot Springs National Park.

Where to Go for a Good Time in

GEORGIA

Events for the Asking

JANUARY
Old Christmas Storytelling Festival, Atlanta.
Rattlesnake Roundup, Whigham.
Peach Bowl Football Game, Atlanta.

FEBRUARY
Georgia Week, Savannah.

MARCH
Cherry Blossom Festival, Macon.
Saint Patrick's Day Celebration and Parade, Savannah.

APRIL
Atlanta Steeplechase, Cumming.
Old South Celebration, Milledgeville.
Masters Golf Tournament, Augusta.
Rose Festival, Thomasville.

MAY
Mayhaw Festival, Colquitt.
Cotton Pickin' Country Fair, Gay.
Designer's Show House, Atlanta.
Georgia Folk Festival, Eatonton.
Scottish Games and Highland Gathering, Savannah.
Masters Water Ski Tournament, Callaway Gardens.

JUNE
Hot-Air Balloon Festival, Helen.
Taste of Savannah Food Festival, Savannah.
Original Dahlonega Bluegrass Festival, Dahlonega.

JULY
Peachtree Road Race, Atlanta.
Shakespeare Festival, Atlanta.

AUGUST
Madison Theatre Festival, Madison.
Georgia Mountain Fair and Country Music Festival, Hiawassee.
Nestlé World Championship of Women's Golf, Buford.
Blue Ridge Mountain Clogging, Gainesville.

SEPTEMBER
Tybee Jubilee, Tybee Island.
Country Fair of 1896, Tifton.
Mountain Music and Crafts Festival, Dahlonega.
Open Bass Tournament/Rodeo, Eatonton.

OCTOBER
National Pecan Festival, Albany.
Okefenokee Heritage Festival, Folkston.
Sorghum Festival, Blairsville.
North Georgia Folk Festival, Athens.
Fall Harvest and Music Festival, Hiawassee.
Southern Open Golf Tournament, Columbus.

NOVEMBER
Fair of 1850, Lumpkin.
Cane Grindings and Syrup Makings, Tifton, Juliette.
Columbus Steeplechase, Pine Mountain.

DECEMBER
Home Tours, Madison, Savannah, St. Simons Island, Athens.
Christmas Festival, Milledgeville.
Christmas at Callanwolde, Atlanta.

NOT ✦ TO ✦ BE ✦ MISSED

An eclectic selection of things to do in Georgia

1. Pay a visit to the Varsity, world's largest drive-in (and eat-in) and renowned mecca for all lovers of "dogs." Nothing else like it anywhere.

2. Take off for a winter quail-hunting weekend to the legendary "Golden Triangle" of the Georgia plains. Experienced or wet-behind-the-ears welcome.

3. Make an Uncle Remus pilgrimage in homage to the beloved Br'er Rabbit tales. Visit the Wren's Nest, Atlanta home of author Joel Chandler Harris; while there, bend your ear toward a resident storyteller for an Uncle Remus tale. Then head to Eatonton, Harris's hometown, to see the commemorative Uncle Remus Museum in a log cabin and the Br'er Rabbit statue.

4. Explore the mysterious Okefenokee Swamp with a guided wilderness canoe trip.

5. Visit Rabun Gap, where the Foxfire tradition was started, and neighboring Dillard for an afternoon of things Appalachian.

6. See where the fate of the Confederate army was sealed at Chickamauga Military Park/ Fort Oglethorpe. Review the events of the decisive 1863 battles and examine an extensive array of weaponry.

7. Witness the delivery and adoption of those huggable Cabbage Patch Kids at Babyland General Hospital in Cleveland.

8. Follow the antebellum trail for a weekend sojourn through the towns and homes of the genteel Old South: Athens, Madison, Eatonton, Milledgeville, Clinton, and Macon.

9. Ferry over to Cumberland Island National Seashore, an undisturbed preserve of seaside flora and fauna. Take your backpack and sleep under the stars. Only 300 people are allowed to visit daily.

10. Spend a weekend in Savannah, a charming and proud seaport city and Georgia's first

settlement. Stroll the historic district, laced with its original twenty-one "squares" of half-acre parks, over 1,100 restored

The riverfront at Savannah.

buildings, and broad avenues lined with live oaks. Tour the waterfront district, rejuvenated center of commerce and shipping (and now shopping). Visit its historic homes and churches, Maritime Museum, and Antique Doll Museum; venture to Skidaway Island's Oceanographic Institute. Explore some of the state's oldest standing forts, Jackson and Pulaski.

11. Come summer, pick your own peaches in orchards around Perry—fresh, juicy, and cheap.

12. Visit a former stronghold of the rich and famous, Jekyll Island, where Rockefellers, Goodyears, Goulds, and so forth, once spent indolent vacations removed from the hoi polloi. Then head to the current stomping grounds of well-bred and well-heeled families from the Northeast to the South, *Sea Island* (take lots of pink and green to wear).

13. Hike the trail up Rabun Bald Mountain to its 4,660-foot elevation. Soak in the pan-oramic view of the Chattahoochee National Forest.

14. Experience firsthand the formidable white waters of the Chatooga River (where the film *Deliverance* was made) with an adventurous raft or canoe trip.

[For the full lowdown on Georgia, straight from the horse's mouth, contact: Georgia Department of Industry and Trade, Post Office Box 1776, Atlanta, 30301.]

GEORGIA CLOSE-UP: *Rebel-rousing Stone Mountain Park*

You might care to go to Stone Mountain Park (outside of Atlanta) for the family recreation this 3,200-acre park and resort offers, and probably to admire its astonishing 825-foot-high mass of exposed granite. As a Southerner, there is another reason you *have* to go. At Stone Mountain you'll encounter two of the most unabashed tributes to the motherland around and, with them, a glimpse into the southern experience: (1) the Confederate Memorial Carving, a massive and inspiring tribute to the Lost Cause on one side of the mountain, featuring Generals Robert E. Lee, and "Stonewall" Jackson, and Con-federate President Jefferson Davis on horseback; (2) the Laser Show, a yee-haw, yahoo crowd-pleasing summertime laser phantasmagoria on the mountain's north face, which concludes with an always rebel-rousing finale of "Dixie" and fireworks.

Stone Mountain.

Where to Go For a Good Time in

KENTUCKY

Events for the Asking

JANUARY
Old Christmas, Prestonsburg.

FEBRUARY
Championship Tractor Pull, Louisville.

MARCH
Storytelling Weekend, Greenup.
Humana Festival of New Plays, Louisville.

APRIL
Kentucky Derby Festival, Louisville.
Hillbilly Days, Pikeville.

MAY
Kentucky Derby, Louisville.
Highland Games and Gathering of Scottish Clans, Glasgow.
Decorator's Showhouses, Bowling Green, Lexington.
Sheep Shearing Weekend, Golden Pond.
Hard Scuffle Steeplechase, Prospect.
Kentucky Mountain Laurel Festival, Pineville.
Big Singing Day (Shaped Note music), Benton.

JUNE
National Mountain-Style Square Dance and Clogging Festival, Slade.
Festival of the Bluegrass, Lexington.
The Egyptian Event (Egyptian-Arabian Horse Show), Lexington.
Appalachian Celebration, Morehead.

JULY
Shaker Festival, South Union.
Junior League Horse Show, Lexington.
State Championship Old Time Fiddlers' Contest, Leitchfield.

AUGUST
Pioneer Days Festival, Harrodsburg.
All-Night Gospel Sing, Renfro Valley.
State Fair, Louisville.

SEPTEMBER
Corn Island Storytelling Festival, Louisville.
Kentucky Highlands Folk Festival, Prestonsburg.
Kentucky Apple Festival, Paintsville.
Cow Days, Greensburg.
Decorators' Show House, Lexington.

OCTOBER
Wool Festival, Falmouth.
National Goose Calling Championship, Bluegrass Waterfowl Festival, Paducah.
Tobacco Festivals, Russellville and Bloomfield.
World Championship Squirrel Dog Hunt, Hoskinston.
State Banjo Playing Championship, Cumberland Mountain Fall Festival, Middlesboro.
Re-enactment of the Battle of Perryville, Perryville.

NOVEMBER
Festival of Trees, Ashland.
Designers' Showhouse, Louisville.

DECEMBER
Home Tours, Louisville, Bardstown, Oakland, Frankfort.
Christmas Tree Exhibition, Owensboro.
Frontier Christmas, Washington.

NOT ✦ TO ✦ BE ✦ MISSED
An eclectic selection of things to do in Kentucky

1. Have yourself a horsey time in Lexington and Louisville, twin hubs of the Bluegrass region. In Lexington head first to Kentucky Horse Park for an all-day tribute to horse history, breeding, raising, riding, and racing. Pay a visit the Keeneland Race Course, Red Mile Harness Track, and, of course, world-famous Spendthrift Farm before you leave. In Louisville make tracks to Churchill Downs and the on-site Kentucky Derby Museum, then wrap up your equine explorations with a wager at the Louisville Downs harness races.

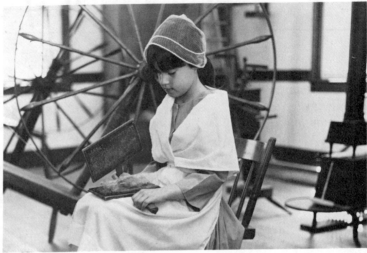

Shaker Village, Pleasant Hill.

2. Spend a back-country weekend of hiking and camping amidst the unsoiled rivers, gorges, and wilderness of Big South Fork National Recreation Area.

3. Angle your way to the annual April crappie runs at Kentucky Lake for some of the best biting you've seen in a long time.

4. Step into Appalachian culture in Berea. See the workings of Southern Highlands life and lore at the Appalachian Museum, admire the traditional handiwork of Berea College crafts, then observe the art of handweaving in the loomhouse of Churchill Weavers.

5. Recount the scouting movement in America at the National Museum of the Boy Scouts, which includes fifty-four original Norman Rockwell paintings of Boy Scout life in its installations.

Liberty Hall, Frankfort.

6. Put Kentucky into historical perspective with a visit to Frankfort. Trace state history at the Kentucky History Museum, Military History Museum, and the Frankfort Cemetery, burial grounds of famous pioneers and politicians. See striking examples of architecture: Beaux Arts (Governor's Mansion), Federal (Vest-Lindsey House), Greek Revival (Ward Hall), and Georgian (Liberty Hall). Check out the early farm implements at Luscher's Farm Relics collection, then head over to see Old Grand-dad at his 1901 distillery.

7. Watch the step-by-step production of the Corvette in Bowling Green at the world's only Chevrolet Corvette facility.

8. View over one hundred of John James Audubon's remarkable "Birds of America" prints at the museum in his namesake state park.

9. Enter the Shaker era at the Shaker Village of Pleasant Hill near Harrodsburg, where twenty-seven original buildings of this 1805 community are preserved. Admire their distinctive architecture, furniture, and tools, observe demonstrations of the Society's life, and walk the peaceful grounds. Stay a while. You can dine and sleep there, too.

10. Descend into the world's largest cave system at the amazing Mammoth Cave National Park, with over 300 miles of mapped passageways. Take a sweater; this is one place the sun never shines.

11. Relive the history and charm of the once-flourishing nineteenth-century town, Bardstown. Tour mansions, museums (including the fascinating Miniature Soldier Museum and Getz Museum of Whiskey History), and a living-history village.

12. Discover prehistoric Indian culture from A.D. 800 to 1350. Burial sites, home sites, temple mounds, and artifacts at Wyckliffe Mounds, Wyckliffe.

[To get the full lowdown on Kentucky, straight from the horse's mouth, contact: Kentucky Department of Travel Development, Capital Plaza Tower, Frankfort, 40601.]

KENTUCKY CLOSE-UP: *Vice Tour*

Kentucky is home state to numerous distilleries and cigarette factories. So why not take a few side trips to see what they're all about? These folks are more than happy to have you pay them a visit. Begin your touring in Louisville at the Philip Morris USA tobacco-processing and cigarette-packing facility. Proceed to Frankfort, home to Ancient Age, Old Grand-dad, and Old Crow distilleries. Resume your vice tour in Bardstown, address for the Getz Museum of Whiskey History, and Jim Beam, Heaven Hill, and Evan Williams whiskies. Should you crave even more, you can find it in Loretto (Maker's Mark), Owensboro (Glenmore), and others.

Maker's Mark Distillery, Loretto.

Where to Go for a Good Time in

LOUISIANA

Events for the Asking

JANUARY
Sugar Bowl Football Classic, New Orleans.
Fur and Wildlife Festival, Cameron.

FEBRUARY
Mardi Gras (occurs some years in March), New Orleans, Lafayette, and other cities.
Boudin Festival, Broussard.

MARCH
Oyster Days, Amite.
Cajun Fun Fest, New Iberia.
PGA Golf Classic, New Orleans.

APRIL
French Acadian Music Festival, Abbeville.
Creole Festival, Houma.
Jazz and Heritage Festival, New Orleans.

MAY
Crawfish Festival, Breaux Bridge (even-numbered years).
Bluegrass Festivals, Bush and Pitkin.
Timberfest, Bastrop.

JUNE
Pirogue Races, Slidell.
Cajun Music Festival, Mamou.
Bayou Lacombe Crab Festival, Lacombe.
Possum Festival, Arcadia.
Jambalaya Festival, Gonzales.

JULY
Northwestern Folk Festival, Natchitoches.
Cajun Bastille Day, Baton Rouge.
Deep Sea Fishing Rodeo, Lake Charles.
Shakespeare Festival, Lake Charles.

AUGUST
South Lafourche Seafood Festival, Galliano.
Le Bal de Maison, Lafayette.
Shrimp Festival, Delcambre.

SEPTEMBER
Festivals Acadiens, Lafayette.
Southwest Louisiana Zydeco Music Festival, Plaisance.
Wildfowl Carvers Festival, New Orleans.
Frog Festival, Rayne.
Sugar Cane Festival and Fair, New Iberia.
Shrimp and Petroleum Festival, Morgan City.

OCTOBER
International Rice Festival, Crowley.
State Fair, Shreveport.
Sauce Piquante Festival, Raceland.
International Alligator Festival, Franklin.
Ark-La-Miss Agri-Industrial Fair, West Monroe.
The Gumbo Festival, Bridge City.

NOVEMBER
Pecan Festival, Colfax.
Plantation Fall Festival, Destrehan.
Festival de Grand Coteau, Grand Coteau.

DECEMBER
Home Tours, Alexandria, Houma, Destrehan, Baton Rouge, New Iberia.
LSU Quarter Horse Show, Baton Rouge.
Christmas in Acadian Village, Lafayette.
Parish Fair and Orange Festival, Plaquemine.

NOT ✦ TO ✦ BE ✦ MISSED
An eclectic selection of things to do in Louisiana

1. Get duded up for an evening of country/western two-stepping at the ever-popular Louisiana Hayride, live radio broadcast and dance every Saturday night in Shreveport. More music-hall dancing (same time) at the Old South Jamboree near Walker.

2. Cook up a Creole meal in short order with a three-hour hands-on class at the New Orleans School of Cooking.

3. Go fish, offshore style, in the coastal waters of the Gulf of Mexico for such gamefish as mackerel, marlin, pompano, snapper, and tarpon. Grand Isle is a favorite charter boat point.

4. Tour the magnificent treasures of Louisiana's plantation country with a drive on River Road (between New Or-

Curtain call at the Hayride.

Jackson Square, New Orleans.

leans and Baton Rouge) or around the town of St. Francisville. See for yourself how good the good life could be if you were a wealthy planter before the War and even experience it in those mansions with bed and breakfast accommodations.

5. See Mardi Gras in the making at Mardi Gras World in New Orleans, where the floats and ornaments of the annual carnival are constructed. Contrast Mardi Gras present with those past by visiting the Presbytere and Old U.S. Mint, which house Mardi Gras exhibits and memorabilia in their collections.

6. Watch the making of a tastemaker on Avery Island, home of the famous Tabasco sauce, with a tour of the cen-

tury-old process. Then explore the 200-acre Jungle Gardens and Bird Sanctuary, exotic living legacy of Tabasco's founding family.

7. Venture into the mystical and mysterious at the Voodoo Museum in New Orleans's French Quarter. Take the museum-guided voodoo walking tour, then visit the grave of Marie LaVeau, legendary voodoo queen of the city, at the St. Louis No. 1 Cemetery.

8. Make a fall excursion to Louisiana's oldest town, Natchitoches, during its open house tour. Sample the charm bestowed by 250 years of prosperous and gracious living with a distinguished French heritage.

9. Stroll the collonaded galleries and shops of the famed Old French Market in New Orleans. Savor every tourist's just reward: steaming hot *café au lait* and those incomparable beignets at Café du Monde.

10. Get face-to-face with the alligators of Bayou Country on a wetlands boat tour. Cruise through the cypress swamplands and marshes for a close-up look at nutria, raccoon, egrets, herons, alligators, and more in their wilderness habitat.

11. Explore Acadiana, heartland of French Louisiana, where French Acadians and expatriates of the French Revolution once settled. Trace the tragedy of Evangeline (immortalized in Longfellow's poem) and her fellow Acadians with visits to the old Evangeline Oak in St. Martinville, her grave at St. Martin de Tours Catholic Church, and the close-by commemorative area, featuring an eighteenth-century Acadian plantation house and period artifacts.

12. Place your bets on thoroughbred racehorses, spring till fall, at racetracks in Lafayette, Vinton, Bossier City, New Orleans, and Kenner.

[For the full lowdown on Louisiana, straight from the horse's mouth, contact: Louisiana Office of Tourism, Post Office Box 94291, Baton Rouge, 70804.]

LOUISIANA CLOSE-UP: *New Orleans's St. Charles Line streetcar*

Ride the tracks of New Orleans history (exact change only, please) on the 150-year-old St. Charles Line streetcar, one of the South's beloved antiques of transit. The sole survivor of a trolley system that once laced the city, the St. Charles line still carries over 20,000 riders daily. You haven't lived until you've ridden the streetcar, so make the best of your outing when you do. Board downtown at Canal and Carondolet streets and settle into a windowside wooden bench for the one-and-a-half-hour circuit. The St. Charles will carry you through the heart of the venerable Garden District, where the gracious architecture of antebellum New Orleans is in plentiful supply, past the campuses of Tulane and Loyola universities, and finally to the end of the line, where there's further fascination for those who choose to disembark: the Audubon Zoo.

St. Charles Line streetcar.

Where to Go For a Good Time in

MISSISSIPPI

Events for the Asking

JANUARY
National Tractor Pull Competition, Jackson.

FEBRUARY
Dixie National Livestock Show and Rodeo, Jackson.
Turkey Federation Calling Contest, Natchez.

MARCH
National Junior College Women's Basketball National Championship Tournament, Senatobia.

APRIL
Natchez Trace Festival, Kosciusko.
Crawfish Festival, Biloxi.
Dulcimer Day, Dennis.

MAY
Jimmie Rodgers Memorial Festival, Meridian.
Flea Market, Canton.
Re-enactment of Civil War Battle at Champion Hill, Edwards.

JUNE
B. B. King Festival, Indianola.
International Ballet Competition (1990 and every fourth year thereafter), Jackson.
Shrimp Festival and Blessing of Fleet, Biloxi.

National Tobacco Spitting Contest, Raleigh.

JULY
Deep-Sea Fishing Rodeo, Gulfport.
World Championship Checker Match, Tupelo.
Rhythm and Blues Festival, Chunky.

AUGUST
Neshoba County Fair, Philadelphia.
Ole Brook Festival, Brookhaven.
Cotton Row on Parade Day, Greenwood.

SEPTEMBER
Delta Blues Festival, Greenville.
Grand Village Indian Festival, Natchez.
Seafood Festival, Biloxi.

OCTOBER
Re-enactment of the Battle of Corinth, Corinth.
Gumbo Festival of the Universe, Necaise Crossing.
Mullet Festival, Biloxi.
State Fair, Jackson.

NOVEMBER
Scottish Highland Games, Biloxi.
Mistletoe Market Place, Jackson.

DECEMBER
Home Tours, Natchez, Jackson, Meridian, Greenwood.

NOT ✦ TO ✦ BE ✦ MISSED
An eclectic selection of things to do in Mississippi

1. See the humble birthplace of a King with a trip to Tupelo, where you'll find the two-room shotgun house in which Elvis Presley was born. See also the next-door Memorial Chapel, legacy of love from the King's loyal followers.

2. Watch a championship checker tournament unfold on a human-sized board at the International Checkers Hall of Fame and Museum in Petal. Then check out checker history and lore around the world at the museum's exhibits.

3. Step back into time—36 million years, that is—with an exploration of the Mississippi Petrified Forest near Flora. The only one of its kind in the eastern United States.

4. Savor the southern wines of the muscadine and scuppernong vines with excursions to wineries around the state: Almaria Vineyards (Matherville), Old South Winery (Natchez), and Thousand Oaks (Starkville).

Elvis Presley's birthplace.

D'Evereux Mansion, Natchez.

5. Travel by boat to explore the islands of the Gulf Coast National Seashore in the Mississippi Sound. Visit Fort Massachusetts, on Ship Island, built by the Confederacy but seized by Union forces and used to imprison Confederate soldiers. Discover the coastal habitats of Horn and Petit Bois islands, both wildlife sanctuaries and nesting places for wintering birds (wilderness lovers can set up camp on Horn island).

6. Make a spring pilgrimage to the magnificent homes of the wealthy Old South in the state that invented the annual rite.

7. Enter the animal world at the Jackson Zoological Park, just-like-home habitat to living creatures from all parts of the planet. Then see suspended animation—of a different sort—at the Museum of Natural Science, repository of mounted wildlife specimens, aquaria, and ecological depictions.

8. Visit the home of a literary giant and favorite native son in Oxford at Rowan Oak, the secluded residence where William Faulkner penned his prize-winning works.

9. Paddle a canoe down the Chunky River south of Meridian for a backwaters pleasure trip (favorite scenic spot: the tiered, fifty-foot-tall Dunn's Falls). Or put in on the banks of Bull Mountain Creek upstate and cast off in search of spotted bass and catfish.

10. Admire the graceful artistry of the pottery of George Ohr and Walter Anderson, both highly sought by collectors and connoisseurs, at Gulf Coast studios: Moran's Art Studio (Ohr), Biloxi; Shearwater Pottery (Anderson), Ocean Springs.

11. Look away to the land of cotton with a visit to the Delta town of Greenwood during the fall harvest. See the bustling cotton market at the height of trading activity, then observe the glory days of cotton re-enacted at Florewood River Plantation (you can even pick your own cotton).

12. Travel by bicycle over the stomping grounds of Indians, DeSoto, and frontier explorers on the ancient and scenic Natchez Trace Parkway. Narrate your overland tour by reading the markers of historic and natural interest.

13. Seek out the memorabilia of Mississippi legends with trips to the Casey Jones Museum in Benton and the Jimmie Rodgers Museum in Meridian.

[For the full lowdown on Mississippi, straight from the horse's mouth, contact: Mississippi Department of Economic Development, Division of Tourism, Post Office Box 849, Jackson, 39205.]

MISSISSIPPI CLOSE-UP: *Vicksburg National Battlefield Park*

For forty-seven days it was the sight of one of the War's fiercest sieges, but the bounty was worth all possible sacrifice to both sides: control of the mighty Mississippi, lifeline of the Confederate States of America. Beyond the river bluffs spread the 1,800 acres of Vicksburg National Military Park, site of the bitter, protracted struggle. Traversing this territory (rent an audio cassette from the Park Service) will put the siege in very human terms, the tragic story unfolding over the battleground of re-created forts, trenches, and artillery installations. More than 1,400 markers, memorials, and monuments (plus the Vicksburg National Cemetery) describe the grim events of spring, 1863, when over 17,000 soldiers of the Blue and Gray fought to the death.

Illinois Memorial, Vicksburg National Military Park.

Where to Go for a Good Time in
NORTH CAROLINA

Events for the Asking

JANUARY
Southeastern Brittany Field Trials, Hoffman.

FEBRUARY
Fiddler's Convention and Buck Dance Contest, Newton.
Great Cardboard Box Derby and Winterfest, Banner Elk.

MARCH
Old Time Fiddlers and Blue Grass Convention, Mooresville.
Carolina 500, Rockingham.

APRIL
North Carolina Azalea Festival, Wilmington.
Designer's Show Houses, Winston-Salem, Pinehurst.
Stoneybrook Steeplechase Races, Tryon, Southern Pines.
Greater Greensboro (PGA) Open, Greensboro.
National Whistlers Convention, Louisburg.
Wilbur Wright Fly In, Kill Devil Hills.

MAY
Winn-Dixie 300 NASCAR Grand National Race and Coca-Cola 600 NASCAR Winston Cup Race, Harrisburg.
Tarheel Storytelling Festival, Winston-Salem.
World Gee Haw Whimmy Diddle Competition, Asheville.

Ramp Convention, Waynesville.
Hang Gliding Spectacular, Nags Head.

JUNE
National Hollerin' Contest, Spivey's Corner.
Annual Singing on the Mountain, Linville.
Blue Crab Derby and Festival, Morehead City.
Seafood Festival and Blessing of the Fleet, Wanchese.

JULY
Shindig on the Green, Asheville (through mid-September).
Grandfather Mountain Highland Games and Gathering of Scottish Clans, Linville.
Brevard Music Festival, Brevard.
Folkmoot USA, Waynesville.

AUGUST
Mountain Dance and Folk Festival, Asheville.
Henredon Golf (LPGA) Classic, High Point.
Shrimp Festival, Sneads Ferry.
National Open Cribbage Tournament, Raleigh.

SEPTEMBER
Masters of Hang Gliding Championship, Linville.
Mountain Heritage Day, Cullowhee.
Collard Festival and Eating Contest, Ayden.

State Championship Charity Horse Show, Raleigh.
Currituck Wildlife Festival, Barco.

OCTOBER
Flora Macdonald Highland Games, Red Springs.
State Chili Festival and Cook-off, Havelock.
Guild Fair of Southern Highland Handicraft Guild, Asheville.
Decorators' Show House, New Bern.
NASCAR Winston Cup Series Stock Car Races, Harrisburg, North Wilkesboro, Rockingham.
Any and All Dog Show, Tryon.

Oyster Festival, Shallotte (South Brunswick Islands).

NOVEMBER
Carolina's Craftsmen's Christmas Classic, Greensboro.
Carolina's Carousel Festival, Charlotte.
Festival of Trees, Wilmington.

DECEMBER
Home Tours, Cape Fear, Wilmington, New Bern, Edenton, Raleigh, Charlotte, Burlington, Fayetteville.
Christmas at Biltmore Estate, Asheville.
Madrigal Christmas Dinners, Cullowhee, Winston-Salem, Boone.

NOT ✦ TO ✦ BE ✦ MISSED
An eclectic selection of things to do in North Carolina.

---

1. Strike out on a wildflower trek in the Blue Ridge Mountains, lofty stage for ever-changing carpets of color, including flaming azaleas and dogwood (spring), mountain laurel (May), and the glorious rhododendron (June).

2. Venture on a vice tour around the state, home to cigarette manufacturers (R. J. Reynolds Tobacco, Winston-Salem; American Tobacco, Reidsville) and brewery (Stroh Brewery, Winston-Salem).

3. Take a waterfall tour (and take a picnic, too) in Nantahala National Forest along U.S. Highway 64. Enjoy the captivating beauty of such cascades as Bird Rock, Toxaway, Whitewater (411 feet), Rainbow, and Bridal Veil Falls. Conclude your tour with sojourns to nearby Dry Falls and Cullasaja.

4. Savor the gingerbread charm of Historic Oakwood neighborhood in Raleigh, tree-lined treasury with over four hundred elegant examples of Victorian architecture.

5. Soar amidst the mountains and amongst the champions. Go hang gliding at Grandfather Mountain near Linville.

Old Salem, Winston-Salem.

6. Review your Revolutionary War history with a stop at Moores Creek National Battlefield near Wilmington, site of a decisive battle that helped insure colonists' freedom from Britain.

7. Scuba a shipwreck (choose from over 400), macabre underwater reminders of the treacherous North Carolina coast.

8. Learn the ways of the Cherokee Indians at Qualla Boundary Reserve with a trip to the Museum of the Cherokee Indian, Oconaluftee Indian Village, and Qualla Arts and Crafts Mutual. Contrast their proud heritage with Cherokee's Magic Water Park and Santa's Land Park and Zoo.

9. Expand your historical horizons with an excursion to Old Salem. This Moravian congregational town founded in 1766 features more than sixty rebuilt/restored structures. Then dig deeper into the past at Historic Bethabara Park, location of the Moravian's first North Carolina settlement and now site of modern Winston-Salem.

10. Learn the lessons of coastal existence for man and nature at the Hampton Mariners Museum in Beaufort. Sign up for a day's guided field trip of birding, fossil hunting, flatland and marsh exploration, shelling, or wildflower excursions.

11. Ski the South's favorite winter slopes at Beech and Sugar Mountains, Cataloochee, and Wolf Laurel.

12. Collect one-of-a-kind examples of mountain-made handiwork with an excursion to the Southern Highland Handicraft Guild's Folk Art Center, east of Asheville, a respected source for the pottery, needlework, crafts, and hand-carved items (like whimmy diddles) of the mountainfolk culture.

13. Discover the historic Atlantic coast settlements of the New World around the Outer Banks: Edenton, a 265-year old colonial coast village brimming with historical sites and architectural treasures; New Bern, a former colonial capital and home to the distinguished Tryon Palace; and Beaufort, charming seacoast town.

[For the full lowdown on North Carolina, straight from the horse's mouth, contact: North Carolina Travel and Tourism Division, Department of Commerce, 430 North Salisbury Street, Raleigh, 27611.]

NORTH CAROLINA CLOSE-UP: *Biltmore House and Gardens*

You'd swear you were in the Loire Valley of France upon sighting the majestic chateau, but you're near Asheville, overlooking the Swannanoa and French Broad valleys at a superlative vantage point: Biltmore House. This is the house that money built—lots of it— to fulfill a dream of Cornelius Vanderbilt's erudite grandson, George. Completed in 1895, the fantasyland mansion, its grand furnishings, and expansive gardens (designed by Frederick Law Olmstead) are all remarkable statements of beauty, design, and ingenuity. You can see the splendor of Biltmore House and Gardens (and its new winery) for yourself; over 50 of its 200-plus rooms are open for exploration if you're willing to spring the price of admission (not cheap, but then again, neither was the house).

The Biltmore House.

SOUTH CAROLINA

Where to Go For a Good Time in

Events for the Asking

JANUARY
Oyster Festival, Charleston.
Grand American Coon Hunt, Orangeburg.
Polo Matches (through April), Aiken.

FEBRUARY
Southeastern Wildlife Exposition, Charleston.

MARCH
Annual Triple Crown (Harness Race, Thoroughbred Trials, Steeplechase), Aiken.
Governor's Frog Jump and Egg Striking Contest, Springfield.
The Carolina Cup Races, Camden.

APRIL
Egg Scramble Jamboree, Lamar.
Heritage Golf Classic, Hilton Head.
Designer's Show House, Charleston.

MAY
Spoleto Festival USA, Charleston.
Flopeye Fish Festival, Great Falls.
Festival of Roses, Orangeburg.
Gullah Festival, Beaufort.
Lowcountry Shrimp Festival and Blessing of Fleet, McClellanville.

JUNE
Watermelon Festival, Hampton.
Catfish Tournament, Eutawville.
Hootenanny, Winnsboro.

JULY
State Tobacco Festival, Lake City.
Hillbilly Day, Mountain Rest.

Great Waccamaw River Raft Race, Conway.
Freedom Weekend Aloft, Greenville.

AUGUST
Little Mountain Reunion, Little Mountain.
Schuetzenfest, Ehrhardt.

SEPTEMBER
Southern 500 Winston Cup Stock Car Race, Darlington.
Harvest Hoedown Festival, Aynor.
Crossroads Festival, Rock Hill.
Scottish Games and Highland Gathering, Charleston.

OCTOBER
State Fair, Columbia.
Gopher Hill Festival, Ridgeland.
Pumpkin Festival, Pumpkintown.
Lancing Tournament, Camden.
Cotton Pickin' Festival, Bishopville.
Hilton Head Seniors International PGA Tournament, Hilton Head.

NOVEMBER
Plantation Days, Charleston.
Colonial Cup International Steeplechase, Camden.

DECEMBER
Home Tours, Aiken, Camden, Charleston, Hilton Head, Pendleton, York.
North-South High School All-Star Football Game, Myrtle Beach.

NOT ✦ TO ✦ BE ✦ MISSED
An eclectic selection of things to do in South Carolina

---

1. Go to seed on the perfect plot with a trip to the George W. Park Seed Company near Greenwood. Gardeners everywhere know their name like the back of their hands. Tour the lush display and test gardens, then take home a fresh supply of *objets d'horticulture*.

2. Make tracks to thoroughbred territory around Aiken, where hopes and dreams and lots of money are pinned on horses. No circus horses here, just the highbrow variety, bred and trained for polo (played eight months a year) or to race to the finish at Aiken's annual Triple Crown events (harness and thoroughbred racing, steeplechasing). If you can't see it firsthand, then see it memorialized at the Thoroughbred Racing Hall of Fame and maybe settle in the saddle yourself for a ride over the bridle paths of

The Charleston Battery.

Hitchcock Woods nature preserve.

3. Get a bird's-eye view of St. Helena Sound from the top of Hunting Island's old lighthouse. Your panorama will include the beaches and marshes of the island (now a state park populated with wild game and migratory birds), the archipelago surrounding Beaufort and Atlantic Ocean horizons.

4. Try for some record smashing of your own at the state's most famous fishing holes, the Santee Cooper lakes (Lakes Moultrie and Marion, near Charleston), home to the world's heftiest landlocked striped bass, channel catfish, and black crappie.

5. Take a slow tour through the capital of fast cars at the Stock Car Hall of Fame near Darlington. Admire the world's largest collection of race cars, buckle up for a simulated raceway ride in Richard Petty's Dodge, and see the ones that didn't get away: illegal parts found in race-ready cars.

Darlington Raceway.

6. Pass into another world in Charleston, refined old city of distinguished history, architecture, and family trees. Prepare to be totally charmed by old Charleston's plentitude of seventeenth- and eighteenth-century dwellings (particularly the indigenous "single house") and gardens; noble churches and offices, shops and marketplaces. Gracious living is the watchword here, and it's practiced expertly. Don't miss strolling on the famous bayside Battery Park, venturing to surrounding plantations (see "Close-Up," below), feasting on sophisticated Low-Country cuisine, or the opportunity to call a historic inn home for a few nights (bring money).

7. Cavort à la Coney Island on the shores of the Grand Strand, endless seaside playland and amusement mecca. If you like crowds, wax museums, water slides, souvenir shops, carpet golf, and the like, you'll be in hog heaven in this neck of the woods.

8. Gather while ye may the popular handiworks of South Carolina's coastal cultures. Pawley's Island hammocks and Low-Country sweetgrass baskets, all handwoven in testament to the state's African and West Indian heritages, are in ready supply.

9. Watch pro-baseball hopefuls sharpen their skills at farm team match-ups with ballpark visits to the Columbia Mets (New York Mets) or the Charleston Rainbows (San Diego Padres).

10. Get there while the getting's still good—to the Bible Belt's own amusement park and dreamchild of Jim and Tammy Bakker, Heritage USA, near Fort Mill. Experience how godly entertainment can be at this "Disneyland for the devout," a combination recreation resort, water park, shopping haven, and religious retreat, all delivered with evangelical aplomb.

[For the full lowdown on South Carolina, straight from the horse's mouth, contact: South Carolina Division of Tourism, Post Office Box 71, Columbia, 29202.]

SOUTH CAROLINA CLOSE-UP: *The Low-Country Plantation Gardens*

They're old, they're big, they're splendid, and they're definitely worth the price of admission. They're the landmark plantations of two distinguished Low-Country dynasties: Drayton Hall and its Magnolia Plantation and Gardens and Middleton Place, gardens, mansion, and stableyard. Within four miles of one another on the Ashley River (near Charleston), both are remarkable heirlooms of early Carolina wealth. At Drayton Hall, c. 1738, you'll find what is considered the nation's finest example of Georgian Palladian architecture, *sans* modernization. Nearby, find the estate's magnificent garden, with its famous tree-sized camellias and abundant azalea beds, plus Drayton's plantation house. There's yet more grandeur and elegance at Middleton Place, Tudor-style home to one of America's founding families and site of Old-World, terraced gardens framed by butterfly lakes and lush ornamental plantings.

Middleton Place Gardens.

Where to Go For a Good Time in

TENNESSEE

Events for the Asking

FEBRUARY
U.S. Indoor Tennis Tournament, Memphis.
National Field Trial Championship, Grand Junction.

MARCH
Mid-South Civil War and Antique Military Show, Memphis.
Southeastern 500 (drag racing), Bristol.
"Wearin' of the Green" Irish Celebration, Erin.

APRIL
State Old Time Fiddlers' Festival, Clarksville.
Dogwood Arts Festival, Knoxville.
Re-enactment of the Battle of Shiloh, Shiloh National Military Park.
Folk Arts Festival, Kingsport.
Designer's Show House, Nashville.

MAY
The Iroquois Steeplechase, Nashville.
Great Smoky Mountains Highland Games, Gatlinburg.
Memphis in May Festivals, Memphis.
International Folkfest, Murfreesboro.

JUNE
Riverbend Festival and Great Tennessee River Raft Race, Chattanooga.
International Country Music Fan Fair, Nashville.
Dulcimer and Harp Convention, Cosby.
Civil War Living History Encampment and Battle Re-enactment, Lexington.

Federal Express/St. Jude's Golf Classic, Memphis.

JULY
Fiddlers' Jamboree and Crafts Festival, Smithville.
Threshermen's Steam Wheat Threshing Show, Adams.
National Mountain Music Festival, Pigeon Forge.

AUGUST
International Grand Championship Walking Horse Show, Murfreesboro.
Tennessee Walking Horse National Celebration, Shelbyville.
Elvis International Tribute Week, Memphis.
National Rolley Hole Marbles Championship, Standing Stone State Park.
Longhorn World Championship Rodeo, Nashville.

SEPTEMBER
National Crafts Festival, Pigeon Forge.
Grassroots Days and Music Festival, Nashville.
State Fair, Nashville.

OCTOBER
National Storytelling Festival, Jonesborough.
Autumn Leaf Special (Steam Train) Excursion, Chattanooga.
Decorators' Show House, Memphis.
Fall Homecoming and Music Festival, Norris.

NOVEMBER
Mid-South Civil War and Antique Military Show, Memphis.
Christmas Festival, Gatlinburg.
Victorian Village Christmas, Memphis.

DECEMBER
Home Tours, Franklin, Murfreesboro, Nashville, Memphis, Columbia.
Liberty Bowl Football Classic, Memphis.

NOT ◆ TO ◆ BE ◆ MISSED
An eclectic selection of things to do in Tennessee

1. Ascend to heights of aged grandeur at the Great Smoky Mountains National Park. Spectacular and beautiful to see and explore, no matter what time of year.

2. Relive the battles of the War Between the States at Tennessee's National Military Parks, including Chickamauga and Chattanooga, Shiloh, Stones River, and Fort Donelson.

3. Tour Jack Daniel's Distillery in Lynchburg or the George Dickel Distillery in Tullahoma and observe the making of Tennessee's famous sour mash whiskey.

4. Head for the thrills. Go hang gliding at Raccoon Mountain Flight Park; take a whitewater rafting trip on the Ocoee, Big South Fork, or Big Pigeon rivers (recommended for the experienced and intrepid).

5. Visit the mecca of every true-blue country music fan in Nashville. Head straight for Music Row, heart of Nashville's recording industry. Proceed to the Country Music Hall of Fame and Museum, Ryman Auditorium (first home of the Grand Ole Opry), and then to Bill Monroe's Bluegrass Hall of Fame and Museum. Tour the homes of country music stars. Spend a day (and night) at Opryland USA theme park; enjoy a long-awaited show at the Grand Ole Opry. Venture out to Music Village USA in Hendersonville, where you'll find the House of Cash, Twitty City, and more music-minded attractions—often live performances, too.

6. Mix the Quaint with the tacky in Gatlinburg and nearby Pigeon Forge. Midst the glory of the Smokies is plenty of the garish, yet there's also year-round snow skiing, fascinating subterranean caverns, and the traditional, widely admired handiwork of mountain craftspeople. Be sure you ride the Gatlinburg Ski Lift for a panoramic view of the Smokies.

7. Do a little energy research of your own at Oak Ridge, where the nation entered the Atomic Age. Visit the American

Point Park on Lookout Mountain.

Museum of Appalachia.

Museum of Science and Energy and take the Oak Ridge Energy Tour.

8. Visit the Tennessee Walking Horse Breeders and Exhibitors Association headquarters in Lewisburg, then tour one of the area's walking horse farms.

9. Explore Memphis. Tour its Victorian Village Historic District, Pink Palace Museum and Planetarium, Botanic Gardens, and Chucalissa Indian Village. Make a summer's day of it at Mud Island, offshore fun-and-folklore tribute to the mighty Mississippi River. Take a riverboat excursion on the *Memphis Queen*. Hang out at Overton Square. Make the pilgrimage of all blues aficianados, Memphis's Beale Street, where the blues play on. And, of course, visit the home of the King, Graceland.

10. Immerse yourself in the ways and lore of Tennessee mountain culture at the Museum of Appalachia in Norris.

11. Spend a winter weekend cross country skiing at Roan Mountain State Resort Park.

12. Cap off your kitsch quotient with a trip to Lookout Mountain, home of Rock City ("See seven states!"), Fairyland, and Mother Goose Village. Don't miss the breathtaking climb up (or down) Lookout Mountain on the steep Incline Railway. Wrap up your excursion with a foray to Ruby Falls and Lookout Mountain Caverns.

[To get the full lowdown on Tennessee, straight from the horse's mouth, contact: Tennessee Department of Tourist Development, Post Office Box 23170, Nashville, 37202]

TENNESSEE CLOSE-UP: *The Peabody Hotel*

According to author Dave Cohn, the Mississippi Delta begins in the lobby of the Peabody Hotel in Memphis and ends on Catfish Row in Vicksburg. At the Peabody "ultimately you will see everybody who is anybody in the Delta." Restored to its glory of old days (and now on the National Register of Historic Places), the elegant Peabody is the place to see and be seen in Memphis. It's also the place to see the "running of the ducks," a daily procession by the hotel's webbed-footed residents to and from the lobby fountain. To the strains of Sousa's "King Cotton March," they waddle to the fountain at 11:00 A.M. (via red carpet) and depart for their roost at 5:00 P.M. with similar fanfare. Naturally, duck motifs abound at the Peabody.

The "running of the ducks."

Where to Go for a Good Time in
VIRGINIA

Events for the Asking

JANUARY

Waterfowl and Wildlife Festival, Newport News.

FEBRUARY

Wildfowl Carving and Art Exhibition, Richmond.

George Washington's Birthday Celebration, Alexandria.

MARCH

Highland County Maple Festival, Monterey.

Children's Kite Festival, Lorton.

APRIL

Historic Garden Week, statewide.

International Azalea Festival, Norfolk.

Designer's Show House, Richmond.

Dogwood Festival, Charlottesville.

MAY

Shenandoah Apple Blossom Festival, Winchester.

Virginia Gold Cup Races, Warrenton.

Virginia Storytelling Festival, Williamsburg.

JUNE

Tidewater Scottish Festival and Clan Gathering, Norfolk.

Virginia Wineries Festival, Culpeper.

Great Rappahannock River White Water Canoe Race, Fredericksburg.

Roanoke Valley Horse Show, Salem.

JULY

Summer Chamber Music Festival, Hot Springs.

Atlantic Ocean Surfing Championships, Virginia Beach.

Shakespeare Festival, Williamsburg.

Chincoteague Pony Penning Day, Chincoteague Island.

Shenandoah Valley Music Fest, Orkney Springs.

AUGUST

Old Fiddlers' Convention, Galax.

Hall of Fame Jousting Tournament, Mount Solon.

Tobacco Harvest Festival, Middleburg.

Highlands Arts and Crafts Festival, Abingdon.

SEPTEMBER

State Fair, Richmond.

Foxfield Races, Charlottesville.

Great Peanut Tour (bicycle), Emporia.

Autumn Gospel Song Fest, Breaks.

OCTOBER

Richmond Newspapers Marathon, Richmond.

Harvest Jubilee and World Tobacco Auctioneering Championship, Danville.

Blue Ridge Folklife Festival, Ferrum.

Battle Re-enactment, Vinton.

Annual Skirmish, Winchester.

NOVEMBER

Charlottesville Fall Festival of Tales, Charlottesville.

Oyster Festival, Urbanna.

DECEMBER

Home Tours, Alexandria, Fredericksburg, Hillsboro, Virginia Beach, Norfolk, Williamsburg, Suffolk, Richmond, Winchester.

Scottish Christmas Walk, Alexandria.

NOT ✦ TO ✦ BE ✦ MISSED
An eclectic selection of things to do in Virginia

1. Observe spectacular showings of migratory birds throughout the year at Assateague Island, including snow geese, swans, hawks, ducks, egrets, herons, plovers, and more.

2. Trace the legacy of Old Salts from the Old and New Worlds at the Mariners' Museum in Newport News. A plethora of artifacts and displays present the history and lore of seafaring through the centuries.

3. Hoof it on horseback over the mountainous back country of the Virginia Highlands Horse Trail at Mount Rogers or the scenic trails of Shenandoah National Park.

Carter's Grove Plantation, Williamsburg.

4. Take a driving tour of the great plantation homes of the Tidewater country, along State Highway 5 from Williamsburg to Richmond. See the stately ancestral homes (some open to the public) of "first families" like Byrd, Harrison, Tyler, and Carter; also visit the nearby historic churches where they worshiped.

5. Treat yourself to a delectable taste of history in Norfolk with an ice cream cone (using original 1905 equipment) from Doumar's famous drive-in, whose patriarch is credited with the wafer cone's concoction.

6. Stand in the footsteps of Patrick Henry in Richmond's Saint John Church, where the patriot made his immortal declaration to the Virginia Convention in 1775. Watch a re-enactment during summer months of this famous moment in American history.

The Barter Theatre, Abingdon.

7. Stage an evening's outdoor entertainment at the popular Barter Theatre, the nation's first state-supported theatre, in Abingdon (regular currency now accepted in lieu of barter).

8. Visit the capital of the Confederacy at Richmond. Tour the Old Hall of the state capitol, where Robert E. Lee was commissioned by the Confederate States of America and the Confederate congress met for three years. Stroll Capitol Square, with memorials to Confederate leaders, then proceed to the nearby Museum of the Confederacy at the Confederate White House.

9. Mix the miracles of nature with the kitsch of man during trips to Luray Caverns in the Shenandoah Valley and the Natural Bridge near Lexington. Take in stride the souvenir shops and attractions—including a wax museum with Adam and Eve and the Seven Days of Creation light show.

10. Board an old logging train in Cass for a ride to the top of Bald Knob in the Allegheny Mountains. Watch for glimpses of wildlife (wild cats and even bears) on your way. Explore the quaint railroad museum for artifacts of the bygone era.

11. Traverse the pivotal theatres of the War Between the States at Fredericksburg and Spotsylvania National Military parks, the sites of four major battles (and the mortal wounding of General "Stonewall" Jackson) and at Petersburg National Battlefield Park, where the ten-month-long conflict eventually yielded the defense of Richmond (and the Confederacy) to the Union.

12. Have your own pheasant under glass after a day's hunt for Iranian black-necked pheasant or Japanese green pheasant in the Tidewater environs.

[For the full lowdown on Virginia, straight from the horse's mouth, contact: Virginia Division of Tourism, 101 North Ninth Street, Richmond, 23219.]

Annual Wild Pony Roundup, Chincoteague Island.

VIRGINIA CLOSE-UP: The annual pony penning at Chincoteague

It's the stuff that storybooks are made of and an event that nearly everyone's heard of: the annual round-up and auction of the wild ponies of Assateague Island. Whether they are descendants of survivors of a shipwrecked Spanish galleon or of prolific herds interred by outnumbered colonists is of folkloric dispute, but they're doubtless the star attraction of a well-attended ritual of over sixty years. Come late July, members of the Chincoteague Volunteer Fire Company become volunteer cowboys, rounding up ponies on the southern end of the island and herding them across a narrow channel for a low-tide swim to Chincoteague. Next day, foals are auctioned to help support the fire company and control herd size. Afterwards unsold ponies swim back to the shores of Assateague. Before you go, read a charming chronicle of the event, *Misty of Chincoteague*.